Hand Tools & Techniques

Handyman Club Library™

Handyman Club of America
Minneapolis, Minnesota

Hand Tools & Techniques

CREDITS

Mike Vail
Vice President, Products & Business Development

Tom Carpenter
Director of Books & New Media Development

Mark Johanson
Book Products Development Manager

Dan Cary
Photo Production Coordinator

Chris Marshall
Editorial Coordinator

Steve Anderson
Senior Book Production Assistant

Kam Ghaffari
Author

Mark Johanson, Chris Marshall
Contributing Writers & Editors

Bill Nelson
Series Design, Art Direction and Production

Mark Macemon
Lead Photographer

Ralph Karlen
Photography

John Nadeau
Technical Advisor and Builder

Craig Claeys
Illustrator

Dan Kennedy
Book Production Manager

Renier Antiques
Historical Tools & Text

> *This book is dedicated to my teacher, Stephen Proctor, who helped me develop the tools to be confident becoming a man who works with his hands*
>
> *And to my grandfather, Frank Lindholm, who worked with his hands all his life, and who helped me develop the tools to be confident becoming a man.*
>
> ~Kam Ghaffari
> Author

ISBN 1-58159-039-3

Handyman Club of America
12301 Whitewater Drive
Minnetonka, Minnesota 55343

Hand Tools & Techniques

Table of Contents

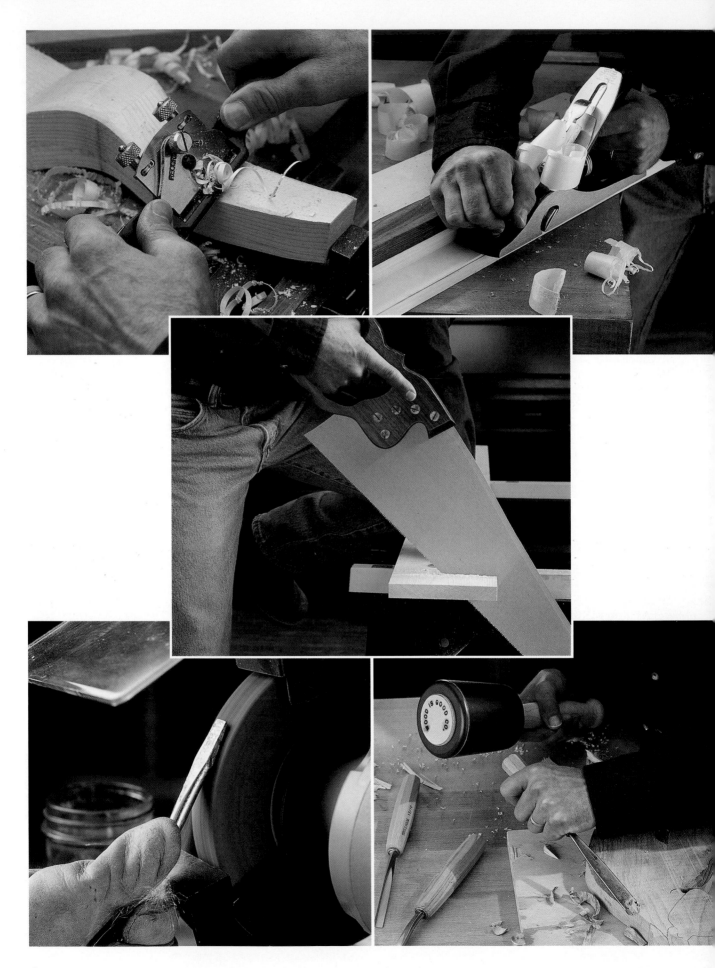

Introduction

Hand tools are not simply curiosities and artifacts from bygone days. While it's true that they do have a rich and fascinating heritage, the fact is they're just as useful today as they ever were—despite the mind-boggling advances in power tool technology that have marked the 20th century. Whether your interests lie in carpentry, woodworking or just tinkering around the house and shop, hand tools can help you.

The casual observer might claim to see a brewing controversy between hand tools and power tools. I see no conflict whatsoever. We will always need both types, and they're not mutually exclusive. And anyone who's ever seen hand tools used as their creators intended will agree. I was taught hand joinery in the British manner by a talented Englishman. Many of my colleagues were instructed very differently by noted Scandinavian masters. I worked alongside quite a few woodworkers on the West Coast who use Japanese hand tools exclusively. I've even visited with Native American artists in the Northwest who use a beaver's tooth as the cutting edge on their carving tools. And through this experience I reached a conclusion: a well-tuned hand tool in skilled hands can accomplish feats of woodworking prowess that even the top of the line power tools cannot approach.

Anyone can learn to operate common hand tools effectively. All that's really needed is a basic interest, a little instruction on proper technique and then some practice. But whether you're picking up a tool for the first time or you've used them for a lifetime, it's important to understand what the tool is meant to do, why it's made as it is, how to hold it and how to best put it to use. In *Hand Tools & Techniques*, developed and published by the Handyman Club of America, we have tried to transmit the fundamentals of hand tool use, together with interesting and helpful information, to serve as a sourcebook you'll enjoy and cherish for years to come.

In addition to helpful information on using hand tools correctly, you'll also find quite a bit of advice on acquiring hand tools in this book. When selecting tools to purchase, consider your skill level, your interests and the work you are likely to be doing—both now and in the foreseeable future. If you plan on doing a few minor repairs around the house, you should be in the market for very different tools than those you'd want if you are a novice woodworker anticipating a lifelong pastime. Deciding what caliber of tools to buy can be a bit of a balancing act, but quality tool manufacturers usually have different lines of tools geared to different needs and skill levels (and priced accordingly).

As with power tools (or automobiles or golf clubs or just about anything, for that matter) you need to keep your hand tools well tuned and well maintained to get the most out of them. That's why this book is filled with straightforward information about taking care of all types of hand tools you're likely to use in your carpentry and woodworking pursuits.

A few words on safety: hand tools don't have the power of an electric motor driving them, but that doesn't mean they can't be dangerous if used carelessly. Cutting tools are sharp and hammers can be heavy. Use them only with care and common sense. And always make sure your workpiece is properly supported, and at a comfortable working height, before taking any kind of tool to it.

Do yourself one more favor: Create a proper storage area for your hand tools (it could be a box, a rack, a series of hooks—it's up to you). And if your workshop space has a concrete floor, lay down plywood or vinyl tiles around your workbench area. Hand tools are the product of centuries of ongoing design evolution—it would be a shame to see them damaged or destroyed by a simple accident.

~K.G.

Measuring & Marking

Whether you're working from sizes and dimensions on a blueprint or sketch, or making it up as you go along, the first step in any project is to transfer your guidelines to your building materials. This procedure, known as laying out, involves both measuring and marking.

No matter what project you are working on—building a tall case clock, replacing a missing part on an antique chair or adding on to your home—the quality of your workmanship depends upon the accuracy of your layout. You need to know the exact sizes and dimensions of all parts. The parts and their joints must be cut and fit straight and true, and at exactly the right angle. And precise marks must be made to guide you in subsequent sawing, drilling and shaping.

While care and precision are key ingredients to measuring and marking success, using the correct tools (and using them correctly) is equally important. The following chapter shows you a wide range of hand tools designed to take measurements, mark workpieces and test your work to make sure it's straight or square.

Measuring Tools

A. Engineer's protractor
B. Outside caliper
C. Inside caliper
D. Vernier caliper
E. Dial caliper
F. Brass pocket caliper
G. Four-fold rule
H. Profile gauge
I. Zig-zag rule
J. Wind-up tape rule
K. Pocket rule
L. Tape measure
M. Steel rule

Rules

The traditional measuring device for woodworkers and carpenters is the folding rule. Modern versions of these time-honored tools are made of wood, metal or plastic and come in two types: the four-fold rule in 2- or 3-ft. lengths, and the zig-zag style that usually opens to 6 ft. Folding rules are compact (6 to 8 in. long when closed) and rigid enough to span long distances without drooping. If you're in the market for a folding rule, buy one with a caliper extension built into the first blade for taking inside measurements (See Photo, right).

One-piece rules, available in lengths ranging from 6 in. to 3 ft., are indispensible in the shop. Six-in.-long pocket rules typically come with a narrow, flexible blade and a sliding-"T" cross-member for taking depth measurements and setting machine blade and bit heights. The longer bench rules serve a variety of uses including general measuring and setting instruments such as a compass or dividers. They also can be used as a straightedge guide. Every shop needs at least a

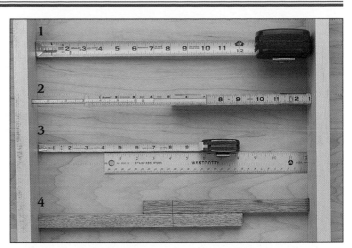

Four ways to take an inside measure. **1: Extend a tape measure and add the length of the case to the measurement on the tape. 2: Using a folding rule with a caliper extension, unfold the rule then extend the caliper out the remaining distance. Add the lengths of the rule and caliper. 3: Lay a metal rule and tape measure together, then add the measurements indicated. 4: Lay two pieces of scrap wood together and draw a reference mark across both scraps where they intersect. Remove the two scraps, realign the marks and measure the combined length.**

Even though the ancient Romans were known to have bronze folding rules, it wasn't until early in the 19th century that folding rules were produced in significant quantities in the United States. During its heyday, the folding rule was produced in more than 100 sizes and lengths for use in numerous trades. They were made of several exotic materials such as ivory, rosewood and ebony, but the most common material was boxwood.

Hinges on the folding rules were usually made of brass and had round, square or arched shapes. Better boxwood folding rules were bound fully in brass. Ivory folding rules usually had hinges and bindings made of German (nickel) silver.

The introduction of the zig-zag rule at the beginning of the 19th century, followed by cloth and steel tapes, essentially phased out the use of bi-fold rules, but they have since emerged as valuable collector's items.

A. Stanley No. 82 carpenter's board scale rule **is a 2 ft., 4-fold rule introduced by Stanley Rule & Level Co. in 1855. Production was stopped in 1917. The brass-bound boxwood rule has a brass arch joint and brass hinges. Both drafting scales and board measure tables are provided.**

B. Al Lufkin No. 2071 rule **is a 1 ft., 3-fold, half bound, narrow boxwood rule with a spirit level mounted in the edge of the center section. The 5/8-in. rule folds to a length of 4 in. and features 1/8-in. and 1/16-in. graduations.**

C. The Stanley No. 40 rule **is a 1 ft., 4-fold, ivory caliper rule, sold from 1855 to 1922. The 5/8-in.-wide rule is fully bound with German (nickel) silver.**

Tips for using tape measures

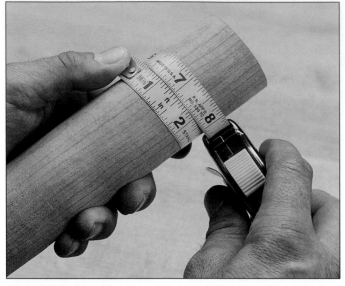

Measuring circumference. **To measure the circumference of a round workpiece, wrap a tape measure around the object and pull it taut so the edges of the tape are side by side. Choose two markings that align, and subtract the smaller tape reading from the larger reading to find the circumference.**

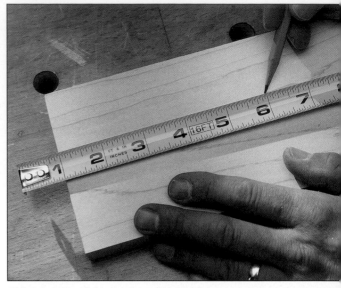

Skip the tip. **If the hook at the tip of your tape measure is worn or damaged, or if you want to be sure you're getting a precise reading, measure from the 1-in. mark instead of measuring off the metal tip. However, don't forget to subtract that 1 in. at the other end.**

12-in. and a 24-in. rule. Purchase these rules as interchangeable blades for your combination square to make your rules even more versatile. Rules are available with metric and standard graduations. A handy combination for standard is 1/8- and 1/16-in. increments on one face and 1/32- and 1/64-in. markings on the other.

Tape measures

Perhaps the most versatile and convenient—and certainly the most popular—measuring tool is the flexible tape rule, better known as the *tape measure.* Tape measures are capable of measuring long distances, yet roll up into a pocket-sized case. And since a tape is thinner than a wooden rule, you can align the tape markings flat against a workpiece to minimize errors.

Wind-up tapes, available in reels up to 100 ft., are useful when you need to measure architectural or landscape projects. The fabric or metal tapes are wound up into a plastic or metal case by cranking a small handle.

For the convenience of everyday use, *retractable tape measures* are the way to go. A good-quality tape is cupped across its width to stiffen the blade when it is extended. A hooked tip, generally with a slot to fit around nail heads, is riveted to the tip of the tape. Retractable tape measures are housed in metal or plastic cases and come in a variety of sizes and marking options for different uses. Most tape measures have layout demarcations for stud spacings (usually marked every 16 in. in red), but you can get tapes with more specialized scales for other uses, such as bricklaying.

Retractable tape measure widths range from 1/4 in. to

1 in., and common lengths vary from 3 to 30 ft. A good general-purpose size is a 16- or 20-ft.-long tape with a 3/4-in.-wide blade. Wider tapes can span greater distances but, unless you're doing carpentry where you need the length, the added weight can be unnecessarily cumbersome.

Maintenance tips:

• Use care when retracting a tape measure blade so the metal tip doesn't snap against the case. This can bend the tip out of shape, and you'll have to readjust it so it reads accurately at zero again.

• Clean metal tapes to keep dirt and debris out of the case, where they'll gum up the winding mechanisms. As you retract or wind the tape into the case, grasp the tape with a cloth that's lightly dampened with soapy water. Position a dry rag behind the cloth to dry off the tape before it enters the case.

"Synchronize" your tapes:

Different tape measures can yield conflicting readings if the angles of their metal tips differ. To synchronize tape measures, hook the tapes side by side on the end of a board, pull out a length of blade, and check to see if the measurements align. If not, carefully bend the tip on one of the tape measures until the readings match.

Calipers

Calipers are precision instruments, capable of measuring inside, outside and depth measurements in fine increments up to 1/1000 in. This degree of precision is unnecessary for rough carpentry (and most woodworking) tasks, but calipers are quite useful for sizing intricate wood joints. Measuring with a caliper can mean the difference between cutting a tenon that will bind or be loose in a mortise, and one that slides in with just enough clearance to form a tight glue joint. Calipers are also great for verifying tolerances in machine and blade setups as well as identifying saw blade thicknesses and router or drill bit diameters.

The most economical and practical caliper for shop applications is a 6-in.-capacity *vernier caliper* with a quick-action thumb clamp and a 1/128-in. scale. A vernier is a gauge consisting of two calibrated scales that slide past one another to measure fine graduations. One scale typically reads in tenths of an inch, while the other scale determines hundredths and thousandths. Align marks on both scales simultaneously to determine a given measurement.

Dial calipers are easier to read than the vernier style, because there's no need to visually align two scales. A sliding scale marks tenths of an inch, and the dial points to hundredths and thousandths positions.

Profile gauge follows contours

Composed of a row of thin, tightly-packed sliding steel or plastic needles, a *profile gauge* can reproduce the contours of complex shapes on moldings or spindles. Just press the needles on the gauge against the shape to create a mirrored profile on the back of the gauge. Use the profile gauge needles as a template for tracing the shape onto another workpiece.

How to measure with calipers

Inside measurements. **Select the caliper blades with flat edges that face away from one another. Set the blades into the opening and slide the caliper jaws apart until they press firmly against the walls of the opening. For the vernier-style caliper shown here, you'll determine the opening width by reading off two scales on the tool handle.**

Outside measurements. **Close the larger caliper jaws (those with flat edges facing one another) around a workpiece. To determine distance between the jaws on a dial caliper, read tenths of an inch off a scale on the caliper handle and hundredths/thousandths of an inch off the pointer in the dial.**

Depth measurements. **Most vernier and dial calipers have a narrow extension probe that slides out of the end of the tool handle to measure depth. Set an edge of the tool handle next to the recess, and open the caliper jaws to extend the probe. Measure depth off the vernier scales or dial just as you would for inside or outside measurements.**

Marking Tools

A. Trammel points
B. Transfer paper
C. Razor blade craft knife
D. Japanese marking knife
E. Spearpoint marking knife
F. Carpenter's pencil
G. White colored pencil
H. Mechanical pencil
I. Pounce wheel
J. Chalking pad
K. Tungsten carbide scribe
L. Spring-action center punch
M. Scratch awl
N. Dividers
O. Compass
P. Chalkline

Pencils & chalklines

For general sketching and layout in carpentry, furnituremaking and cabinetry, a standard *No. 2 pencil* is an indispensible marking tool. The No. 2 lead is soft enough that it won't dent the wood along your layout line, as harder lead can. If you expect to erase a layout line on wood, use a light touch when drawing. If your project requires finer pencil lines, use a *mechanical pencil* with replaceable leads in .5 mm and finer .3 mm lead thicknesses. Mechanical pencils maintain consistent line width and do not need sharpening.

A *carpenter's pencil* is ideally suited for framing and other rough carpentry tasks, but its fat mark is too vague for even moderately accurate furniture work. Use it in the workshop for making general reference marks when jointing, planing or aligning boards for glue-ups. A carpenter's pencil has a flat body, so it won't roll off your workbench. The lead is broad and thick to resist breaking if dropped or crammed into a pants pocket, and it is usually made of soft, dark graphite that shows up well on dark lumber. The heavy lead can withstand the rigors of marking rough lumber, where an ordinary pencil point would break. Sharpen the lead with a few strokes of a utility or pocket knife, or tack a piece of medium grit sandpaper to a flat surface for sharpening.

For darker materials like walnut or hardboard, pencil lead can be difficult to see. In these instances, a white colored pencil comes in handy. The hard ones keep their points nicely, but they transfer almost no pigment to the work surface and the lines are difficult to see. Choose one with a soft lead, and between sharpenings twirl the tip on a piece of fine sandpaper to rejuvenate the point.

Chalklines, a mainstay in carpentry and remodeling, have their woodworking applications too. Use a chalkline for snapping rough layout lines on sheet stock and wide lumber before breaking it down into smaller workpieces with a saw.

Transfer paper

Transfer paper is used to trace patterns or templates onto wood. It is coated on one side with a pressure-sensitive colored pigment (usually black) that lifts off the paper and bonds to hard surfaces. To transfer a pattern, lay the transfer paper pigment-side-down on your workpiece. Place your paper template on top of the transfer paper and trace over the outline of the pattern with a pen or pencil, applying light pressure. The pigment erases easily with a pencil eraser.

Marking knives

The best way to mark accurate layout lines on wood is with a sharp knife. A knife produces a narrower and

Marking dark worksurfaces like hardboard or walnut with a white colored pencil produces layout lines that are easier to see than pencil lines.

more precise line than a pencil or an awl, and it severs, rather than scratches or tears through, wood fibers. Use a knife to mark layout lines for chiseling or sawing to eliminate tearout next to the layout lines.

Marking knives (also called *striking knives*) are woodworking tools made specifically to mark tenon shoulders, mortises and sharp layout lines for hand sawing and chiseling. A marking knife is beveled on only one face, and the blade is ground to a point in one of three positions: at the left corner, right corner or the middle of the blade width (called *spearpoint*). Choose the blade style that allows you to pull the knife against a straight-

Transfer paper works like carbon paper for duplicating layout lines from a sketch to a workpiece. Lay your sketch over the transfer paper and tape both into position on a workpiece. Then trace along the lines of the drawing to transfer the image.

Transferring patterns with a pounce wheel

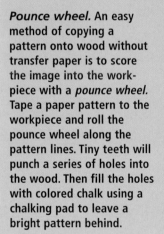
Chalking pad

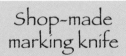

Pounce wheel. An easy method of copying a pattern onto wood without transfer paper is to score the image into the workpiece with a *pounce wheel.* Tape a paper pattern to the workpiece and roll the pounce wheel along the pattern lines. Tiny teeth will punch a series of holes into the wood. Then fill the holes with colored chalk using a chalking pad to leave a bright pattern behind.

Use a marking knife for precision work. Marking knives have a flat face to follow a straightedge, and a sharp, beveled face that slices through wood fibers to scribe very precise layout lines. A spearpoint marking knife is shown above.

Awls, punches & scribers

An *awl* is used to mark centerpoints, as when drilling pilot holes in wood. The indentation it creates also serves as a starter hole for small nails. To drive the pointed tip for marking holes, tap the wood handle of the awl with your palm. Awls can also be used to scribe layout lines that stand up better than pencil lines, but aren't as precise as lines scribed with marking knives. Keep an awl point sharp by honing it on a sharpening stone or sandpaper.

A *centerpunch* is an alternative tool for marking starter holes on hardwoods or metal. Tap manual centerpunches with a hammer to make a mark. *Automatic centerpunches* employ a spring-loaded mechanism that provides the hammering action.

To etch lines on metal or plastic, use a *scriber* with a tungsten carbide tip—it holds a point longer than an awl. The carbide tips can be replaced when they become dull.

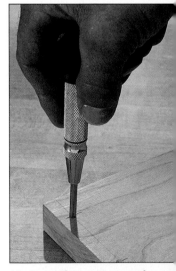

'Automatic' centerpunch. Make starter holes for drilling or nailing using a centerpunch. "Automatic" centerpunches have spring-loaded points that create deep, uniform starter holes when activated (the mode shown above is activated by pressing down on the handle).

edge with the bevel edge facing you.

To use a marking knife, place the flat back of the knife blade against a straightedge so the beveled edge faces out. Draw the knife toward yourself, keeping the blade held tightly against the straightedge.

Some marking knives come with wood handles, while others, such as Japanese marking knives, are simply a length of steel sharpened on one end without a handle.

Another handy knife to keep around the shop is a slim, pen-style craft knife with a disposable #11 razor blade. It will earn its keep many times over for cutting veneers or trimming cardboard templates.

Shop-made marking knife

Make a low-cost marking knife by grinding the teeth off an old hack saw blade. Grind the blade to a point, bevel an edge on one face, and hone the bevel sharp.

Compasses & dividers

Compass and dividers are really two names for the same tool, but with one distinction: dividers have a metal point on the ends of both legs, while a compass has a metal point on one leg to serve as a pivot, and a pencil or piece of lead on the other leg for marking. The tools can be used somewhat interchangeably.

The main purpose of a compass is to scribe perfect circles and arcs by holding one leg in place and pivoting the other leg around the first. They are equally handy for scribing a line to match an irregular contour, as when fitting countertops or shelving in a restricted area. Better compasses are precision instruments that employ a finely machined nut on a threaded rod to secure the legs in position.

Dividers are sturdy tools that feature a locknut to set the leg opening and a knurled knob for fine adjustment. Dividers come in different lengths, and some have a removable point that can be replaced with a pencil. Use these tools to transfer a dimension from plans to a workpiece, to step off equal measurements along a straight or curved line or to divide a line into a number of equal segments.

For instance, if you need to lay out a number of lines 3 in. apart along a board—as for dowel or shelf holes—set the tool legs 3 in. apart, lock the legs in position, then step off and scribe as many marks as you need.

Conversely if you have an odd distance like 11 13/16 in., and you need to divide it into seven equal parts, simply set the dividers to roughly what you think the fractional distance should be and step off the distance a few times, adjusting the setting each time, until you establish a setting that yields seven equal divisions.

Scribing with a compass. **To fit a workpiece tightly into an unsquare wall corner, set a compass wider than the gap between the workpiece and the wall and draw a line, using the pointed leg as a tracing guide. Cut along the line. The workpiece should form a perfect fit against the wall.**

Stepping off equal distances. **Set dividers to the distance you need to repeat along a layout line. Use one leg as a pivot, and scribe a short arc with the other leg. Use each arc as the starting point for successive marks. Be sure to tighten the divider securely to keep the leg opening from changing as you proceed.**

Trammel points

For drawing larger circles, use a pair of *trammel points* instead of a compass. Trammel points are sets of clamping fixtures that mount onto a wooden bar. The distance between the points determines the radius of the arc or circle being drawn. Trammel points typically are outfitted with removable metal tips, but one of the points also accepts a pencil or pencil lead. To draw a circle or arc, clamp both trammels onto a wooden bar and set the radius distance between the metal pivot point and the pencil point with a ruler. Hold the pivot point steady at the center-point of the circle or arc while you rotate the pencil around it slowly.

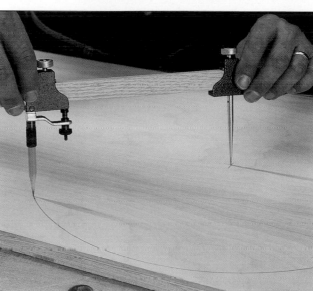

Use trammel points **for scribing larger circles. Set the distance between the trammel points to match the circle's radius. Hold the metal point in position at the center of the circle and swing the pencil point around to draw the circular layout line.**

Cutting gauge

Combination marking
& mortising gauge

Marking & Cutting Gauges

Combination gauges combine the functions of marking and mortising gauges in one tool. The post has a marking pin on one side and mortising pins on the other side. One of the two mortising pins is adjustable by way of a sliding rod that runs in a channel along the post.

Cutting gauges look like marking gauges but are outfitted with a tiny bevel-edged knife, rather than a pin, for scoring cleanly across wood grain. The knife is held in place by a brass wedge.

Marking gauges

Gauging is a woodworking term that refers to marking guide lines parallel with an edge, end or surface of a board. Gauging is used for—among other things—marking lumber to width and to thickness, marking out joints, and scribing layout lines for chamfers. Tools used for this purpose, called *gauges,* are easy to use and produce accurate, repeatable lines, enabling you to mark both sides of a joint with the same setting.

A *marking gauge* is used for marking wood with the grain or on end grain (if used across the grain it scratches or tears like its primal cousin, the awl). Roughly 8 in. long and usually made of beech or rosewood (sometimes steel), it consists of a fence (also called a *head*) that slides along a post. The fence is locked in position with a thumbscrew. A pin projects through the post near one end to serve as a scribing point. The pin should be sharp and set so the point projects out 1/16 to 1/8 in. from the face of the post.

To set a marking gauge, use a rule or the depth rod on a calipers to adjust the fence the proper distance from the pin. NOTE: *Although some marking gauges have a graduated scale on the post, don't count on its accuracy for critical work, especially as the tool gets used and worn—it's better to check your setting against a rule.* Set the thumbscrew lightly, and make fine adjustments by grasping the fence and tapping one end or the other of the post against your workbench. Then, tighten the thumbscrew securely.

A *mortising gauge* is essentially a marking gauge with two pins, rather than one. The outer pin is fixed and the inner pin is adjustable by means of a brass pull slide or a threaded rod that runs along the post.

When buying a marking gauge, choose one outfitted with a thumbscrew made of metal or wood, not plastic. Plastic screws tend to break. Unless you're doing a lot of laying out and like to keep several tools adjusted to different settings, buy a combination gauge rather than a marking gauge. This gauge has double mortise pins on one side of the post and a single marking pin on the other, which allows it to serve double-duty for both marking and mortising functions.

Methods for setting a gauge

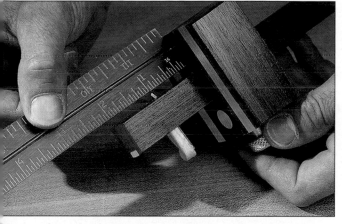

Use a rule or the depth rod on a calipers to adjust the gauge fence so it's the proper distance from the pin. Although some marking gauges have a graduated scale on the post, don't count on its accuracy for critical work, especially as the tool wears.

Use a chisel to set the distance between the pins on your mortise gauge when cutting a mortise. Select the chisel that you'll use to cut the mortise. This way, the layout lines will match the chisel width. Then adjust the gauge fence to center the mortise.

Cutting gauges

A *cutting gauge* is similar in form and use to a marking gauge, except that instead of a pin it is fitted with a small knife blade held in place in the post by a tiny brass wedge. This enables it to slice fine, crisp lines in wood, either across or with the grain.

The cutting gauge blade is pointed and beveled on one side. Typically, it is sharpened to a point like a marking knife, but the tool is more convenient to use if you sharpen the blade to a spearpoint instead so the tool can be both pushed and pulled. Reshape the blade with a metal file and sharpen it to a keen edge on a whetstone. Mount the blade with only enough of the blade protruding as is necessary to score the wood. Set the blade with the bevel facing the fence; this way the blade will tend to pull the fence tight against the work, preventing the knife from running with the grain.

On new cutting gauges, check to be sure the blade wedge fits tightly in the post mortise from top to bottom. Otherwise, the blade could shift positions while in use. Chisel the post mortise, if necessary, to improve the fit of the wedge in the mortise.

Cutting gauges are used for all kinds of marking, including laying out the width and thickness of a rabbet for butt hinges and marking out for inlaid stringing and banding in veneer work. They can even be used to slice up strips of veneer.

Marking gauge

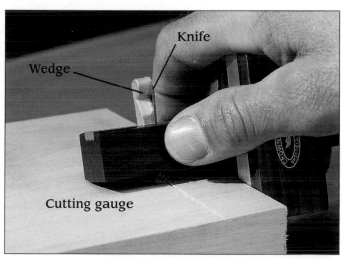

Knife

Wedge

Cutting gauge

Using marking gauges and cutting gauges. To apply a marking or cutting gauge to your workpiece, grasp the fence with your palm and fingers as though it's a baseball you're about to pitch. Extend your thumb so it backs up the cutter in the post. Tilt the tool forward slightly, and make the mark by pushing the tool. Your thumb provides forward pressure while your fingers push downward with just enough force to press the pins or blade into the wood. Keep the fence pressed tightly against the workpiece. Choose a marking gauge with pins (left) for cutting along the grain, and use a cutting gauge outfitted with a wedge and bevel-edged cutting knife (right) for scoring clean layout lines across the grain.

Squares & Straightedges

A. Try square
B. Engineer's square
C. Double square
D. Dovetail squares
E. Speed square
F. Graduated straightedge
G. Carpenter's square
H. Protractor head
I. Center-finding head
J. Combination square
K. Japanese miter square

Try square techniques

Marking layout lines. Butt the try square stock-first against an edge and draw a line along the face of the workpiece, using the blade as a guide. Use this line as the reference for marking lines on the adjoining edges and opposite face.

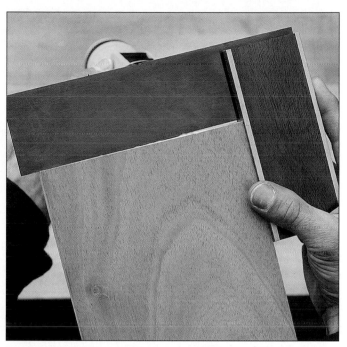

Testing for square. Set the square against a workpiece so the stock and blade rest snugly against two flat planes (edges, ends or faces). Shine a light behind the joint between the blade and the workpiece. Any gap reveals that the workpiece is not square.

Squares

The basis of carpentry, furnituremaking and cabinetry—as well as many other trades such as metalworking, glass cutting, masonry and tile work—is the 90°, or right, angle. The secondary angle is half this angle, or 45°. Since so much of construction and fabrication is centered around the rectangle, it's not surprising there are so many types of squares—devices that ensure those angles are a true 90°.

Try squares. For furnituremaking and carpentry, the traditional tool for squaring is the *try square.* It is a straightforward tool, consisting of a thin blade attached at 90° to a thick, square handle (called a *stock*). Its essential purpose is to mark right angles prior to cutting and to check (or "try") those cuts and joints for squareness. Most try squares also have ruler graduations on one or more blade edges. Because the role of squaring is so fundamental to woodworking and carpentry, the try square remains an essential shop and worksite tool. In fact, the try square has become somewhat of an icon of woodworking, and has been raised into the realm of tools-as-art. Some try squares continue to be fashioned by master craftsmen to the highest standards of function and beauty and offered to the public as limited-edition showpieces. Antique try squares are also popular collectibles.

There seems to be an endless number of aesthetic and functional variations on this simple tool. Inexpensive try squares with lightweight plastic stocks and steel blades are available for rough work. Quality models usually have a steel or brass blade and a hardwood stock (traditionally, rosewood) faced with brass to prevent wear. They should be precision-tested for accuracy, and the stocks should be riveted solidly to the blades to resist shock. Common try square sizes have blades ranging from 6 to 12 in. Most craftsmen own a try square in both 6 and 12- in. sizes. For miniature or model work, you may want a 2 or 3- in. try square.

Try squares generally have blades permanently fixed to the stocks, so they cannot be adjusted if the tool should fall out of square. For this reason, avoid dropping a try square, as the impact could throw the blade and stock out of square with one another. Some deluxe versions of the wood/brass/steel try square are made to be shockproof.

The *engineer's square* is an all-steel try square that's finely ground and tempered for extreme accuracy. It is valuable for metalworking and for various shop duties, such as squaring table saw blades and building jigs.

A variation on the wood/brass/steel try square is the *miter square,* with its blade fixed at 45° to the stock. The stock on a miter square is located about halfway along the blade so the square can be used for marking and checking both halves of a miter cut: 45° and the complementary 135° angle.

Uses for combination squares

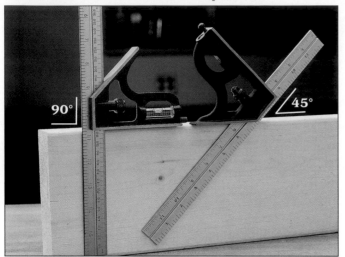

Marking 90° and 45° angles. A combination square can be used as both a try square and a miter square simply by changing the orientation of the head to the blade.

Combination squares. A major innovation in the design of the square occurred in 1879 when Leroy S. Starrett patented an invention he called the *combination square.* Starrett went on to found the renowned precision tool company that bears his name, based on the success of this brilliant device. The combination square is a reformulated try square, with features that make it more versatile. Most combination squares are composed of a blade (a metal rule inscribed with several different measurement graduations) mounted in a metal stock, also called the head, that has a 90° face and a 45° face. The head slides in a channel along the blade and can be locked in any position or removed altogether. In addition, the head contains a built-in spirit level and, on many versions, a hardened scribing pin for marking layout lines.

As well as handling the standard duties of a try square and a miter square, the combination square can serve as a depth gauge, a height gauge and, with the use of its level, as a plumb gauge. Since its blade

Checking for plumb. A combination square can be used as a level for framing work. Set the rule's blade against a vertical surface and use the spirit level in the head of the square to check the vertical member for plumb. For greatest accuracy, use a level instead for checking level and plumb.

Squaring rebates. Check rebates (such as rabbet grooves) for square using the end of the blade as a miniature square. Set the 90° face of the head against the front edge of the rebate and extend the blade until it is just short of the back of the rebate. The blade end and the back of the rebate should be parallel to one another.

Measuring depth. Set the 90° face of the square's head against a flat surface and extend the blade down until it touches the bottom of the recessed area. Measure the depth of the recess by reading off the blade where it intersects the head at the top of the recess.

Marking parallel lines. Set the combination square so the end of the blade extends past the head the same amount as the distance you want the parallel line to be from the edge of the workpiece. Tighten the head on the blade. Hold a pencil against the end of the blade and slide the square and pencil together along the board.

length is adjustable, you can team it with a pencil to form a marking gauge for scribing a line parallel to an edge. The tool also can be disassembled into its basic components to provide a ruler and a small level. And if all that isn't enough, you can purchase combination square accessories that slide onto the blade, such as a center head that can locate the

Choosing a combination square

The combination square is such an adaptable tool, you may find it's the only square you need for shop work. The popularity of this tool means there is one available in every price range, with an accompanying range of qualities. The least expensive models, some with plastic heads, would be suitable for non-critical rough work. For more intricate work, only the higher-end precision tools have suitable tolerances. Because you'll come to depend on the tool, a top-quality combination square is a wise investment.

The most basic (and most useful) model has a 12-in.-long blade—but look for one with an interchangeable 24-in. blade that can be mounted in the same head. Choose a square with blades marked in eighths, sixteenths and thirty-secondths increments.

A good combination square has a tempered steel rule blade with machined (not printed) graduations and either a plain-ground finish or satin chrome plating that makes the graduations easier to read. Chrome plating also makes the rule more rust-resistant. The head should be of cast iron or hardened, forged steel. Squares are available with blades ranging in length from 4 to 24 in. Square heads are sized proportionately to match the rule.

center of a circular workpiece, and a protractor head that can be swiveled to any angle.

Double squares. A *double square* is a cross between a try square and a combination square, used mostly for small jobs. Like a combination square, the head slides along a graduated steel blade and can be removed for complete access to the blade. However, the head on a double square is fixed at 90° to the blade, so it can't measure or produce 45° layout lines.

Specialty heads for combination squares

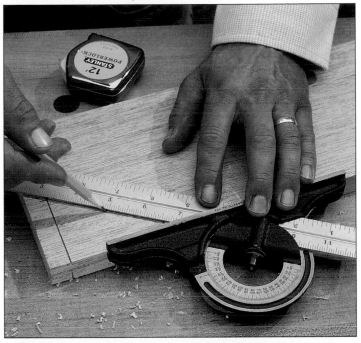

Protractor head. **For drawing or verifying angles other than 90° or 45°, the protractor head swivels and clamps the blade at any angle within a 180° range.**

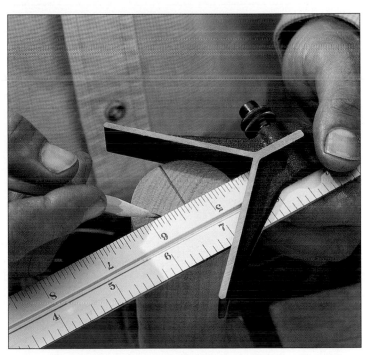

Center-finding head. **The center-finding head forms a 90° inside angle and holds the blade so the blade bisects the head at its midpoint. Its purpose is to find the center of a circle, such as the end of a large dowel or spindle. To use the head, insert the rule and rest the circular workpiece inside the crook of the head. Draw several lines across the workpiece along the blade, turning the workpiece a quarter turn or so for each line. The intersection of the lines marks the center of the circle.**

Carpenter's squares. The carpenter's square, also called a framing square or a rafter square, is an L-shaped right angle of flat steel or aluminum with embossed graduations in ⅛- or 1/16-in. increments. Since it can lie flat, a carpenter's square is a great layout tool, much like a drafting triangle. The most common size has a 2-in.-wide, 24-in.-long side—known as the body—and a 1½-in.-wide, 16-in.-long side—called the tongue. The large size of this tool is necessary when working with long framing lumber and full-sized sheets of plywood.

Despite its simple form, this is a truly versatile tool for building construction, as you might guess from its various names. As well as checking the squareness of inside and outside corners, a carpenter's square can simplify a whole slew of mathematical tasks—including laying out numerous angles, calculating rafter work, and marking rise and run layouts on stair stringers. There are also assorted tables and formulas marked on the face of the square to simplify carpentry mathematics even further. In fact there are so many things you can do with this tool that it usually comes with an instruction booklet when you buy one.

Dovetail squares. The dovetail square makes quick work of marking angles for cutting dovetail pins and tails. Usually made of aluminum or brass, this square provides a template for the common 1:6 ratio angle for softwoods and 1:8 ratio for hardwoods. There are several different dovetail square designs but they all do basically the same thing. Some are sold as combination tools with both ratio angles on the same square or as a set of squares outfitted with one ratio angle on each tool.

Buttons

Carpenter's square. **Graduations along both the body and tongue of a carpenter's square make it possible to establish two measurements at once, as when determining the rise and run of stair layouts on a stair stringer. Brass buttons can be attached to the tool edges to speed the layout process.**

Dovetail square. **There's no need to calculate the correct angle for dovetail pins and tails if you use a dovetail square. Simply set the lip of the square against the workpiece and mark a line along the preset 1:6 or 1:8 ratio angle of the square.**

Speed squares

Speed squares were designed with carpentry in mind. Essentially a 45° triangle, this square is marked with roof pitch graduations to serve as a quick reference for cutting rafters and other angles for rough framing.

A device variously called a rafter layout square, protractor square, or angle square—but more commonly known by the trade names speed square or quick square—is a standard layout tool for carpentry. It comes in steel, plastic or aluminum versions and is shaped like a right triangle, with a perpendicular flange along one edge to butt up against a workpiece like a try square. Speed squares are used as both rafter squares and protractors, thanks to various scales printed on the body of the tool. Some carpenters use them as circular saw guide fences for cutting the ends of boards square. The 45° and 90° edges also make speed squares handy for setting blade angles on a table saw. Most speed squares come with instruction booklets to explain their many scale features.

Straightedges

An accurate steel straightedge is a wise investment for anyone interested in pursuing fine woodworking or cabinetry. It will serve as the shop standard of reference for flatness and straight lines. A straightedge is the tool to use for checking the flatness of cast machine surfaces; setting the infeed and outfeed tables and knives on your jointer; testing the flatness of your hand plane soles; spotting wind or twist in a board; drawing or scribing straight lines for layout; cutting veneers; and a multitude of other tasks.

True straightedges are not the same as straight rules that can be purchased at any home center or hardware store for a few dollars. Rather, they are precision-ground, hefty machinist's tools (the thickness of a 3- or 4-ft. straightedge made of tool steel is almost ¼ in). Some straightedges come with numbered graduations stamped into the metal, but many are simply beveled on one or both long edges. Good-quality steel straightedges will be guaranteed flat on edge to within a few thousandths of an inch.

If investing in a good straightedge, buy a 4-ft.-long model that's lengthy enough to stretch across table saw and jointer tables or to verify longer straight lines and flat surfaces in layouts. While not cheap, with careful use and good care, a good straightedge will last a lifetime. In addition to the 4-ft. straightedge, you may want to look into purchasing a 2-ft. blade for your combination square to serve as a shorter straightedge for smaller jobs. Considering the cost of these tools, pull

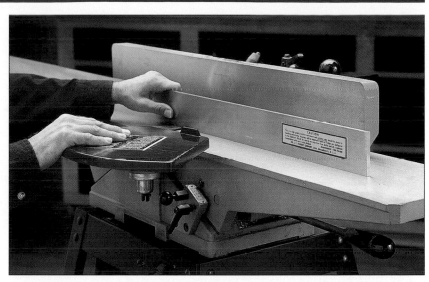

A precision steel straightedge can introduce a new level of accuracy to your woodworking. Use it for testing and adjusting stationary tool beds, as well as for any layout task that requires you to scribe absolutely straight, flat lines.

your precision straightedges out only for those instances where achieving absolute accuracy and flatness is a must. Build several long shop-made straightedges for everyday use (See *Tip,* below).

Take great care to avoid dropping steel straightedges on hard surfaces. Once an edge is dinged, you compromise the accuracy of the tool. Store a straightedge in its original box, or secure it with tape to a wooden backer board that is wider and longer than the straightedge to protect the edges and ends.

Since these tools are made of unpainted raw steel, make sure your straightedge stays dry, and apply an occasional coat of light machine oil or wax to protect it from rusting.

Tip: Shop-built straightedges

Some form of straightedge is essential in any workshop. Buy a precision steel straightedge to keep on hand as a reference tool. Then build several shop-made straightedges, using your steel straightedge to test the shop-built versions. Use ¾-in.-thick medium-density fiberboard, plywood or stable hardwood to make your own straightedges in several sizes (4, 6 and 8 ft. are common lengths). The straightedges should be at least 3 in. wide so they'll stay flat along the edges.

Improve the accuracy and durability of your shop-made straightedges by covering the faces and edges with plastic laminate.

Cut your own straightedge guides and test them with a quality steel straightedge before and after covering them with plastic laminate.

Bevel Gauges

A. Cast aluminum & steel bevel gauge with locking screw in the end of the handle

B. Bevel gauge with brass-bound rosewood handle & wing nut lock knob

C. Bevel gauge with high-impact plastic handle

D. Steel bevel gauge with knurled lock knob

Bevel gauges

Bevel gauges, also called *sliding bevels* or *sliding T-bevels,* are essentially modified try squares with blades that can be adjusted to any angle. These simple gauges are extremely valuable when you need to replicate an angle from one workpiece to another or to a tool. Bevel gauges also are handy for laying out cutting lines when cutting base and cove molding. And they make quick work of marking repeated angles, such as marking pins and tails for dovetail joints. A bevel gauge is a useful set-up tool for establishing blade angles on your table or band saw or bit angles for portable drills and drill presses.

Bevel gauge blades, usually made of steel or brass, are machined with a longitudinal slot so the blade can slide along a bolt in the handle stock and form angles on either side of the handle. Blades can be locked to

any angle by tightening a wing-nut, lever, screw or knurled knob on the end of the bolt. The blade folds conveniently away into the handle when not in use.

Handles are made of high-impact plastic, wood, metal or a combination of wood and metal. As with the try square, higher-end bevel gauges often feature fine and exotic woods such as rosewood. Some tool makers also fabricate the blade out of wood. Bevel gauges come in different lengths. Longer blades are generally more useful, since the blade can provide a longer reference line for marking. But smaller 3- or 4-in. blade sizes are handy for working in confined spaces—a typical problem in restoration or remodeling situations.

To replicate an angle, set the gauge handle against one surface and pivot the blade until it rests against the adjacent angle surface, then secure the blade. Use the gauge in this locked position to transfer the angle. Be careful not to jar the blade when transferring the angle.

For those instances when you know the exact degree of angle you need, use a steel protractor as a reference for setting the blade angle on your bevel gauge. Set the bevel gauge against the protractor, align the blade to the proper angle on the protractor, and tighten.

Something to be aware of when choosing a bevel gauge is the projection of the locking device. On some models the wing nut or tightening lever extends beyond the edges of the handle when it's tightened and could interfere with some set-ups. An easy solution is to buy a bevel gauge with a knurled knob or screw tightener instead.

The simplicity of these tools makes them equally accurate, from one tool to the next, regardless of style or blade and handle composition. Important attributes to look for are a secure locking mechanism and a straight blade and handle. The blade should remain sheathed in the handle when not in use.

Marking dovetails with a bevel gauge. Use a bevel gauge for marking repetitive angles such as dovetail layouts. Bevel gauges are a suitable alternative to dovetail squares because they can be set to any angle and locked in position. Be sure to tighten the blade securely so the angle doesn't shift while you mark layout lines.

Setting miter angles for cutting molding

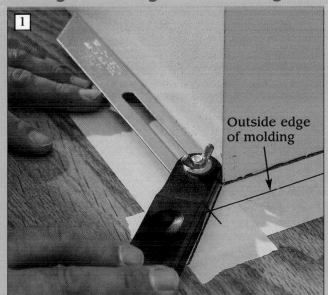

Outside edge of molding

Setting miter angles. Most walls do not meet at a 90° angle, which can make miter-cutting difficult when installing base molding. One solution is to lay masking tape on the floor on either side of the corner and mark reference lines on the tape that represent the thickness of the molding you are installing. Extend the reference lines so they intersect at the corner. Set a bevel gauge blade against the wall and pivot the handle until it aligns with the intersected base molding reference lines. Lock the blade. Transfer this angle to your miter saw to set the miter angle, and cut the molding.

Levels & plumb bobs

When building furniture and smaller objects, squares and rules are basically the only tools you need to establish that angles between parts are correct and that the overall project is square. But when building large structures such as a house, fence or deck, however, you'll need to beef up your measuring and marking tool arsenal a bit. You'll need some absolute references to determine true vertical (plumb) and horizontal (level): you'll need at least one level and a good plumb bob.

Levels. In addition to larger construction projects, levels are essential for installing cabinetry or bookshelves. Any kind of stationary machinery or appliance, from power jointers to washing machines, work more efficiently if they are leveled.

Traditional levels contain one or more glass or plastic tubes, called vials, that contain liquid and a trapped air bubble. The vials are mounted in the frame of the level to be precisely parallel or perpendicular to the edges of the level. Each vial is marked with two lines near the center. When the air bubble floats between these lines, the tool is said to be level or plumb, relative to the surface of the earth. Most levels have three vials: one mounted along the center of the tool to measure level readings with the tool held horizontally and two other vials located near each end to test for plumb when the tool is held vertically. Some levels also contain a vial mounted diagonally at a 45° angle to help establish this angle.

To use a level, set a long edge against the surface to be checked and read off the appropriate vial. Always position yourself squarely in front of the vial to determine the position of the bubble. Just as with other measuring tools, levels are subject to parallax distortion; taking a visual reading from the side will render an inaccurate reading.

Levels come in a variety of different sizes and

Levels & Plumb Bobs

A. **Two-ft. aluminum I-beam carpenter's level**

B. **Four-ft. brass-bound mahogany carpenter's level**

C. **Torpedo level**

D. **16-in. high-impact plastic carpenter's level**

E. **Two-ft. aluminum carpenter's level with electronic readout and spirit plumb vial**

F. **Steel plumb bob**

G. **Brass plumb bob with removable steel tip**

H. **Aluminum plumb bob**

Hand Tool Heritage:
Stratton Spirit Level

Spirit levels that we know and use today were not commonly adopted by the building trades until early in the 19th century, although they were invented almost 200 years earlier.

Antique level collectors are constantly hunting for small levels that are still in the original box—often made of exotic wood with decorative brass trim. Small levels usually command the highest prices. Distinctive filigreed iron levels made by the Davis & Cook Level Co. are the most desirable of all spirit levels.

Common materials used for manufacturing spirit levels included cherry, rosewood, laminated mahogany, boxwood, aluminum, pressed steel, iron and even sheet metal and sugar pine. Spirit levels have ranged in length from 4-in. pocket and line levels to 5- and 6-ft. mason and railroad levels. Some have built in peep sights, used to establish grades and batter boards; miner's levels even have a built-in light.

The Stanley Rule and Level Co. and the Stratton Brothers Level Co. have been two of the largest spirit level producers in the United States. The Stratton Brothers Level Co. produced the carpenter's spirit level shown here. It is a 10-in.-long, fully brass-bound mahogany level. Patented in 1870, the plumb spirit is located on one end.

Tip: Checking & adjusting level calibration

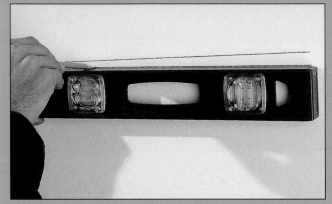 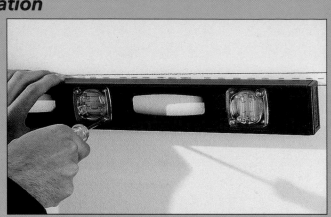

Calibrating a level. Don't assume that a level right out of the carton will actually produce level lines. Unless the vials are perfectly parallel to the edges of the level, all readings are inaccurate. To check the calibration, hold a level against a wall and shift it until the center vial reads level. Draw a line along the top edge of the level. Then, flip the level end for end and align one end of the level with the line you just drew. Pivot the level until the center vial reads level. If the level is correctly calibrated, the top edge of the level should align with the reference line on the wall. If it doesn't, draw a second line like the first to mark this new position. Neither pencil line is level. Rather, the distance between the lines is double the amount the level is out of calibration. Draw a third dashed line midway between the other two lines to establish true level. Set the level along this dashed line, loosen the set screws that hold the center vial in place, and shift the vial until it reads level. Tighten the screws. To adjust the end vials for plumb, follow the same procedure, holding the level vertically on the wall instead of horizontally and reading off the end vials. Flip the level edge for edge instead of end for end.

styles, depending upon the intended application of the tool. Better-quality levels are fitted with removable vials that can be replaced if they become damaged or fall out of calibration. Some levels also have adjustable vial holders that can be reset if the vials get jarred out of alignment (See *Tip,* above). Carpenter's levels and torpedo levels are the two types we're most accustomed to seeing, but a wealth of specialty levels, such as line levels and post levels, have been created—mostly for exterior construction work. Electronic and digital levels are becoming increasingly popular with contractors. As the prices of these new versions of the old tool come down, many weekend do-it-yourselfers are acquiring them as well.

Carpenter's levels are the all-purpose choice for larger construction and landscaping tasks. They come in 2-, 4- and 6- and 8-ft. lengths. Two- and 4-ft. sizes are most common for general duty. Carpenter's levels have long been and continue to be available in hardwoods like mahogany, cherry or teak, bound with brass edges and ends for durability. Some are even made of cast iron. However, lightweight aluminum I-beam levels are the most common and reasonably priced carpenter's levels today.

Torpedo levels are tapered on either end and about 9 in. long—a handy length for working in tight quarters. They come with aluminum, wood or plastic bodies and usually contain a 45° vial. Some torpedoes are outfitted with magnetized edges and are popular with plumbers, who affix them to cast-iron or galvanized pipes to establish slopes for drain and waste pipes.

Line levels, just a few inches long, are made of lightweight plastic and contain one vial. These inexpensive levels are hung beneath mason's string lines for landscaping, masonry and other construction applications.

Post levels have plastic bodies that form a 90° corner to wrap around two faces of vertical posts or framing members. These levels are equipped with a vial on either face and one on the corner to ensure that fence posts are both level and plumb. Most styles are held in position with a rubber band so your hands are free to shift the post while setting it in the ground.

Plumb lines & plumb bobs

When something is plumb, it describes a vertical line directed toward the gravitational center of the earth. A *plumb line* is a length of cord outfitted with a pointed weight called a *plumb bob* on one end.

To use a plumb line, tie the cord to a support point (for example, a nail) and suspend the plumb bob to within about ¼ in. of the surface below the suspension point. Allow the bob to swing freely and come to rest. Mark the position of the bob's point. The line formed by the string from the support point to the tip of the plumb bob represents *true plumb* in three dimensions.

A plumb line is used in constructing foundations, framing walls and in surveying. However, plumb lines are also useful around the house and shop. For instance, you can suspend a plumb bob to establish a vertical line on a wall for aligning decorative objects, stencils or sheets of wallpaper. You can also use a plumb line in conjunction with a carpenter's square to determine a level line when a level isn't available: Hang the plumb line near a solid vertical surface, like a wall. Once the bob comes to rest, mark the line formed by the plumb line on the wall. Be careful not to shift the plumb line as you mark the reference line. Then, align one long edge of the carpenter's square with the line you drew and mark along one of the horizontal edges of the square to create a level line.

Although the word "plumb" comes from the latin word for *lead,* modern plumb bobs are usually made of brass, steel, aluminum or cast iron. Since the pointed tips can become damaged or bent from use, some bobs have replaceable tips. Plumb bobs are available in a variety of weights. Heavier ones are intended for longer plumb lines or for outdoor use, particularly in windy conditions. For most indoor uses you shouldn't need one heavier than 2 or 3 ounces.

Hand Tool Heritage: Plumb Bobs

(A) "Perfect" shaped, 4¾-in.-long, 1⅝-in.-dia. plumb bob weighs 22 ounces. Made of bronze, it has a removable steel point. (B) "Transitional" shaped, 4⅛-in.-long, 2-in.-dia. plumb bob weighs 30 ounces. Composed of brass, this bob has a steel point and removable cap. (C) "Turnip" shaped, brass 8-in.-long, 3¼-in.-dia. plumb bob weighs 8 pounds, 2 ounces. Plumb bobs weighing over 6 pounds are sometimes referred to as "bridge bobs."

Plumb bobs have been an essential building tool for centuries. Egyptians used stone plumb bobs as early as 2600 B.C. Since that time, plumb bobs have been fabricated from a variety of metals, ivory and wood. At one time, plumb bobs were hollowed out and filled with mercury to increase their weight without changing their overall size.

More than 150 patents have been issued for plumb bobs in the United States. The plumb bobs' long history and extensive variety of sizes, shapes, materials and uses have been of interest to antique tool collectors for years.

Sawing

Sawing is the first step in shaping a piece of wood into a finished project. Obviously, electric power saws are the best cutting tools for many operations, especially when you need to make a number of repetitive cuts. But hand saws still occupy an important place in the workshop. They're quieter, safer, less expensive and more portable than power saws. And since your strength alone supplies power to a hand saw, you have complete control over the cut, making possible some very fine work that simply can't be done with power tools.

When making curved cuts, a coping, fret or bow saw cuts just about as fast as a power scroll saw or jig saw. Sometimes it's easier to grab a hand saw for an awkward cut in large, unwieldy work than trying to figure out supports and jigs to accomplish the same task with a power saw. But for many woodworkers, the most important reason to use hand saws is the simple pleasure experienced by making a cut by hand. Once you master hand saw technique, a good, sharp saw is a real pleasure.

When you consider new hand saws, it's surprising how primitive these tools look. Hand saws have been around for centuries in one form or another, but their basic function has stayed largely the same. Even in these *high-tech* times, in which much of what is produced quickly becomes obsolete, it's hard to improve on the elegant simplicity of hand saws.

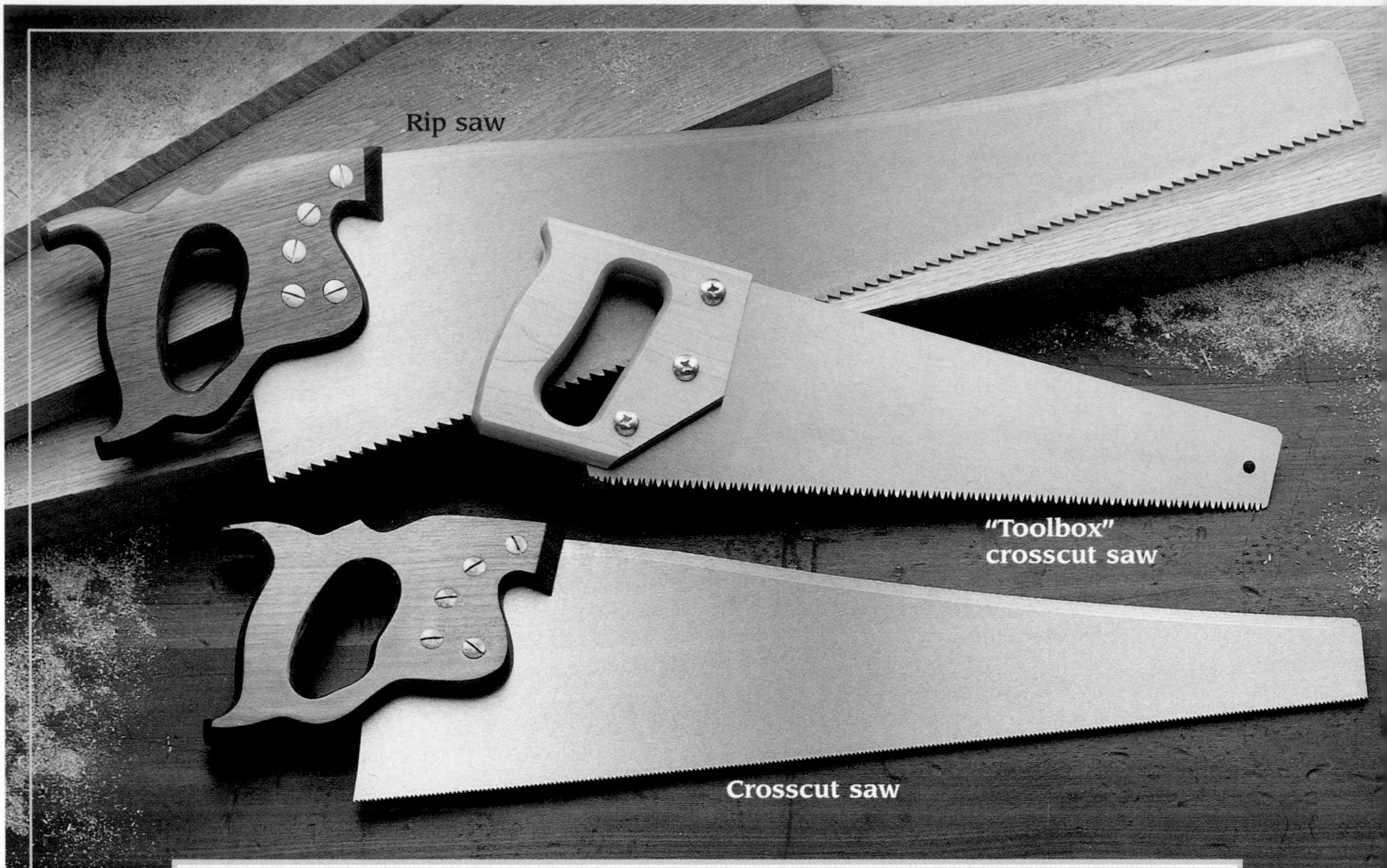

Rip saw

"Toolbox" crosscut saw

Crosscut saw

Crosscut & Rip Saws

Rip saws have long blades designed to make quick, clean cuts that follow the grain of the board.

Crosscut saws have shorter teeth with beveled cutting edges that slice through the wood fibers when cutting across the grain of the board.

"Toolbox" saws are all-purpose crosscut saws sized to fit into standard toolboxes. They're suitable for most wood cutting tasks encountered in general carpentry.

Crosscut & Rip Saws

Crosscut and rip saws are more widely used and better-known than other styles of hand saws. At first glance, it can be hard to distinguish a crosscut saw from a rip saw because their overall shapes are quite similar. But a close inspection of the saw teeth will reveal the main difference between the two types. Because they are designed to cut wood quickly and aggressively along the grain, rip saws have fewer, larger teeth than crosscut saws. Crosscut saws cut with smaller teeth, sharpened like knives, that slice cleanly through wood fibers when cutting across the grain.

Most hand saws are characterized using two measures: the length of the blade and the size and spacing of the saw teeth. Tooth size is noted in one of two ways: number of teeth per inch (*tpi*), measured at the low points between teeth (called *gullets*); or points per inch (*ppi*), measured from tooth-tip to tooth-tip.

Rip saw blades tend to be longer than crosscut saw blades (typically 26 in.) and usually have from 4 to 6 *ppi*. Longer blades with larger teeth require you to take fewer strokes to complete a cut. Shorter blades are preferred for finer, more controlled work. Crosscut saws range in length from 24 to 26 in. and typically have 8 to 12 ppi. Shorter versions of crosscut saws, called "Toolbox saws," can have blades as short as 15 in., allowing them to fit into a standard toolbox.

As general-purpose tools, crosscut saws outperform rip saws. The smaller, finer teeth produce smoother cuts on most woods, including plywood, which is prone to tearout. Crosscut saws can also do a respectable job of rip-cutting, although they're not as fast as rip saws. If you cut mostly soft framing lumber, however, rip saws can handle ripping or crosscutting with superior speed.

Because the teeth are designed to cut on the push stroke, both rip saw blades and crosscut saw blades need to be stiff. Otherwise, the blades would buckle in the saw cut. Manufacturers stiffen the blades through a process of hammering and cooling the metal (called *tensioning*). A properly tensioned saw blade should remain straight, without flexing, when the saw is held out horizontally.

Quality saws are forged so the line of the "spine" forms a very shallow, concave curve. This improves the saw's balance. The blades on top-dollar saws often are *taper-ground,* so the blade is actually thinner near the back than at the cutting edge. Taper grinding helps prevent the blade from binding in the saw kerf.

Rip saw teeth are made to to plow aggressively through wood, like tiny chisels, and are filed straight across to provide maximum cutting surface. Crosscut saw teeth, on the other hand, are filed with edges that bevel (usually 45° to 60°) in alternating directions so they slice through wood cleanly as they cut across the grain (See illustrations, below).

Rip saw and crosscut saw teeth have a *set:* that is, they are bent away from the line of the blade in opposite directions. Set determines the width of the saw *kerf* (the slit that the saw blade makes in the workpiece). If the kerf is wider than the thickness of the blade, the blade is less likely to bind as it cuts.

A saw with sharp, properly set teeth requires much less effort than a dull saw. If your saw bogs down in a cut, it may need to be sharpened; binding or buckling may mean the teeth need to be reset (See page 155).

Anatomy of a crosscut saw

Blade back may be flat or concave and even ground to a thinner taper than the cutting edge to minimize binding.

Fasteners on better-quality saws are machine screws fitted into tubular nuts to ensure a tight fit between the blade & the handle.

Handle typically made of a hardwood like beech or maple but may also be high-impact plastic.

Heel

Saw tooth styles & sizing

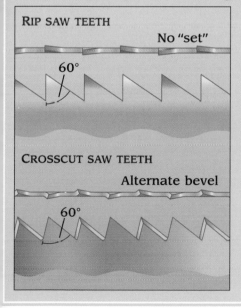

RIP SAW TEETH

No "set"

60°

CROSSCUT SAW TEETH

Alternate bevel

60°

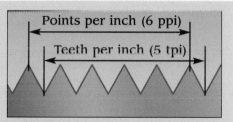

Points per inch (6 ppi)

Teeth per inch (5 tpi)

Saw teeth bodies for both rip saws and crosscut saws form 60° angles, but notice that the leading edges of ripsaw teeth are perpendicular to the blade edge, while the leading edges of crosscut teeth pitch back about 15° from vertical. Rip teeth are filed straight across so they're cutting edges are perpendicular to the blade, while the cutting edges of crosscut teeth are filed at 30° angles to the blade. Saw teeth are measured in points per inch (ppi) or teeth per inch (tpi). A blade's ppi will exceed the tpi by one.

Saw buying tip

Before buying a rip saw or crosscut saw, make sure the handle is firmly fastened to the blade. The best saws use heavy machine screws attached to tubular nuts that pass through the blade and handle. Avoid saws with handles and blades that are attached with wood screws alone. Wood screws may allow the blade to loosen in the handle over time.

How to cut with a hand saw

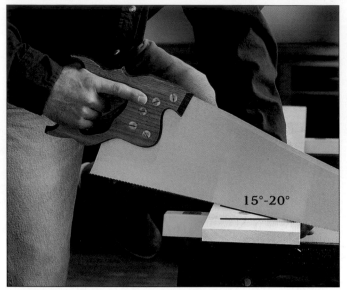

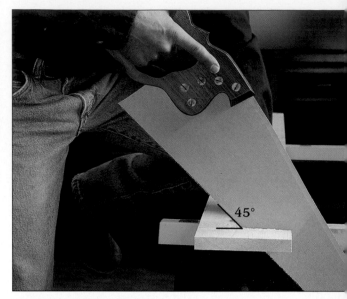

1 Grip the saw like a pistol with your index finger extended straight along the handle. Cut a starter notch, guiding the blade with the thumb of your free hand. Hold the saw at a low angle (15 to 20°) to cut the notch, then move your thumb away.

2 Raise the blade in the starter notch and begin to cut with long, smooth saw strokes. Use your knee to steady the work-piece. For crosscuts, as we show here, saw at about a 45° angle to the workpiece. For rip-cuts, saw at a higher, 60° angle.

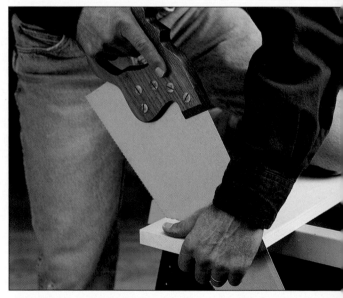

3 Inspect your cuts for square using a try square or speed square. As you gain experience, you'll eventually develop a "feel" in your wrist for making square cuts.

4 When you near the end of a cut, reach around the blade with your free hand to support the waste piece. Finish up the cut with light strokes to avoid chipping out the end of the cut.

Using hand saws

While it may look simple, sawing wood with a hand saw is certainly not an intuitive activity. However, with a little practice and a sharp saw, you'll quickly get the feel of efficient and accurate sawing.

Supporting your workpiece. Before you start cutting, make sure the workpiece is well supported and held securely in a vise, on sawhorses or on the workbench. Many hand tool users find it helpful to use low

sawhorses (24 to 28 in. high) so they can position themselves squarely over the workpiece, using a knee as a hold-down. Standing directly over the workpiece gives you a good line of sight down the blade and max-imizes your range of motion for each saw stroke. How-ever you set up your workpiece, allow enough clear space below the work so the blade toe doesn't strike the floor at the bottom of the stroke. As you saw, antic-pate the weight of the waste piece as you near the end of the cut and be sure to support it adequately so it doesn't break off prematurely and splinter the workpiece. To accomplish this, you may need to shift the position of the sawhorses partway through the cut, especially when making a long cut or removing a large, unwieldy waste piece.

> Sawing should be relaxed, not stressful. Don't try to break any speed records or attempt to rush the cut with short, hard strokes. Hurried cutting will only tire you out and make it difficult to keep the cut straight.

Grip the saw handle as if you're shaking hands, grasping firmly but not too tightly. Extend your forefinger along the handle to help guide the saw and keep it aligned with your hand and forearm.

Starting the cut. If you're working on a fine woodworking project, do not try to cut right to the cutting line with a handsaw. You'll get the most accurate results by cutting just on the waste side of the line, then planing down to the cutting line. For rough carpentry tasks, a cut made exactly at the cutting line is more typical. If you're sawing with your right hand, grasp the board on the left side of the blade, using your left hand, and place your left thumb against the side of the blade where it meets the wood to act as a guide for getting the cut started. Draw the saw backward with a couple of short strokes, near the heel of the blade, to score a starter notch. Move your thumb out of the way before you begin sawing.

An accurate start is critical to a successful cut. If the saw blade strays out of line when you begin the cut, angle it slightly to get it back on track as you saw, but be aware that too much arc in the cut will cause the blade to bind. Make the first few strokes with the blade at a low (15° to 20°) angle to the wood, so you have an unobstructed view of the cutting line.

Making the cut. After the initial notch is made and the blade is tracking correctly, begin to raise the blade to a normal cutting angle. For ripping, saw at about a 60° angle relative to the wood; for crosscutting, try to maintain a shallower, 45° angle. As you saw, make sure the blade is cutting perpendicular to the workpiece. Check the cut for square by occasionally positioning a try square or speed square against the blade and the workpiece.

If you are a right-handed sawyer, keep the waste side of the board on your right, so you are looking down the left side of the blade at the cut line. Blow off the sawdust when it accumulates to keep the cutting line visible. For best control of the saw cut, keep your right eye, shoulder, elbow, arm and the saw in the same vertical plane.

Tips for rip-cutting

Clamp a straightedge cutting guide along your layout line to guide the saw blade as you cut. A straight piece of 2× lumber will provide enough bearing surface to guide the saw.

Insert a wood shim in the kerf behind the blade to keep the saw kerf from closing, which can cause the blade to bind in the cut. You'll find this tip particularly helpful when making long rip-cuts and when cutting wavy-grained or wet lumber.

Saw with smooth, long, even strokes, using almost the full length of the blade to get the most out of each stroke. Keep your arm motions fluid. Apply light pressure on the push stroke, letting the saw teeth do the hard work of cutting. Relax your arm on the return stroke, since the return provides little cutting action. If the blade binds, don't force it to continue cutting. Back the saw up in the kerf, realign it, and begin making a straighter cut, using light strokes.

As you near the end of the cut, reach around and support small waste pieces with your free hand to keep them from breaking off. If the waste piece is large, you may need to provide additional support from beneath with another sawhorse. If you're making a stopped cut, rather than cutting all the way through a workpiece, draw the last few strokes with the blade held vertically so the cut ends squarely. Use very light pressure and small strokes to finish the cut.

Hand Tool Heritage: Crosscut & Rip Saws

25-in. *Disston* rip saw

Disston rip saw with thumb hole

26-in. *Atkins* crosscut saw

The saw pictured at the top of the photo is a 25-in. Disston rip saw, made between 1840 and 1855. It is sharpened to 5½ points at the toe, and widened to 4½ points at the heel. The closed handle is carved from applewood and is fastened to the blade with three brass screws and a brass, Henry Disston & Sons, medallion screw. The blade features a small nib near the toe, which is characteristic of early crosscut and rip saws. The purpose of the nib is the subject of much speculation among tool collectors: one leading theory holds that the nibs were intended to be used to score cutting lines. The closed-handle Disston rip saw in the lower left of the photo above features a thumb hole at the top of the handle. Disston patented the closed handle, thumb recess design in 1874. The third saw above (below right) is an E. C. Atkins & Co. 26-in. crosscut saw.

Prior to the 17th century, hand saw blades weren't tensioned in the forging process as they are today, so saws required wooden or metal stretcher frames to keep the blades from buckling. Advances in steel technology during the mid-18th century allowed toolmakers to begin forging stiffer, non-reinforced crosscut and rip saw blades that resemble the modern hand saws we use today.

Until 1855, the steel used in American saw blades was imported from England. Then, Henry Disston of Philadelphia built the first crucible steel melting plant in this country for producing saw-quality steel. The company went on to become the largest saw maker in the world.

Tenon saw

Gent's saw
(offset handle)

Dovetail saw
(open handle)

Slotting saw

Dovetail saw
(straight handle)

Back Saws

Tenon saws are the general-purpose members of the back saw family, capable of cutting larger tenons and miters smoothly and accurately.

Dovetail saws are shorter, narrower versions of tenon saws that feature smaller crosscut teeth perfect for fine dovetail and tenon work.

Gent's saws perform the same joint-cutting functions as dovetail saws, but have slightly larger teeth for faster cutting. Some gent's saws have a reversible offset handle for cutting into restricted areas where an in-line handle would interfere with the work.

Slotting saws, the smallest back saws, have ultra-fine crosscut teeth for cutting miniature wood joints.

Back saws

Back saws are fundamental to accomplishing fine woodworking with hand tools. The name *back saw* refers to a family of saws designed primarily to cut dovetails, tenons and miters. Unlike the tapered blade style of crosscut saws and rip saws, back saws have rectangular blades with stiff, reinforced spines, and most have fine crosscut-style teeth with minimal tooth set. Some back saws have teeth cut in a modified rip-tooth style, but the tooth set is still slight to keep the kerf narrow. The number of teeth per inch varies from 12 to more than 30 tpi, depending upon the kind of work each saw is intended to do. Saws with higher tpi have the smallest teeth so they produce the smoothest (and slowest) cuts.

Back saw blades are thinner than either crosscut or rip saw blades, so they need to be reinforced with a brass or steel spine that extends the full length of the blade. Without a spine, back saw blades, which cut on the push stroke, would surely buckle. The spine does limit the depth of cut a back saw can make, but the blades are plenty wide to suit most joint-cutting tasks.

Deep cuts that the spine would interfere with are better done with larger saws with more aggressive teeth.

Back saw handles vary in style, from closed or open-handled *pistol* grips on the larger tenon and dovetail saws, to the straight, in-line handle style employed with gent's saws and slotting saws. Particular handle styles will vary by manufacturer, but pistol grip handles tend to be used with saws suited for larger cutting tasks, while in-line handles are outfitted on saws with fine teeth for slow, precise cutting.

Using back saws

Learning to use a back saw skillfully is not difficult, but it does require a little practice. Back sawing tech-

Proper back sawing stance and technique. Set up your workpiece so your forearm and hand are aligned with the saw blade as you cut. If you are right-handed, stand with your right foot in back of your left. Support the workpiece in a bench hook (shown here) or in a vise. Saw in a piston-like motion, keeping the blade parallel to the benchtop.

Bench hook

nique differs from cross-cutting or rip-cutting in that the saw remains horizontal throughout the cut, rather than being angled downward. Cutting on a horizontal plane increases the number of teeth in contact with the workpiece during the stroke, which actually slows down cutting speed. However, the weight of the blade spine decreases the amount of downward pressure you need to apply on the saw. This way, you can grip the saw gently and concentrate your efforts on guiding the saw, rather than powering it.

Preparing to cut. Secure your workpiece firmly at a comfortable working height. How high depends on your own height: Standard workbench height should be suitable for most people. Add blocking beneath the legs of the bench if you need to raise the workpiece to a more comfortable height. Position the workpiece so your forearm will stay aligned with the saw as you cut.

When laying out your saw cuts (especially for dovetails and tenons, where tolerances are critical) score your layout lines with a marking knife or a utility knife. Clamp the workpiece in a vise when you need to make tenon or dovetail cuts on the end. If cutting tenon shoulders or rabbets, secure the workpiece against a *bench hook* to keep the workpiece from shifting as you cut (See photo, left, and illustration, next page). A bench hook also provides a backer board beneath the workpiece so you don't cut into the benchtop. To use a bench hook, press down on the workpiece with your free hand. Set the bench lip against the front edge of the workbench.

Making the cut. Grip the saw handle comfortably. If you grip the handle too tightly, you'll be inclined to put too much force on the cut, which could make the blade swerve away from the cutting line. Use the thumb of

Get a "feel" for sawing horizontally

If you're new to back-sawing, here is a simple exercise that can help you establish a proper grip and get the "feel" for sawing horizontally to the bench. First, lift the saw by the spine, using your free hand. Place the crook of your sawing hand (the webbed part between thumb and fingers) against the back of the handle and point your thumb and all four fingers forward. With a kerf already established, practice cutting by making several open-handed push strokes with the saw. When cutting dovetails and other intricate joints, this is all the pressure you need to apply to the saw; the weight of the saw does the cutting. Now, close your fingers loosely around the handle, keeping the your index finger pointed, but trying to recapture the feel of the open hand.

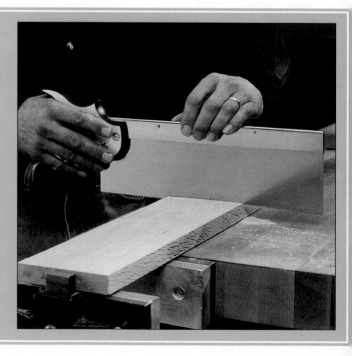

your free hand to guide the side of the blade when you start the cut. Or, cut a V-channel (see *Tip,* below). To establish the kerf, raise the heel of the saw blade about 10° off the workpiece and make a couple of push strokes with the toe end of the blade until it is seated about ⅛ in. into the wood. Then, pivot the saw downward to a horizontal cutting plane. As you begin to saw, pull your thumb away from the blade to prevent an accident if the blade should jump out of the kerf.

Keep the blade as close to horizontal as possible, so the depth of cut remains even. Keep your shoulder aligned with the saw and your forearm aligned with the blade. Your sawing arm should pump back and forth smoothly, cutting with almost the full length of the blade.

Tenon saws

Tenon saws are used for general bench work, including cutting tenons, miters, rabbets

Build-it-yourself bench hook

Back block supports the workpiece from behind.

Base, made of scrap plywood. Use glue and wood screws to attach it to the back block and bench lip.

Cutting area, 2 to 3 in. wide

Bench lip wraps around the front edge of workbench.

Bench hooks are hold-down devices designed to steady your workpiece when sawing on a workbench. The base should be wide and deep enough to support the workpiece: a 10- to 12-in. square base is large enough for most tasks. The back block should be shorter than the width of your backsaw, so the spine of the blade won't interfere with the saw cut. Set the workpiece on the bench hook so the cutting line is in the cutting area. Use your free hand to hold the workpiece steady against the back block while you make your cut.

Tips for back sawing

Create a V-channel to guide the blade. Cut a shallow V-channel along your layout line with a utility knife and a straightedge. The channel functions as a starter notch to ensure that the saw blade will follow the layout line cleanly.

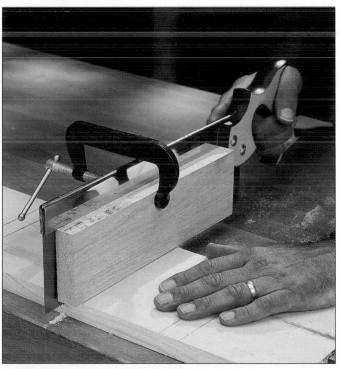

Cutting kerfs. Clamp a guide block to the side of your backsaw blade so the bottom of the block will rest against the workpiece when the blade reaches the depth of cut you need. This way, the cut will be uniformly deep across the board.

and other parts for making wood joints. Because they have fine saw teeth, they're well suited for cutting plywood. Tenon saws also can be used in miter boxes.

In the past, cabinetmakers who hand-cut all their tenons would have utilized many different tenon saws having both rip cutting and cross cutting teeth to handle the various cutting situations they'd encounter, including making cross-grain and end-grain cuts. But most woodworkers today prefer to use a single tenon saw that's suitable for all cutting tasks, so the majority of modern tenon saws are equipped with versatile crosscut-style teeth.

Tenon saws are manufactured with blade lengths ranging from 10 to 14 in., although a 14-in. blade can get a little unwieldy. A 10- or 12-in. length is more comfortable for most uses and offers better overall cutting control for making more precise cuts. Choose a saw with 13 to 15 tpi; the teeth are large enough to cut quickly, while still small enough to provide a reasonably smooth cut.

Dovetail saws

The dovetail saw is a shorter and narrower version of the tenon saw. Dovetail saws are outfitted with

Cutting tenons with a tenon saw

Tenon saws are uniquely equipped for hand-cutting tenons to make mortise-and-tenon joints. First, mark layout lines for cheek and shoulder cuts on your workpiece. Then, clamp the workpiece at about a 45° angle to the benchtop. Begin by making the cheek cuts: For each cheek, make a series of three cuts along the cheek layout line to reach the tenon shoulder (See *Illustration*, below). Make the first diagonal cheek cut. Pivot the workpiece 45° on the other side of vertical to make the second diagonal cheek cut. Finally, saw down to the shoulder layout line with the workpiece clamped vertically in the bench. Then, cut the tenon shoulders along the shoulder layout lines.

Use a bench hook to secure the workpiece as you make the shoulder cuts, sawing along the tenon shoulder to the kerf that was cut for each cheek. Use a plane or chisel to smooth and shape the tenon as needed.

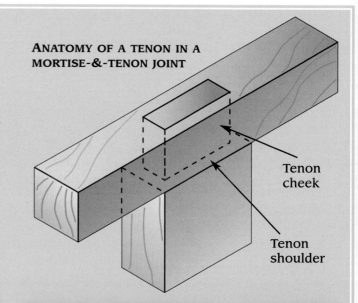

ANATOMY OF A TENON IN A MORTISE-&-TENON JOINT

Tenon cheek

Tenon shoulder

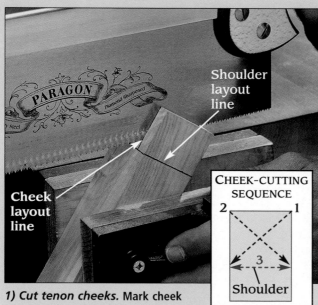

Shoulder layout line

Cheek layout line

CHEEK-CUTTING SEQUENCE

2 ————— 1

3

Shoulder

1) Cut tenon cheeks. Mark cheek and shoulder layout lines on the workpiece. To cut each cheek, saw diagonally from each corner of the waste area to the endpoints of the shoulder layout line. Tilt the workpiece in a vise before each cut so the diagonal cuts along the cheek layout lines can be made with the saw parallel to the workbench.

Bench hook

2) Cut tenon shoulders. Complete the tenon by cutting along the shoulder layout line to release the waste material created by the cheek cuts. Make the shoulder cuts with the workpiece laying flat and held firmly against a bench hook. Rest your index finger against the side of the saw blade to guide the cuts as you start. Work carefully to keep the cut perpendicular and to avoid cutting too deeply.

either straight or pistol-grip style open handles, and the blades generally are 8 in. long, with 18-20 ppi (20 being preferable). The dovetail saw excels at making a variety of small cuts for fine wood joinery, such as cuts for dovetails, tenon shoulders and small miter cuts. Use the same cutting technique as you would for sawing with a tenon saw.

Smaller back saws

A number of smaller back saws with straight, rather than pistol-style handles are available for cutting tasks that require little or no tearout. This category includes the *gent's saw* and *slotting saw* (sometimes called a *hobby saw*). These saws have extremely fine teeth, so they excel at making smooth cuts with minimal tearout on all kinds of woodworking joints, including dovetails.

Some manufacturers offer gent's saws with an offset handle that allows you to saw nearly flush to a vertical surface. The handle is removable and can be installed on either the left or right side of the blade.

The differences between these diminutive back saws lie mainly in blade length and tpi count. Blades range in length from 4 to 10 in., and tpi counts vary from 15 to 20. "Slotting" or "bead" saws have ultra-fine teeth, ranging from 25 to 32 tpi. The teeth and blade size make slotting saws impractical for large cutting tasks, but they are the right choice for delicate applications like model-making and miniature work.

Cutting dovetails. A straight-handled dovetail saw makes quick work of cutting dovetail joints. Fine, crosscut teeth and minimal tooth set produce smooth, even cuts with very little tearout. Saw with careful, controlled strokes, letting the saw teeth (not heavy downward pressure on the blade) do the cutting.

Miterbox saws

Miterbox saws are the largest back saws, with blades ranging from 14 to 30 in. long and up to 6 in. wide. These saws are made specifically for use in a miter box. Their extra length permits longer strokes and faster cuts, while wider blades make it possible to miter-cut 2 × 4s and wide moldings without bottoming out the saw cut on the blade spine. Most miterbox saws are sold with the miterbox. A tenon saw is a suitable alternative for those miter boxes that do not come with a miter saw.

A miter box is a wood, metal or plastic cutting guide that makes sawing quick, true miter joints simple and foolproof. Basic miter boxes consist of a U-shaped trough with slots cut across it at angles of 45°, 90° and 135° to the saw blade. More elaborate and accurate miter boxes are made of heavy cast metal. The saws that come with higher-end miterboxes look more like hacksaws than back saws, with narrow blades that fit into a tubular or bar-style frame. The saw frame slides in a track above the miter box, which guides the cut and keeps the blade perpendicular to the workpiece.

Saw maintenance

In order to cut efficiently, a saw needs to be sharp and well-tuned. Use a straightedge to check that the blade is straight. If the blade is loose in the handle, you may have to remove the bolts and insert paper or cardboard shims around the blade where it fits into the handle.

Wipe the blade periodically with light oil or paste wax to prevent rust. Accumulations of rust will pit the blade over time and cause the blade to drag in the saw kerf as you cut.

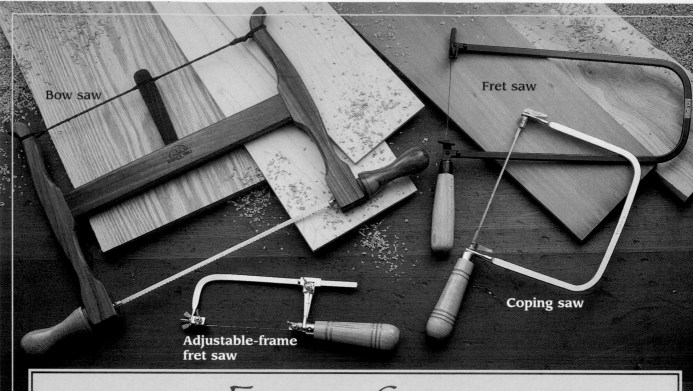

Bow saw

Fret saw

Adjustable-frame
fret saw

Coping saw

Frame Saws

Bow saws: *Surely the tool that inspired power band and scroll saws, bow saws excel at cutting gradual curves as well as making rip cuts and crosscuts.*

Fret saws: *The saw of choice for marquetry and inlay work, these saws hold extremely thin blades with fine teeth that can cut tight curves without binding.*

Fret saw frames have either a deep throat for removing inset cutouts or an adjustable frame that allows you to salvage broken blade sections.

Coping saws: Highly maneuverable, coping saws cut both insets and molding profiles with ease.

Bow saws

Bow saws are traditional European tools of uncommon beauty. They excel at making intricate, curved cuts and can be used for most types of delicate wood joinery. They cut with a longer stroke and greater depth of cut than can be accomplished with a back saw. Learning to use a bow saw correctly takes time and practice, but the advantages make it worth the effort.

Bow saws consist of a three-piece hardwood frame and a pair of wooden handles. Two arms (called *cheeks*) are connected to a central crossbeam (called a *bridge*), and the cheeks pivot slightly at the connection point. Bow saw blades resemble oversized coping saw blades and are strung between the cheeks, then connected with pins to metal shafts in the handles. Turning the handles realigns the blade to any angle—a handy feature for cutting curves or getting the frame out of the way when making long cuts that exceed the depth of the saw beam.

Multiple strands of wire or string stretch between the top ends of the cheeks, forming a tensioning device for the blade. Wire-tensioned bow saws are tightened by turning a turnbuckle. Bow saws strung with string are tightened with a stick of hardwood (called a *toggle*) that's threaded between the strands to serve as a lever for winding the twisted string tight. Removing the blade is a simple matter of unwinding the string or loosening the turnbuckle to release the tension on the blade.

Bow saws are measured by blade length, which ranges from 12 to 27 in. Smaller and larger sizes are also made in Europe, but they aren't commonly available in the United States. Blades are interchangeable within a given length, and tooth counts vary from 6 to 14 tpi, in both rip-cutting and crosscutting profiles. Blade widths range from ⅜ to 1½ in. Narrower blades with more tpi are made for cutting curves, while wider blades with larger teeth are meant for accomplishing straight rip-cutting and crosscutting tasks.

Longer bow saws generally are used with a two-handed grip, wherein both hands are intertwined around the cheek and handle. The index finger of one hand should be held straight and set against the side of the blade to help guide the cut. Shorter (12- or 18-in.) bow saws can be powered and guided with one hand only. Bow saws are *unidirectional:* they can cut on either the push stroke or the pull stroke, depending upon which handle you grip.

For general sawing, a bow saw offers several advantages over a rip or crosscut saw. The blade is held in tension between the handles, so it resists buckling. Bow saw blades are narrow and thin, so they cut more quickly and are more maneuverable if the cut should stray from the layout line. Plus, bow saws can produce either straight or curved cuts with equal ease and precision. In fact, before the advent of small electric band saws, bow saws were the primary tools used for resawing, ripping and other cutting functions that are now reserved largely for stationary, electric band saws.

It's possible to make inset cuts in a workpiece with a bow saw. Simply release tension on the blade, feed the blade through a pilot hole in the cutout area, then reconnect it to the saw frame. Pivot the blade by turning both handles to help keep the frame of the saw clear of the workpiece as you cut.

Coping saws

The coping saw is a small, inexpensive frame saw used to cut tight, intricate curves in carpentry. Blades are only about ⅛ in. wide, and they can be swiveled in the saw frame so the frame is not obstructed by the workpiece during a cut. Coping saws are indispensible for cutting contours in base and cove moldings, in order to fit mating pieces together tightly (a technique called *coping*). Coping saws are also good tools for removing the pesky waste pieces between

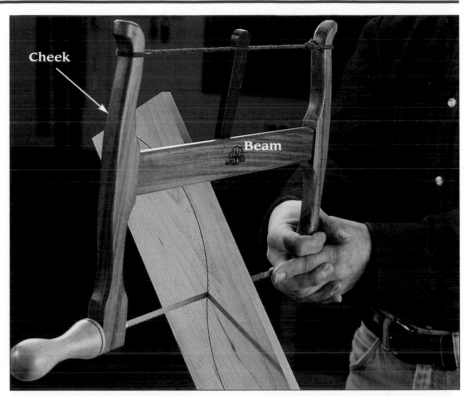

Bow saw technique. When using larger bow saws, interlock the fingers of both hands around one handle and one cheek so the handle rests in the palms of both hands. Don't grasp both handles to make a cut. Extend one index finger along the side of the blade as a guide. Work the saw through the cut with smooth, sweeping strokes. Rotate the blade as needed by turning the handles to keep the saw frame clear of the workpiece.

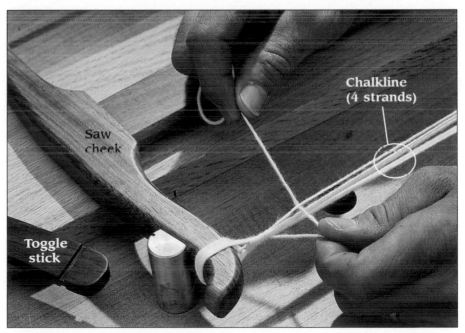

Stringing a bow saw. Eventually, the tensioning string on a bow saw will need to be replaced. First, remove the old string. Install the saw blade and clamp the bow saw cheeks between bench dogs to impart tension to the blade. Wrap four loops of fresh chalk line between the saw cheeks, then wind string around each cheek. Weave the end of the string back and forth through the long strands to secure it. Trim off the excess. Thread the toggle stick between the strands near the middle of the saw, and wind the string up with the toggle stick (as you would a tourniquet) to tension the blade.

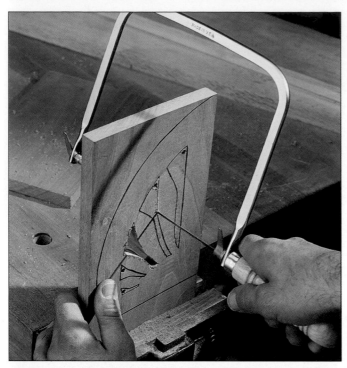

Making interior cutouts. Any frame saw can be used to make interior cutouts. First, drill a pilot hole in the waste area. Remove the blade and thread it through the pilot hole. Reattach the blade and make the cut, turning the blade in the frame as necessary so the frame clears the edges of the workpiece.

Coping. Profiled molding, such as base or crown molding, typically is installed using miter joints at the corners. To miter-cut profiled molding, first cut the end of one piece of molding at a 45° angle, using a miter box. Then trim off the beveled edge of the cut board along the profile line with a coping saw held perpendicular to the workpiece. The blade teeth should face the handle when making this cut.

Molding profile

pins when cutting dovetails, or for making any cut with tight-radiused curves.

The metal frame on a coping saw imparts the tension that holds the saw blade taut. The blades have tiny cross pins running through each end. One pin slides into a notch on a swivel fitting at the leading end of the frame; the other pin fits into a notch on the end of a metal rod that threads through the frame and into the handle. Turning the handle clockwise while holding the threaded rod in place increases tension on the blade. Releasing the tension on the blade is done by turning the handle counterclockwise.

The typical coping saw takes a standard 6½ in.-long blade, regardless of the depth of the *throat* (the distance from the top of the frame to the blade). Coping saw throat capacities range from 4 to 7 in. Blades are meant to be disposable, so they aren't suitable for resharpening. Tooth counts range from 10 to 20 tpi.

When cutting curves, particularly those that are inset within a workpiece, you'll need to rotate the blade in the frame periodically to keep the frame clear of the workpiece. To turn the blade, twist the notched fittings on each end of the blade equally. Try to keep the blade from twisting unnecessarily as you do this, or it could break. Once you've rotated the blade, be sure to straighten it lengthwise. If the teeth "spiral," the blade will catch in the saw kerf or skew as it cuts.

A coping saw generally is used with the blade mounted so the teeth point away from the handle, which means the tool saws on the push stroke. However, you can also mount the blade so the teeth point toward the handle and cut on the pull stroke. To keep your cutting layout lines clear of sawdust, install the saw blade so the teeth will exit the wood on the side opposite the lines.

When cutting curves, keep the coping saw perpendicular to the workpiece when possible to avoid twisting the blade. Although a coping saw can negotiate intricate curves, it still has a flat blade and the the tightness of the radii it can follow is limited. If the blade binds in a curve, don't force it further. The curve is probably too tight. Back the blade up a bit in the kerf, widen the kerf with a few additional strokes (just enough to allow the blade room to turn) and try cutting the curve again.

Fret saws

Fret saws resemble coping saws closely, but they accept even finer blades and usually have greater throat capacity. They're commonly used to cut extremely thin materials such as wood veneer for marquetry projects. Because fret saw blades are so thin, they can break easily. Care must be taken to avoid sawing too fast or twisting the blade. Thanks to the deep throats available (which range from 2½ to 20 in. deep), fret saws can accomplish fine scrollwork deep within a wide panel. Like coping saws, fret saw blades can be mounted with the teeth facing either direction, as dictated by the work at hand.

Fret saws are fitted with plain-end blades that are clamped at each end between two metal blocks and tightened with a thumbscrew. Some fret saws, also called *jeweler's saws*, have adjustable frames that accommodate blades of different lengths (and in a pinch, even broken blades).

Most fret saw blades are 5 in. long and can be used for both manual fret saws and power scroll saws. Thickness and tooth configuration vary from a ¼ in. wide, 7 tpi blade used to cut thick lumber down to a whisper-thin 32 tpi blade used to cut veneer. Blades are also available for cutting a variety of non-wood materials, including bone, shell, plastic, rubber, metal, stone and glass. There's almost no limit to the tightness of radius you can turn with a fret saw. You can even outfit the saw with a spiral scroll saw blade that will cut in any direction.

For most fret-saw cutting tasks, hold the saw vertically with the handle beneath the workpiece. The teeth should face down toward the handle. The most convenient setup for sawing this way is to make a *saddle jig* from scrap lumber (See *Photo*, above). The "V" cutout in the saddle jig allows you to cut deeply within the workpiece, while still supporting the workpiece near the blade throughout the cut. Size the saddle jig and the depth of the "V" cutout so the workpiece can be rested on the bearing surface of the jig without need for a clamp.

To use the saddle jig, clamp it to the bench so the legs of the "V"

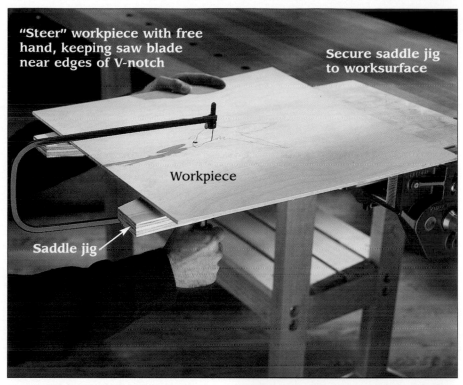

"Steer" workpiece with free hand, keeping saw blade near edges of V-notch

Secure saddle jig to worksurface

Workpiece

Saddle jig

Use a saddle jig. When making deep inset cutouts with a fret saw or coping saw, support the workpiece on a saddle jig clamped to the bench. The saddle jig is simply a sturdy piece of scrap plywood with an elongated "V" cutout that creates access for the saw when the workpiece is rested on the jig.

Frame saw blades are very delicate and almost impossible to sharpen, so be sure to keep a few extras on hand in case the blade you're using breaks or becomes dull during a cutting project.

extend beyond the surface of the bench. The saw should remain inside the "V" area for the entire cut. Instead of moving the saw along the layout lines as you would when using other types of saws, "steer" the workpiece with your free hand so the saw follows the layout lines. Since the blade teeth face the handle, each time you pull the saw through the cut the blade will help hold the workpiece against the V-block. The saddle jig also works with coping saws using the same technique.

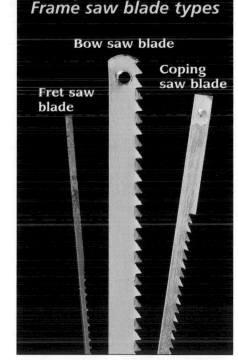

Frame saw blade types

Bow saw blade

Coping saw blade

Fret saw blade

Frame saw blades are attached to the saw in three different ways, depending upon on the type of saw. Bow saw blades are secured in the bow saw frame with pins that pass through holes on each end of the blade. Coping saw blades are fitted with crosspins that slide into notched fittings on the saw. Fret saw blades are secured with small clamps mounted on the saw frame.

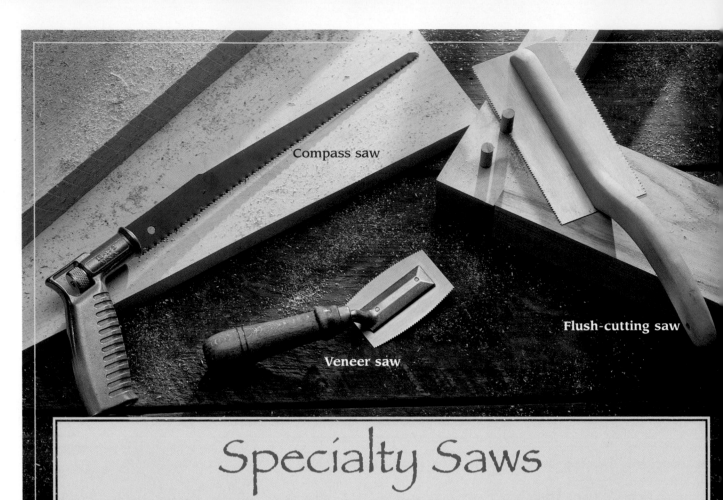

Compass saw

Flush-cutting saw

Veneer saw

Specialty Saws

Veneer saws have convex cutting edges and straight teeth to score veneer against a straightedge.

Flush-cutting saw blades have teeth on four edges. The handles are offset and the teeth have no set, which allows

the saw to trim dowels and other joint details flush to the surface of the workpiece.

Compass saw blades taper to a point—perfect for making inset cutouts in wallboard or paneling.

Veneer saws

Veneer saws are made for one purpose—to rip and crosscut veneer. The saw blade has two convex cutting edges with teeth running along the full length of each edge. Curved cutting edges provide greater control over the cut by limiting the number of teeth that come in contact with the veneer during a cut. The teeth on each curved edge run in opposite directions so the blade can be detached and reversed on the handle when one edge becomes dull. The back of the blade is flat and the handle is offset so the saw can be used vertically against a metal straightedge or wood guide. The teeth have no set and are flat on the back side but bevel to a point along the front edge. Veneer saws generally have 12 to 14 tpi and cut on the pull stroke.

Flush-cutting saws

Flush-cutting saws have a row of teeth on all four edges of the blade, and the teeth have no set. Because there is no tooth set, flush-cutting saws enable you to

trim dowel pins and wooden plugs nearly flush to the surface of the workpiece without marring the surrounding surfaces. One long edge of the blade typically has a tooth count of 11 tpi for making faster, coarse cuts, while the other long edge usually has around 14 *tpi* to produce smooth cuts that require minimal sanding.

Compass saws

Compass saws are intended to cut curves or cutouts in wood and wallboard where a jigsaw would be bulky or cumbersome and a frame saw can't reach. They consist of a handle, made of wood, metal or plastic attached to a narrow crosscut blade that tapers nearly to a point. Hold the saw perpendicular to the workpiece for cutting, and work in short, stabbing strokes.

Since the blades are wider than those of a coping or fret saw, compass saws cut more gradual curves; but the fact that the blade is not held in a frame makes these saws more convenient for making cuts that are not near an edge. The pointed compass saw blades can

Cut with the finer teeth when trimming with a flush-cutting saw, especially if you're cutting hardwood. The finer teeth will yield a smoother cut with less risk of tearout than the coarser teeth on the opposite edge of the saw blade.

Use a straightedge guide when cutting veneer strips with a veneer saw. Rock the saw along the curved edge of the blade when making longer cuts. For greater control, position the blade so only a few teeth cut at one time.

be "punched" through soft gypsum wallboard or started in a small pilot hole for making cuts through one side of a finished wall or panel. This feature makes compass saws popular with carpenters, plumbers and electricians who use them to create openings for pipes and receptacle boxes. Compass saws are inexpensive additions to any homeowner's toolbox.

Compass saw blades range from 10 to 14 in. long and have 8 to 10 tpi. The teeth are pitched forward on the blade, so the saw cuts on the push stroke. The disadvantage to this tooth configuration is that the slender blades and large teeth are more prone to buckling or breaking if they are pushed too aggressively.

To make a cutout in wood using a compass saw, drill a pilot hole large enough to accommodate the pointed

tip of the blade. Insert the blade into the hole and saw carefully to avoid catching and bending the blade. Since compass saws produce a coarse cut, make sure to cut on the waste side of the layout line and remove any remaining waste with a spokeshave or file.

Although compass saws can be used for cutting holes in wallboard, inexpensive wallboard saws made just for this purpose are worth purchasing if you do a lot of wallboarding. Wallboard saws have a short, straight handle permanently fixed to a 6 in. blade. The blade comes to a sharp point at the tip so it can be poked through wallboard without a starter hole. Wallboard saws have fewer tpi and produce a coarser cut than compass saws, so they are not intended for cutting wood.

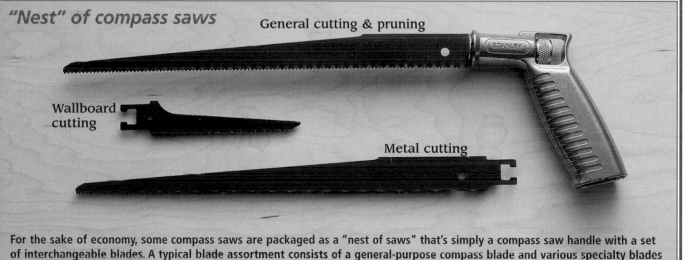

"Nest" of compass saws

General cutting & pruning

Wallboard cutting

Metal cutting

For the sake of economy, some compass saws are packaged as a "nest of saws" that's simply a compass saw handle with a set of interchangeable blades. A typical blade assortment consists of a general-purpose compass blade and various specialty blades for cutting non-wood materials, such as soft metal and wallboard.

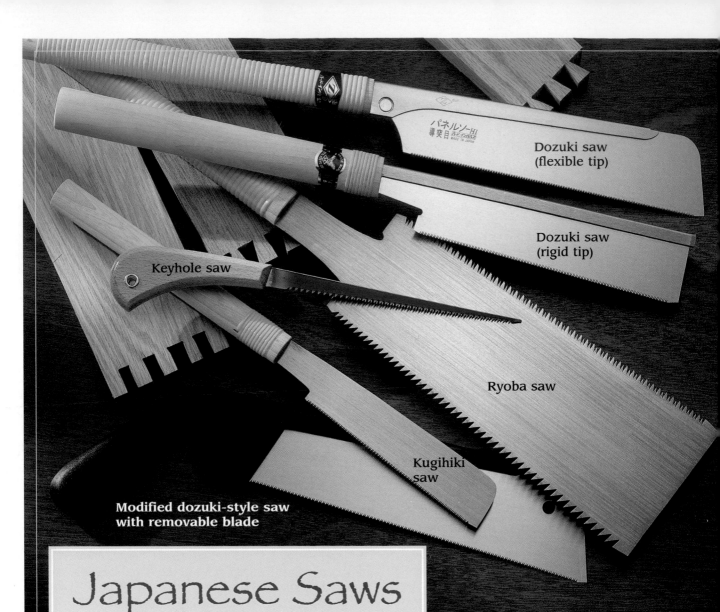

Dozuki saw
(flexible tip)

Dozuki saw
(rigid tip)

Keyhole saw

Ryoba saw

Kugihiki
saw

Modified dozuki-style saw
with removable blade

Japanese Saws

Dozuki saws: Japanese versions of Western back saws, intended for general joint-cutting tasks; blades come in various shapes, but all are reinforced with spines.

Keyhole saws: Tapered blade and aggressive teeth pattern for cutting inset holes quickly in wood.

Ryoba saws: Two saws rolled into one—blade is outfitted with rip teeth on one side and crosscut teeth on the other.

Kugihiki saws: Flexible blade and minimal tooth set for flush-trimming dowels and through tenons.

Modified dozuki-style saws: Hybrid Western saws modeled after traditional Japanese dozuki has high-impact plastic handle and quick-release disposable blade.

Back saws and bow saws for woodworking evolved from the early furnituremaking practices of British and European cultures. Japanese saws developed out of a very different tradition. Furniturebuilding was not as

central to woodworking in Japan as it was in Europe. Carpentry, on the other hand, became elevated to an art form, and master craftsmen devised ever more intricate, complex and beautiful joints for the construction of houses and temples.

Most Japanese saws were designed for cutting particular parts of wood joints, though many saws still used today were created to satisfy the needs of other specialized artisans, such as the shoji maker, the sandal maker and even the maker of sword scabbards.

Because Japanese woodworkers customarily saw lower to the ground than at waist height, Japanese sawmakers designed their saws with shorter blades that cut on the pull stroke. While this may seem strange to Westerners at first, it certainly makes sense. A shorter blade requires less clear space beneath the bench for sawing. Plus, pulling a saw through the wood rather than pushing it tensions the blade, so there is less tendency for the blade to bend. Without the need for extra stiffening, the Japanese have developed thin saw blades, which enable their saws to cut quickly and leave a small kerf. Handles are typically straight and are longer than those on Western saws, to allow for a two-handed grip a comfortable distance up from the blade.

Japanese saws are manufactured from very hard grades of steel, so the teeth tend to stay sharp for a long time. However, the steel used in Japanese saws is also more brittle, so the blades can break if they buckle. But buckling shouldn't be a problem if the saws are used properly.

Tooth configurations

Crosscut teeth—the tooth pattern found on most Japanese saw types—are bevel-ground on three edges like miniature knife blades, and the bevels alternate from tooth to tooth. A three-bevel design allows the teeth to slice through wood with minimal tooth set. Tooth design, combined with a thin-kerfed blade, adds up to saws that cuts aggressively, yet are easy to control. Japanese crosscut saws are capable of great accuracy, and the teeth leave a smooth finish. The three-bevel crosscut tooth pattern is so efficient, some American saw manufacturers offer Western-style crosscut saws with a similar tooth design.

The teeth on Japanese rip saws look more like Western rip saw teeth, but Japanese rip saws come in two styles—one for cutting hardwood and another for cutting softwood. Since native softwoods are the most common construction material in Japan, rip saws are traditionally made for softwoods. However Japanese do use hardwoods, such as native red oak. In recent years more and more saws are being made with hardwood rip teeth to accommodate the growing Japanese saw export market.

Ripping teeth for softwoods are narrower from base to tip than those for hardwoods, and the teeth are pitched at a sharper angle on the blade to cut more aggressively. Hardwood ripping teeth are wider at the base, which makes them stronger than softwood teeth. They are pitched at a more gradual incline to the blade, making them less likely to dig into the wood.

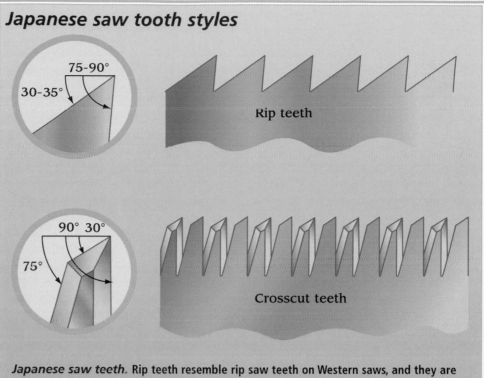

Japanese saw tooth styles

75-90°
30-35°

Rip teeth

90° 30°
75°

Crosscut teeth

Japanese saw teeth. Rip teeth resemble rip saw teeth on Western saws, and they are filed straight with no bevel edge. The tooth pitch varies from 75 to 90°, depending upon whether the saw is intended to cut soft- or hardwood. Crosscut teeth are radically different from rip teeth. Crosscut teeth are sharpened with three distinct bevels to slice wood like a knife.

Ryoba saws are two-sided cutting tools, with rip teeth on one side of the blade and crosscut teeth on the other. The traditional method of sawing with a ryoba is to position the workpiece low to the ground and grip the saw handle with both hands.

Dozuki saws perform the same cutting tasks as Western back saws and even bear some resemblance—the blade is stiffened with a metal spine along the back. Saw with one hand on the handle, index finger outstretched to guide the blade. Keep the blade parallel to the worksurface as you cut.

Kugihiki saws have thin, flexible blades intended for trimming dowels flush without marring the surrounding wood. Grip the saw with one hand and exercise care when cutting to keep from buckling the delicate blade.

For both rip saw styles, the sizes of the individual teeth increase from the heel of the blade to the toe. This is because the saw stroke begins on the heel of the blade and ends at the toe. Smaller teeth help to start the cut, while larger teeth remove progressively more material once the cut is underway.

Japanese saw types

There are many styles of *noko giri* (Japanese woodworking saws), which can be divided into the following five categories.

Ryoba & kataba. The *ryoba,* or double-edged saw, is Japan's standby, akin to Western rip and crosscut saws in American woodshops. Ryoba saws are really two saws in one—the blades are outfitted with rip teeth along one edge and crosscut teeth on the other edge. Blades are square at the end and wider at the toe than at the heel. The handle shaft is usually a native softwood, wrapped with rattan.

The sizing and number of teeth on a ryoba are dependent on the blade length: longer blades have larger and fewer tpi. Saws with 7½- to 9½-in. blades are suitable for cabinetry, furniture and finish carpentry. Ryobas with 10½- to 11½-in. blades are made for larger carpentry work, like cutting tenon joints on timber-frame houses.

To minimize binding in the saw kerf, ryoba blades are thinner along the center and the teeth are set along both edges. However, for deep crosscuts where the whole blade is buried in the wood, the rip teeth can engage in the workpiece at the same time as the crosscut teeth. On rough cuts this may not be a problem, but two sets of teeth in a cut can scratch the walls of the kerf or bind and bog down the cut. To avoid this situation, spread the kerf with a wedge, or make a series of relief cuts in from the closest edge so the waste can be removed in chunks. The *kataba,* a one-sided version of the ryoba, has rip or crosscut teeth on one side of the blade only. It's a good alternative to the ryoba if you often have many deep cuts to make.

The common grip for a ryoba, particularly in the medium to large sizes, is two-handed, spacing your hands apart near the two ends of the handle.

Dozuki. The dozuki is a single-edged crosscut saw with a steel or brass spine along its back to reinforce and stiffen an extremely thin blade. In this respect the dozuki resembles the Western back saw, and it serves essentially the same purpose: cutting fine miters, dovetails and tenons for precise wood joints. The name dozuki means "tenon shoulders."

Dozuki saws may be the finest cutting saws available. The 8- to 11-in. blades range from 17 to 32 tpi. Modified crosscut tooth patterns are available for either softwoods or hardwoods. The tiny teeth have very little set, yielding a cut that is extremely smooth and seldom requires further planing. Since dozukis are used to

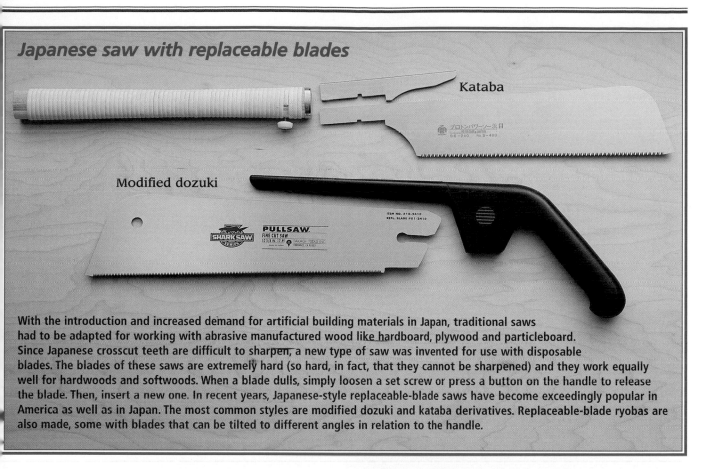

Japanese saw with replaceable blades

Kataba

Modified dozuki

PULLSAW.
FINE CUT SAW
SHARK SAW

With the introduction and increased demand for artificial building materials in Japan, traditional saws had to be adapted for working with abrasive manufactured wood like hardboard, plywood and particleboard. Since Japanese crosscut teeth are difficult to sharpen, a new type of saw was invented for use with disposable blades. The blades of these saws are extremely hard (so hard, in fact, that they cannot be sharpened) and they work equally well for hardwoods and softwoods. When a blade dulls, simply loosen a set screw or press a button on the handle to release the blade. Then, insert a new one. In recent years, Japanese-style replaceable-blade saws have become exceedingly popular in America as well as in Japan. The most common styles are modified dozuki and kataba derivatives. Replaceable-blade ryobas are also made, some with blades that can be tilted to different angles in relation to the handle.

make fairly shallow cuts, binding isn't a problem. A light coating of wax on the blade will smooth the cutting action even more.

A dozuki is used one-handed, with the index finger along the top of the handle to press down and guide the blade while sawing. Keep the blade parallel to the benchtop when sawing, just as you would a back saw.

Kugihiki. The name kugihiki means "to cut nails," and indeed this saw was designed to trim off Japanese wooden nails (dowels), as well as plugs and through-tenons, so their ends are flush with the surface of the wood. The blade has no spine and starts out wider at the toe, then tapers down to the heel. The thin blade can be flexed to sit next to a workpiece without the handle or your hand getting in the way. The teeth (usually 20 to 26 tpi) have no set.

Keyhole. Japanese keyhole saws resemble their Western cousin, the compass saw. The handles are contoured for a one-handed grip, and the blades taper to a point. However, Japanese keyhole saws feature a more aggressive, modified crosscut tooth design, which helps them cut faster through wallboard or through wood. These saws cut on the pull stroke, so the slender blades are less likely to kink than a compass saw blade. The spine of the blade is thinner than the cutting edge and the steel used is not as hard as other Japanese saws, so it isn't as brittle and stands up to more abuse.

Keyhole saws are very similar in function to Western compass saws (See page 47). Use them for making interior cutouts in a variety of building materials: wood and nonwood alike.

Chiseling & Carving

Chisels are among the most used (and misused) tools in any toolbox. Chisels are sharp steel blades mounted to stout handles, but too quickly they become emergency screwdrivers, paint scrapers and pry bars. And that's okay. The cheap chisels in sets most of us own are practically disposable. If they get more use as a dried glue scraper than a mortise cutter, good for them. But there is another kind of chisel out there: a precision instrument that can slice smoothly into the hardest hardwood and never waver from its cutting line. Once you've come to know the virtues of a fine chisel, you can bet it won't be going anywhere near a paint can lid.

If you've had bad luck working with chisels in the past, don't give up on them quite yet. Well-honed and applied with some skill and dexterity, they can accomplish things in the woodshop you never would have thought possible.

Woodcarving is a popular pastime that's attracting more followers all the time. But you don't have to be a great artist to take up woodcarving. Sure, creating a prizewinning wood sculpture would be a lot of fun, but there are plenty of other ways to take advantage of woodcarving skills: repairing furniture, making custom molding and even setting up a little side-line business selling driveway signs are just a few. In this chapter, you'll find a good introduction to the tools that the woodcarver uses to pursue his craft.

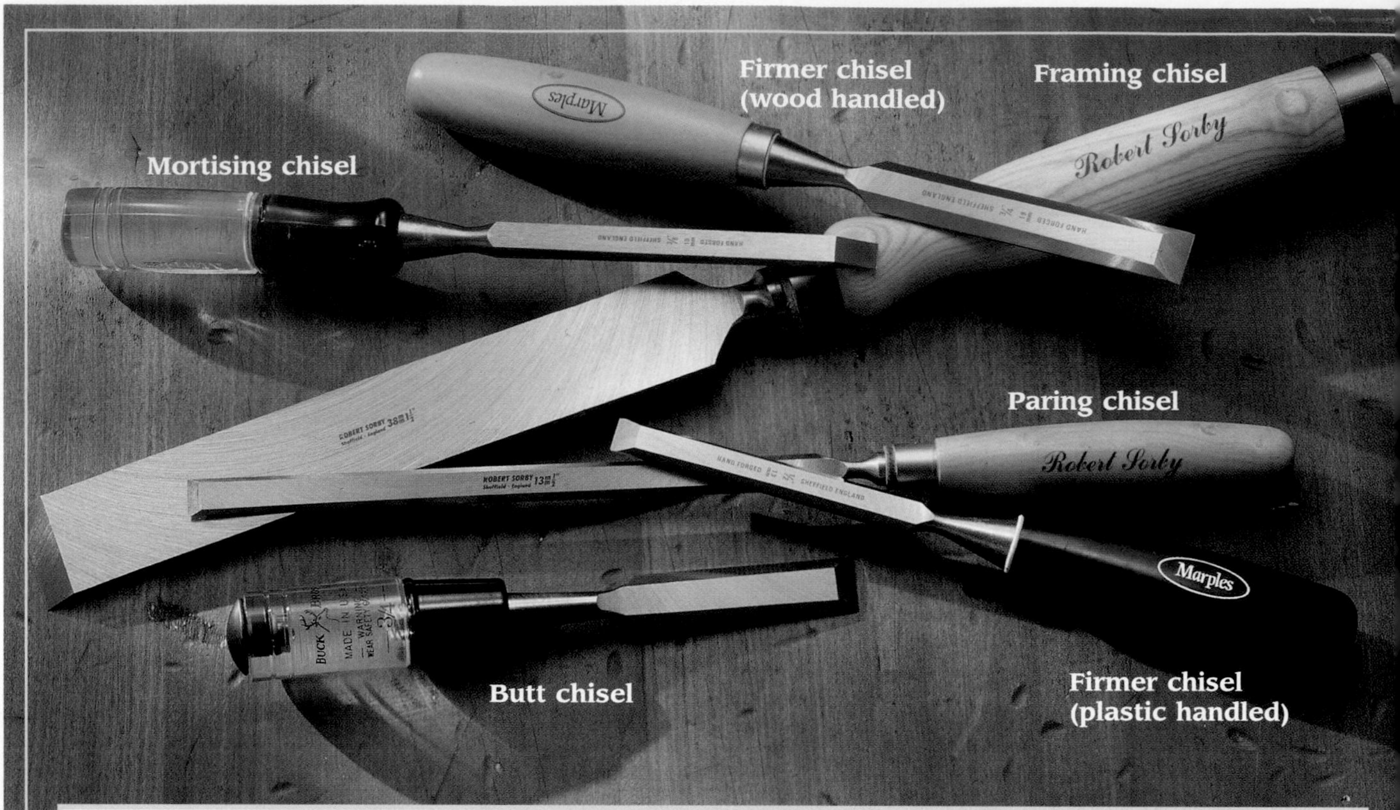

Mortising chisel

Firmer chisel
(wood handled)

Framing chisel

Paring chisel

Butt chisel

Firmer chisel
(plastic handled)

Common Chisel Types

- **Firmer chisels** are intended for general hand-chiseling and paring tasks; blades are beveled on both the cutting edge and sides.

- **Paring chisels** have elongated, beveled blades for making deep or long paring cuts.

- **Mortising chisels** are used with a mallet to chop deep mortises; blades are tapered and square on the sides and range in widths from ⅛ to ½ in.

- **Framing chisels** have thick, square-edged blades that come in widths up to 2 in. Handles are reinforced with a metal hoop that reduces the risk of splitting when struck with a mallet.

- **Butt chisels** are short, bevel-edged firmer chisels, often equipped with a metal cap on the handle that can be struck with a metal hammer or a mallet. Inexpensive, they are an economical tool for general rough carpentry.

Wood chisels

It's safe to say that some type of chisel is used by everyone who works extensively with wood. Timber framers and carpenters, boatbuilders, patternmakers, fine furniture makers, cabinetbuilders and carvers all have one or more types of chisels that are absolutely essential to their work.

The chisel has been in existence for a long time, yet its basic form has been basically unchanged by evolution—despite the number of power tools that have been created to replace hand tools, the chisel continues to stand out as one hand tool that hasn't been motorized.

The chisel performs a host of trimming, shaping, paring and chopping functions. Lightweight and easy to use, they're sturdy enough to withstand aggressive pounding and gouging. Yet, the chisel remains capable of performing the most delicate and precise work.

Most chisels used today fall into one of four common chisel families: firmer chisels, butt chisels, paring chisels and mortising chisels. Because the concept of a chisel is so simple, the basic design has been adapted to perform innumerable special tasks. A few of the more common specialty chisels are shown and discussed on pages 60 to 62.

Chisels are sized by blade width, which ranges from ⅛ to 2 in. Other than blade width, the main differences between chisels are in composition, shape and handle

Anatomy of a wood chisel

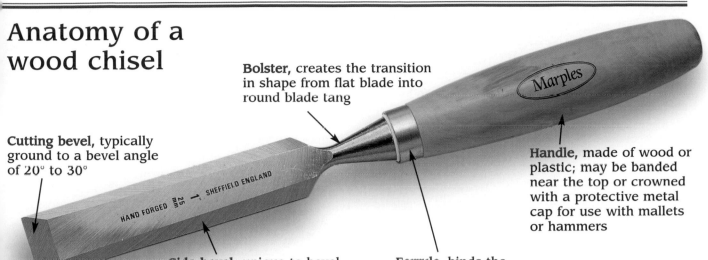

Bolster, creates the transition in shape from flat blade into round blade tang

Cutting bevel, typically ground to a bevel angle of 20° to 30°

Side bevel, unique to bevel-edged chisels, helps blade fit into tighter spaces

Ferrule, binds the handle to the bolster

Handle, made of wood or plastic; may be banded near the top or crowned with a protective metal cap for use with mallets or hammers

(Blade engraving reads: HAND FORGED 25 mm 1" SHEFFIELD ENGLAND)

(Handle logo reads: Marples)

style. Traditionally, chisels have been made with wood handles. Those designed for striking generally have a protective cap or a metal hoop at the butt of the handle. Many chisels are now available with handles fashioned from reinforced acrylic or high-impact plastic. These artifical materials are quite durable and perfectly serviceable in most situations. The only real rap on them, however, is that they can become slippery when used for extended periods of time—unlike wood, plastic will not absorb perspiration.

Use the the chisel categories on the following pages as a guide for building a set that's right for you, basing your choices on your own needs and interests. Buy the best-quality chisels you can afford. It's better to have a few good chisels than a whole rack of substandard tools with steel too soft to hold an edge. If you're considering making an investment in a higher end chisel or chisel set, make sure to actually hold the tools before making any purchase—each chisel has its own weight and balance, and holding it is the only way to know for sure if it's a comfortable fit for you. Another good test is to examine the back of the blade with a straightedge. Chisel backs need to be flat, both for ease of sharpening and to make paring possible. The flatness of the back is a good indicator of how carefully the chisel was machined at the factory and serves as one way to measure overall chisel quality. For most people, chisels with smooth, plain handles are the most comfortable. I prefer a simple oval boxwood or beechwood handle, common on many brands of English chisels.

Packaged sets that include a variety of chisel sizes are a good way to start building your chisel collection. If you plan to use chisels mostly for rough carpentry, look into a set of butt chisels with hardened steel blades in the following sizes: 1/4, 3/8, 1/2, 3/4 and 1 in. For woodworking, a set of wood-handled firmer chisels in the following sizes will meet most chiseling needs: 1/4, 3/8 or 1/2, 3/4 and 1 or 1 1/4 in.

Firmer chisels

Firmer chisels are versatile, popular tools for general-purpose paring and chiseling on furniture and carpentry projects. Generally, their blades are beveled on the cutting edge as well as the sides, although a few have square (non-beveled) sides. Square-edged firmers are made to take heavy pounding with a mallet, yet they can perform delicate paring cuts as well. Bevel-edged blades are not as strong as square-edged blades, but beveled firmers can be tapped lightly with a wooden mallet with little risk of breakage or splitting the handle. The best tool for hand or "push" chiseling, a sharp firmer chisel can glide through a workpiece with minimal effort.

Paring chisels

Though bevel-edged firmer chisels are used commonly for paring, a better tool for the job is the special paring chisel. Equipped with long, thin blades that provide plenty of bearing surface for making long or deep cuts, bevel-edged paring chisels are great for cleaning up corners and chiseling joints, such as tenons and dovetails. While their slender profile allows the blade to fit into angled or undercut corners, paring chisel blades are delicate, so the tools should never be struck with a mallet—apply hand pressure only.

Mortising chisels

Mortising chisels are struck with a mallet to chop deep mortises for wood joinery. The thick blades won't bend when levering out waste wood from the mortise. Mortising chisel blades taper in thickness from the ferrule to the cutting edge. Non-beveled blade edges maintain alignment within the walls of the mortise. Most mortises employed in furnituremaking can be cut with either ¼ or ⅜ in. mortising chisels.

Framing chisels

Framing chisels (also called registered chisels) are longer and stronger than mortising chisels and usually have a metal hoop on the end of the handle to keep the wood from splitting or mushrooming. Designed for tim-ber-frame construction, framing chisels have blades that are square on the edges and up to 2 in. wide.

Butt chisels

Butt chisels are shorter variations of the firmer chisel. Their short, beveled blades and small handles make them handy for use in tight spaces, but their small size and generally lower quality standards make butt chisels the least useful chisel type for fine woodworking. Butt chisels are perfectly adequate for general carpentry tasks, such as cutting shallow mortises for hinge plates and strikeplates. The handle on most butt chisels has a crowned metal cap on the end, so the chisel can be struck with a mallet or metal hammer.

Chiseling techniques

Chiseling techniques are fairly intuitive once you have a few guidelines under your belt. After that, skill-building is simply a matter of practice.

The two basic cuts made with a chisel are: paring (finer cuts to reduce the workpiece in size by slicing away shavings of wood), and chopping (making deep, vigorous cuts, often with a mallet, as when cutting deep mortises). Paring can be accomplished with the chisel in a vertical or a horizontal position; chopping is best done working on a vertical plane.

The key to successful chiseling is to remove wood in manageable amounts—the most common chiseling mistake is trying to remove too much stock in a single pass. Shallower cuts are easier to control. When possible, save time and effort by using other tools, such as saws, drills and planes, to remove as much wood as you can before applying your chisel to the workpiece.

Whether you're chopping or paring, always direct the initial cuts away from your layout line, on the waste side of the workpiece. Then, gradually work toward the layout line with shallow strokes. Cut away from your body and keep your fingers well behind the cutting edge of the blade. Before you begin to chisel, secure your workpiece firmly, so it won't move while you chisel. This also frees up both hands to guide the chisel.

Paring. **Paring is a basic cutting task that can be accomplished with any sharp chisel. For rough paring, position the chisel at a moderately low angle (around 30°) to the workpiece, with the beveled cutting edge down. If making a cut in a defined area (such as a shallow mortise like the one being cut above) score a line along the outline first. Move the chisel forward, cutting away from your body. Once the cut is pared to rough size, flip the chisel so the bevel is facing up and smooth off the cut with the chisel held close to parallel to the workpiece.**

Chopping. **Remove as much wood as you can in the cutting area with a drill, then select a mortising chisel (or a sturdy firmer chisel) that's the same width as the mortise—when planning your project, design the mortises to match your tool widths. Position the chisel so the beveled edge is facing into the opening, then drive it at a perpendicular angle to square the walls of the mortise. Then, tip the chisel at a slight angle and drive it toward the center of the mortise, from each end, to flatten the bottom of the cut (as shown above).**

Chopping (mortising)

Chopping is a chiseling technique used mostly in wood joinery to make joints that require internal cutouts (primarily mortises for mortise-and-tenon joints). Since chopping normally is done by striking the chisel with a mallet, use a sturdy chisel designed for this purpose (a mortising chisel or a square edge firmer chisel). See the photo on the previous page (right) for a description of chopping technique.

Paring

Paring is the most frequently used chiseling technique. It is simply the controlled slicing of fine shavings to reduce a wood part in size, alter its shape or create a smooth surface. Paring correctly requires that you use both hands on the chisel, so be sure to secure the workpiece adequately before starting work. If you are right-handed, hold the handle with your right hand to power the cut. Grip the blade near the cutting edge with your left hand to serve as a guide and to help restrain the cutting force supplied by your right hand. For initial cuts, hold the chisel with the bevel on the cutting edge facing down. Tilt the chisel blade at about a 30° angle to the workpiece and skew the edge of the blade as you push it forward (called oblique paring). Doing so will produce a shear-

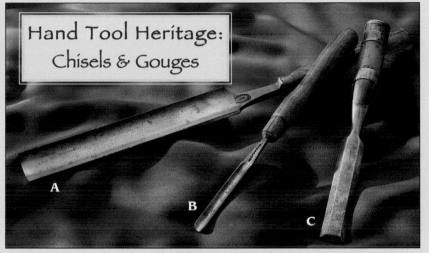

Some of the finest antique chisels were manufactured in Sheffield, England, and in the United States in the late 19th and early 20th centuries. Collectors are especially interested in chisels made by the English firms W & S Butcher, I & H Sorby, Spear & Jackson, and J. Howorth and U.S. manufacturers Buck Brothers, D. R. Barton, James Swan, and L & J White, among others.

Hand Tool Heritage: Chisels & Gouges

(A) 15¼ in. long by 1 in. wide, tanged gouge with an iron ferrule on its 5¼ in. hickory handle. It is marked with the *D. R. Barton, 1832, Rochester, N.Y.* trademark. (B) 10 in. long by ⅜ in. wide tanged gouge, also part of a plane-maker's set, has a 5½ in. long hickory handle. (C) 9½ in. long by 13/16 in. wide, all-steel firmer chisel that was part of a plane-maker's set of chisels and floats. Made in Germany, it was used to smooth cheek sides and throats of wooden bench planes. The rare, hand-forged, steel-caged handle has a boxwood insert.

ing cut that shaves more easily and smoothly than a parallel cut. For fine paring, position the chisel so the non-beveled face of the cutting edge is lying nearly flat on the workpiece.

Horizontal paring. Cutting cham-

fers, beveling board ends, and even rounding over corners are all typical chiseling operations that are normally done working on a horizontal plane. Hand positions for horizontal chiseling will vary, depending upon the cut you're

Chiseling & grain direction

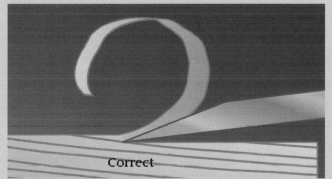

Correct

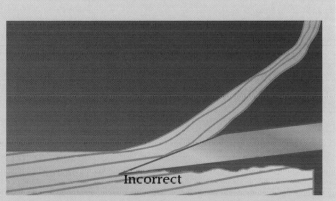

Incorrect

Where possible, chisel with the grain. Examine the grain direction on the edge of your workpiece to determine which direction it is angled in relation to the surface. Chiseling with the grain will give a smooth cut, while going against the grain will cause the blade to dive into the workpiece, tearing up or splitting the wood fibers and leaving a rough surface.

Proper stances for chiseling

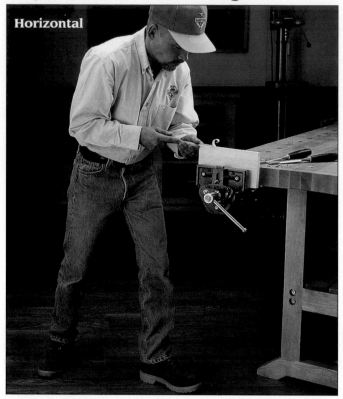

Horizontal

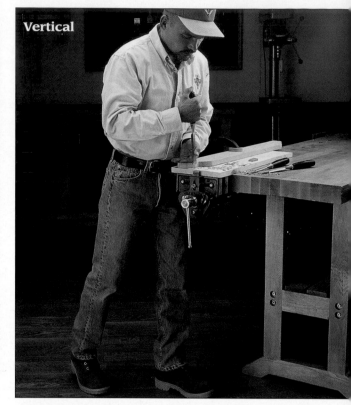

Vertical

Correct stance for horizontal paring: Extend the index finger of your right hand so it rests against the chisel bolster. Align your index finger and forearm with the blade. Stand with your right foot to the rear and bend at the waist slightly. To make the cut, roll forward on your right foot so the driving force comes from your feet and legs, not your upper body.

Correct stance for vertical paring: Stand with your upper body over the workpiece, Grip the chisel handle with your right hand and guide the blade with the thumb and index finger of your left hand. Bend at the waist and, when you make the cut, keep your arms locked so all the cutting force comes from your shoulders and hips. Rock the chisel back and forth along the cutting line with your right hand to make your shavings.

making. Generally, grab the blade with your left hand and drive the chisel with your right when you need to remove large amounts of waste. For delicate chiseling like paring and chamfering, control the blade with your your left thumb and first few fingers, steering the blade closer to the cutting edge. Adopt the stance shown above (left photo) for good balance and to enable your lower body to provide much of the chiseling force.

Vertical paring is a technique used most frequently for trimming tenons to size and shape. It is generally done either across the grain or to cut end grain (as when trimming a tenon). Both tasks are accomplished in much the same way. With the workpiece secured, lean over the cut and use your upper body weight to press down on the chisel handle and drive the blade (right photo, above).

Wood grain direction

Chiseling wood is easier when your cut follows the path of the wood grain, as shown in the illustration on the previous page. When chiseling with the grain, you can use the chisel with the bevel down to make

meatier roughing cuts. The bevel prevents the blade from wandering upward, so it won't drive into the wood too deeply. For finishing cuts, always pare with the bevel facing up. Whenever possible, cut with the grain, even if it means chiseling from several directions to finish a cut.

Chiseling end grain. It's not uncommon to encounter situations where you need to chisel across the grain or along the end grain of a board. When chopping end grain, especially with a mallet, remember to leave a thin shaving to be removed on the final pass or two, since cutting quickly or powerfully across end grain can easily tear out chunks of the wood fiber, leaving voids that are difficult to conceal. A fine finish cut, pared with the chisel at a skewed angle, should shear the end grain fibers cleanly and leave a smooth surface. Check to make sure the chisel is truly vertical for these last cuts (See photo, following page).

Chiseling across the grain is required in many wood joinery situations, including paring lap joints and dadoes. The best way to make cross-grain cuts is to remove most of the waste material with another tool,

Chiseling across the grain. To keep the edges of a workpiece from tearing out as you chisel across the grain, cut out the waste from both sides of the joint first, working your way in toward the center. Once the edges of the workpiece are chiseled to your layout lines, pare out the waste in the middle.

Paring chamfers with a chisel. Guide the chisel blade near the cutting edge with your left hand, while driving the chisel with your right. Use your left index finger as an edge guide beneath the chisel blade to keep stock removal consistent and ensure that the chamfer is even along the workpiece edge.

such as a saw, then pare to the cutting line. If you need to make a cross-grain cut using only a chisel, rough out the waste first, chiseling with the bevel facing down. Keep in mind that the grain along the far edge will split off if you try to cut straight across. To remedy this kind of tearout, chisel halfway into the cut from one direction, then chisel in from the other side of the workpiece, keeping the blade angled slightly upward so the area at the center of the joint or dado is leveled last. Then, chisel away the center area. If you are paring across end grain horizontally, as when cutting dovetail shoulders, pare from both sides toward the center to keep from splintering out the back face.

How to chisel along end grain

Smoothing end grain. Using a firmer or butt chisel, hold the chisel blade bevel-up at a low angle to the workpiece. Skew the blade edge to the workpiece as you push the blade forward in a scraping motion. You'll need to switch chisel direction frequently to make sure the tool is always directed toward the center of the board, not toward any of the faces or edges, which can tear out.

Chiseling end grain. If you need to chisel end grain that will remain exposed, do your chopping on the waste side of your layout line. Then, pare by hand up to the layout line. Chopping shy of the layout line will keep the chisel blade from tearing out end-grain wood fibers, which would leave a rough edge.

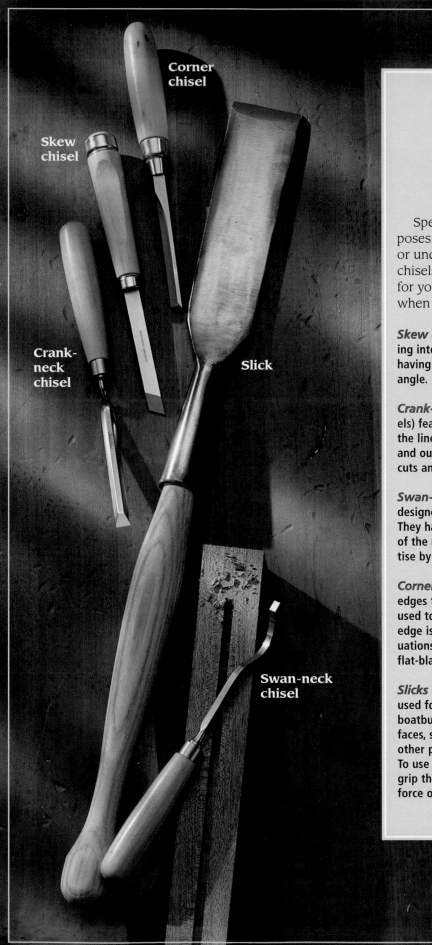

Corner chisel

Skew chisel

Crank-neck chisel

Slick

Swan-neck chisel

Specialty Chisels

Specialty chisels are created for unique purposes, such as cleaning out recesses in joinery or undertaking large-scale paring tasks. These chisels likely won't be the first you'll purchase for your shop, but they can be indispensable when the need arises.

Skew chisels have an angled cutting edge for reaching into tight corners. They're usually sold in pairs, one having a right-hand and the other a left-hand skew angle.

Crank-neck chisels (sometimes called dog-leg chisels) features a neck that's bent so the handle is above the line of the blade. This offset gets the handle up and out of the way when you're paring long interior cuts and housings.

Swan-neck chisels are specialty mortising chisels designed to smooth the bottom of a deep mortise cut. They have a hooked blade that rides along the bottom of the mortise so you can flatten and smooth the mortise by levering against the curve of the blade.

Corner chisels have blades with two inside cutting edges that meet at a 90° angle. Although they can be used to clean out inside corners, the double cutting edge is designed to help the blade track straight in situations where a wavy grain or knot would throw a flat-blade chisel off course.

Slicks are about the size of a baseball bat, but can be used for making fine paring cuts. Timber framers and boatbuilders use slicks for leveling hand-hewn surfaces, smoothing the sides of large mortises and any other paring work they can't get at with a hand plane. To use a slick, you tuck the handle under your arm, grip the chisel handle with the same arm and use the force of your body to push the chisel into the cut.

Simplify tricky tasks with specialty chisels

Flattening dado bottoms. Crank-neck chisels with offset blades allow you to follow the bottoms of dadoes and other grooves without the handle or your hand getting in the way.

Corner cleanup. The angled cutting edge and square sides of a skew chisel make it a good tool choice for removing waste from corners and sharply angled cuts.

Methods for storing chisels

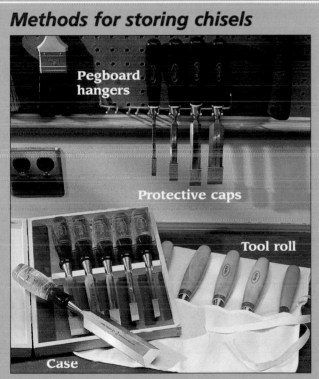

Pegboard hangers

Protective caps

Tool roll

Case

Proper storage protects the cutting edges of chisels (and makes it easier to locate chisels as you work). In the shop, the best storage system is a rack with a hole for each chisel, so you can group by type and arrange your chisels in order of size. If you need to transport your chisels, buy a canvas or leather tool roll with individual pockets. Each blade is protected, and the whole set of chisels rolls up into a small package. If your chisel set was purchased in a case, save the case for storage.

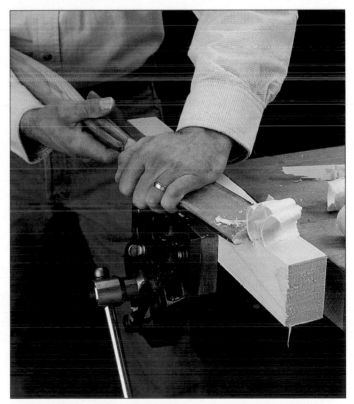

Heavy-duty chiseling tasks. Slicks are designed to be held under one arm, while you guide the blade with your other hand. Use your legs to drive the chisel forward, keeping your arms and upper body locked in position. Pare with the bevel side of the cutting edge facing up, skewing the tool edge slightly as you push the chisel forward.

Japanese dovetail chisels. Japanese dovetail chisels feature three blade bevels that converge along the top and center of the blade. This design makes for an extremely tight blade profile, perfect for removing waste between dovetail pins and tails.

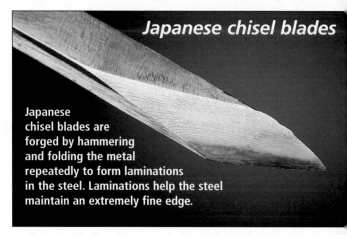

Japanese chisel blades

Japanese chisel blades are forged by hammering and folding the metal repeatedly to form laminations in the steel. Laminations help the steel maintain an extremely fine edge.

Concave vs. flat backs. Japanese chisel backs are ground concave, unlike Western chisel backs, which are ground flat. The advantage to concave backs is that they minimize the amount of surface area to be flattened on the blade back.

Japanese chisels

Japanese saws have become quite popular in America in recent years, but to date only true hand-tool enthusiasts are familiar with Japanese-style chisels. Where Japanese saws are distinguished from Western types by the fact that they cut on the pull stroke rather than the push stroke, Japanese chisels are worked in the same way as their Western counterparts.

Japanese chisel blades are made of soft steel or wrought iron for strength, with a layer of extremely hard, high-carbon steel laminated to the softer metal to form the cutting edge. The blade bodies are then heated and hammered flat, then repeatedly folded and hammered to form actual laminations in the steel, which are almost invisible to the naked eye. This process means the blades can be sharpened more keenly and will last longer between sharpenings than most Western chisel blades.

Another big difference between Western and Japanese chisels is that the backs of Japanese chisels are ground slightly concave rather than flat (See photo, above left). The hollow reduces friction and speeds the sharpening process. Some chisels have multiple hollows with a long, thin flat area between each hollow.

The standard Japanese bench chisel has beveled edges and commonly has an oak handle with a steel hoop on the end. The hoop keeps the wooden handle from breaking down under mallet blows. The usual blade variations are available, such as: firmer, mortise and paring styles. But one practical Japanese style I've yet to see from Western manufacturers is a dovetail chisel. Its edges are beveled all the way down to create a triangular cross-section that really performs for cleaning up dovetail joints, pins and tails (See photo, above right).

Anatomy of a gouge

Metal hoop, reinforces the end of the gouge handle for striking with a mallet

Leather washer, absorbs shock transmitted from mallet blows through the handle

Cutting edge, bevel faces on the convex (out-cannel) or concave (in-cannel) side of blade

Metal ferrule, locks handle & bolster together

Bolster, marks transition of blade body into tapered tang that seats inside handle

Gouges

A gouge is essentially a chisel with its blade bent into a channel to create a curved cutting edge. If you can imagine a firmer chisel rolled up, you've got what's called a firmer gouge. Firmer gouges are heavy-duty tools with straight, parallel edges. The common style, called out-cannel, is used for grooving and hollowing and has its cutting bevel on the outside of the curve.

If a chisel blade were rolled up the other way, its bevel would be on the inside. Gouges with this blade style are called in-cannel scribing or paring gouges. They are used for work in which perfectly perpendicular curved cuts are needed. However, in-cannel blades are difficult to sharpen, which makes them the less-preferred style for most serious gouge users.

Carving gouges are numbered according to their curve, or sweep, from #2 through #11. The lower numbers are shallow (a #1 blade is dead flat); as the numbers increase, the sweep becomes more curved. The narrow, U-shaped #11 is called a *veiner,* used for fluting and deep cuts where you don't want the corners to dig in.

In general, the deeper gouges

are used for roughing out large amounts of wood. The shallower sweeps serve to level out and smooth ridges and hollows left by deeper tools. Carving gouges can have parallel sides, or the sides can

taper toward the handle to give clearance behind the cutting edge. Fishtail gouge blade bodies taper back drastically. They are delicate tools, useful for cleaning out corners and undercutting, particularly

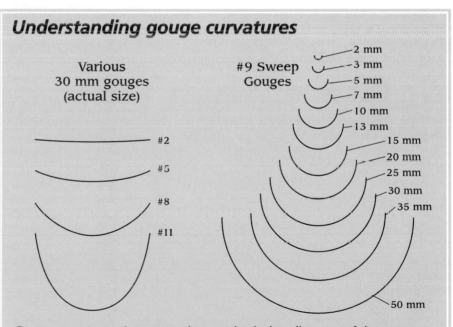

Understanding gouge curvatures

Various 30 mm gouges (actual size)

#2
#5
#8
#11

#9 Sweep Gouges

2 mm
3 mm
5 mm
7 mm
10 mm
13 mm
15 mm
20 mm
25 mm
30 mm
35 mm
50 mm

Gouge curvatures. A common misperception is that all gouges of the same number have curves of the same arc. Actually, same-numbered gouges have the same relative curvature in proportion to their size. For example, the curve of a #9 gouge is shaped roughly like a half circle. A 50 mm # 9 will have its semicircle taken from a 50-mm-dia. (2 in.) circle, while a 3 mm #9 will have a much tighter curve, namely that of a 3 mm (⅛ in.) circle. In this way, all #9 gouges are deep-sweep tools; whereas if the 3 mm gouge were to have its arc taken from a 50 mm circle, the blade would be almost totally flat.

SWISS MADE 1 5/12

SWISS MADE 1/8

SWISS MADE 5F/6

SWISS MADE 11/3

SWISS MADE 13/10

SWISS MADE 9a/7

SWISS MADE 2 8/6

SWISS MADE 3/20

SWISS MADE 8/7

H

I

J

K

L

M

N

A

B

C

D

E

F

G

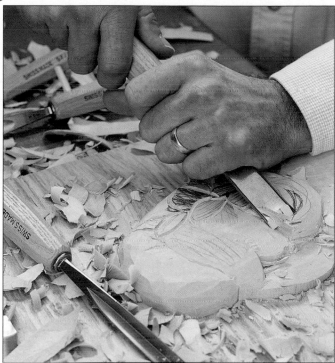

Rough-in with a mallet. To remove large amounts of waste wood and shape a rough carving, use a carver's mallet with carving chisels and gouges. Hog out material on the waste outside of your layout lines to keep from tearing out more wood fiber than you need. Mallets are helpful primarily when carving hardwood.

Rough-in with hand pressure. For carving softer woods like basswood, hand power and sharp carving tools are all you should need to rough in your shape. Grip the chisel or gouge with the bevel facing down and apply force with your right hand as you guide the blade with your left hand.

Gouges & Carving Tools

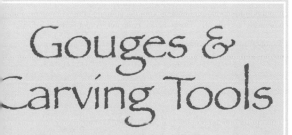

A. #8 Heavy bent carving gouge (18 mm)
B. #8 Carving gouge (13 mm)
C. #3 Carving gouge (20 mm)
D. 1-In. Out-cannel gouge
E. #5 Palm-handled fishtail
F. ¼-in. Palm-handled skew
G. ⅛-in. Palm-handled V-parting
H. Skew-cut carving chisel (12 mm)
I. Straight-cut chisel (8 mm)
J. #5 Fishtail (20 mm)
K. #11 Veiner (3 mm)
L. #13 V-parting tool (10 mm)
M. #9 Spoon gouge (7 mm)
N. #8 Back bent gouge (6 mm)

when side-to-side clearance is limited. Heavy-duty fishtails with 2- to 3-in.-wide blades are made to be used with a mallet for log building and for roughing large carvings like totem poles, carousel horses and life-size figures.

The standard straight gouge is the most often-used carving tool, but there are circumstances where the straight shank won't work. A bent gouge has a curve along the length of the blade that enables it to reach down into concave areas, deep depressions and bowls. The spoon gouge has a sharp bend near the front section of the blade for cutting tighter, narrower recesses. The back-bent gouge is like the spoon, but with its bend reversed so the cutting edge is on the convex side of the "spoon."

Carving tools

To add or refine details in wood requires a different set of tools specially designed for carving. Carving can be done in "relief" (carving into a flat surface), such as in signs, plaques, illustrations, rosettes and other applied decorations. Carving can also be done "in the round" for three-dimensional objects like figures, decoys and sculpture. And many styles of traditional furniture have heavily carved elements that require carving tools to make repair parts.

Rough carving can be done with a mallet and gouge to

Reading handle numbers

Many carving tools are stamped with two numbers on the handle, separated by a slash. The first number relates to a standard numbering system based on the curvature (or sweep) of the blade. The second number identifies the width across the blade, either in fractions of an inch or in millimeters. For instance, a tool stamped "13/10" means it is in the #13 sweep family with a blade that is 10 mm wide (See chart, page 63).

remove stock quickly until your project is close to the shape you want. But for refining details and doing finish cuts, use carving tools applied with hand pressure. This allows a very fine degree of control over depth, angle and length of cut. The idea is to leave extremely smooth surfaces on the wood, ready for your oil or finish, since you can't go back over a detailed carving with sandpaper. Keep the tools razor-sharp and be alert to sudden changes in grain direction. You may need to change the direction of your cuts periodically as you progress across your workpiece to avoid chipping out the grain.

If you are just starting your foray into woodcarving, you don't need to invest a great deal of money on carving tools. Every manufacturer sells value-priced sets with assortments of the most basic and useful tools, often pre-packaged with a tool roll for storage and protection—sometimes even with slipstones and a mallet. A set of 10 to 15 tools will get you off to a good start. Individual tools can be added later when you discover the sizes and shapes you need for your type of work. The tools shown on the preceding page represent a good, complete starter set.

Even if you don't plan on doing any carving, a 13 or 16 mm #8 gouge is a handy tool to have in the workshop. It has a moderate curvature that makes it useful for getting into the odd details you find on moldings, and it can also be used for paring off plugs on a curved surface.

Buy quality tools from reputable toolmakers and distributors. Inexpensive "student" sets in art supply stores may be adequate for a single wood-block print in pine, but they're not very comfortable to use and, more importantly, the steel is usually soft and won't hold a sharp edge.

Standard straight-handled carving tools are used with two hands, like a chisel. One hand guides the blade and the other hand supplies the driving force behind the tool. Shorter "mushroom"-handled tools are intended to be used with one hand only. Simply nestle the handle in your palm and guide the blade with your fingers.

Carving chisels differ from ordinary woodworking chisels in that the cutting edge is beveled on both faces. The edge can be straight across or skewed. Carving chisels are also available with bent blades so they can be maneuvered into tight recesses.

V-parting carving tools have a V-shaped cutting edge, available in a variety of sweep angles, which makes them effective for outlining corners, grooving and adding details and textures. Parting tools can also be obtained with bent or spoon-shaped blades. Most of these tool styles are also available in "micro-sized" versions, often packaged in sets for extremely fine detail and miniature work.

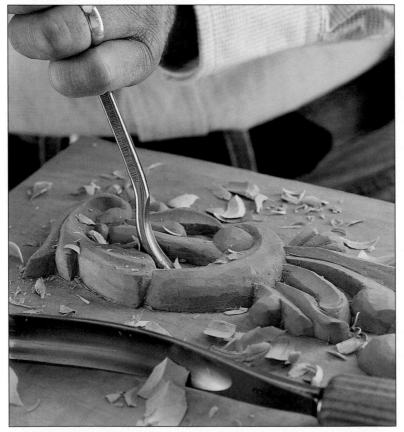

Bent gouge to clean out recessed area. Use a bent or spoon gouge to clean out deep recesses in tight areas on a carving project. Use only hand pressure on the tool, and carve out very thin shavings to avoid tearing or chipping the grain.

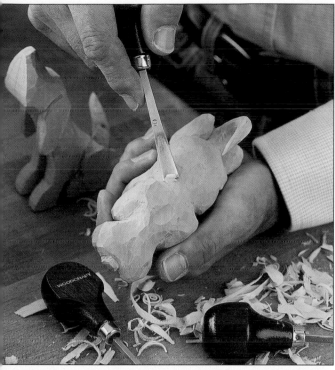

Mushroom-handled carving tools. Mushroom-handled tools are designed to be gripped in the palm of your hand. Their small blades come in a variety of shapes that are designed for producing fine details in carvings. Change your grip on the workpiece as needed to keep your hand clear of the blade.

Veining carvers. Veining tools have narrow concave blade sweeps and are intended to be used for making long, flowing cuts, such as flutes. You'll know your blade is sharp enough if the shavings curl away as you cut.

Fishtail gouges. Fishtail gouges feature slender, tapered blades that make them perfect for cleaning out waste from tight inside corners. Guide the tool with your left hand, gripping it close to the blade, with your thumb pointing toward the handle. Drive the tool with your right hand.

V-parting tools. Use a V-parting tool to start layout lines on a rough carving. These tools also can be used to cut wide grooves. Grip the tool as you would a fishtail gouge, with your left thumb facing the tool handle.

All-purpose shears   **Utility knife**

Jack knife

Chip carving knife

Lock-blade shop knife

Knives & Shears

- **Utility knives** are intended for general paring and cutting tasks. Disposable blades are razor sharp.

- **Jack knives** are made in a variety of blade lengths and configurations suited for cutting and carving. Blades typically fold and store in handles.

- **Chip carving knives** are specially designed for carving. Short blades do not fold or retract.

- **Lock-blade knives** use a locking mechanism in the handle to hold the blade open for cutting and carving. The blade can be unlocked and folded into the handle for storage.

- **All-purpose shears** are intended to cut many materials, including paper, cardboard, fabrics and string. They're made in a variety of styles suitable for heavy-duty cutting applications.

Knives

Knives have already been discussed in this book as marking tools, but their obvious primary purpose is for cutting. A utility knife (or razor-blade craft knife, depending on the strength or delicacy required) can be used in place of a saw for cutting innumerable thin materials, including wood veneer, paper, cardboard and sheet-vinyl flooring. Often a blade can follow a curved layout line easier and more smoothly than a pair of scissors can. And a slender knife blade can clean out sharp corners in wood joints where a chisel just won't reach.

Carving knives come in an ever-expanding array of specialized types for chip carving, relief carving and whittling. Some carving knives are fashioned with blades that fold into the handle to protect the cutting edge, while the blades on other models are permanently extended.

When selecting knives for carving, pay particular attention to how the handles fit your hand. The diameter of the handle should be large enough to grip comfortably when you make a loose fist with your hand. You'll spend many hours handling these tools, so even minor annoyances in how the handle fits your hand could lead to hand fatigue.

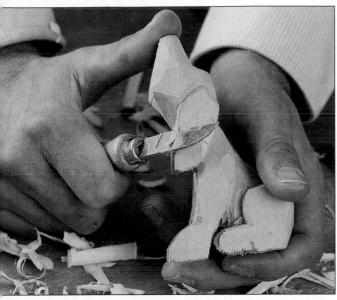

Chip carving knives. **Chip carvers feature shorter blades in a variety of shapes to suit small or detailed carving projects. Blades are sharpened along one edge only. Most chip carving knives must be honed first before they can be used.**

Utility knives. **A tool with innumerable uses, the utility knife makes quick work of everything from outlining hinge mortises to stripping wire, cutting floor tile and sharpening shop pencils. The razor blades are disposable and store inside the handle.**

Shears

Every shop should be equipped with at least one pair of shears near the bench. Household scissors make quick work of cutting paper templates to shape, and most are capable of also cutting thicker materials such as cardboard, felt and cloth. Some heavier-duty shears are designed with oversized handles and stout blades, which allow you to cut through thick or abrasive materials like carpet, linoleum and leather. Choose shears with self-sharpening stainless-steel blades; they'll be corrosion resistant, and the cutting edges will stand up to years of abuse. Pick a style with comfortable, ergonomically-shaped handles and a screw-type pin that secures the parts together, so you can loosen or tighten the screw to adjust the shearing action.

Sharpness test for knife blades

A variety of tests can be applied to determine the sharpness of a knife blade. Some, such as shaving off a thin layer of finger nail or the hair on your arm, should be avoided. A safer and easier method is simply to inspect the blade edge under a bright light. If you see areas where light glints off the cutting edge, you've actually located dull spots. The edge on a sharp blade should reflect no light. For more on sharpening a knife blade, see page 154.

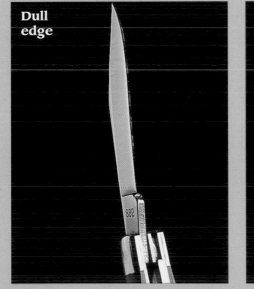

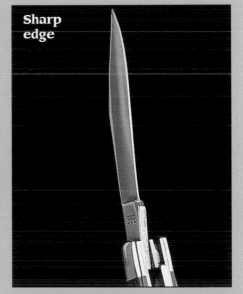

Identifying a dull edge. **Shine a bright light against the cutting edge of a knife blade. Light will reflect off dull spots.**

The mark of a sharp edge. **Sharpen the cutting edge until it reflects no light.**

Drilling

*A*dvancing technology has provided us with amazingly powerful cordless drills and specialty power drills that can blast through just about any task in no time at all. As a result, the hand-powered drill has become an overlooked tool in recent years. That's too bad, but not too surprising. It's easy to forget that the many hand drills still available today are the result of thousands of years of tool evolution. And despite their reliance on old-fashioned elbow grease for their power, they have set a standard for controlled power and brilliant engineering. From skilled professionals who depend on precise control, to contractors who can't afford to sit around waiting for their power packs to recharge, to collectors who simply appreciate great design, you don't have to look too far to find people who still depend on old-fashioned hand-powered drills.

Still not convinced? Here are a few more reasons to resist the urge to toss your old brace-and-bit onto the table at your next tag sale:

• Their safety, ease-of-use and quietness make these the perfect tools for kids to learn woodworking with—plus, the coordination developed through the proper balancing of cranking and applied pressure is fundamental to hand tool basics.

• Using a manual drill is a more deliberate operation than power drilling, but it can also be more precisely controlled. Tiny drill bits that would break almost instantly when powered by an electric drill can be carefully bored by hand, and the depth of cut can be stopped on a dime.

• Large holes that would require a drill press to bore electrically can be safely and accurately drilled freehand, at any angle, with a brace.

• A gear-driven hand drill is quick to set up, cordless and perfect for work where a power drill would be too bulky or inconvenient. And working in tight quarters, a push drill can fit in anywhere a screwdriver can.

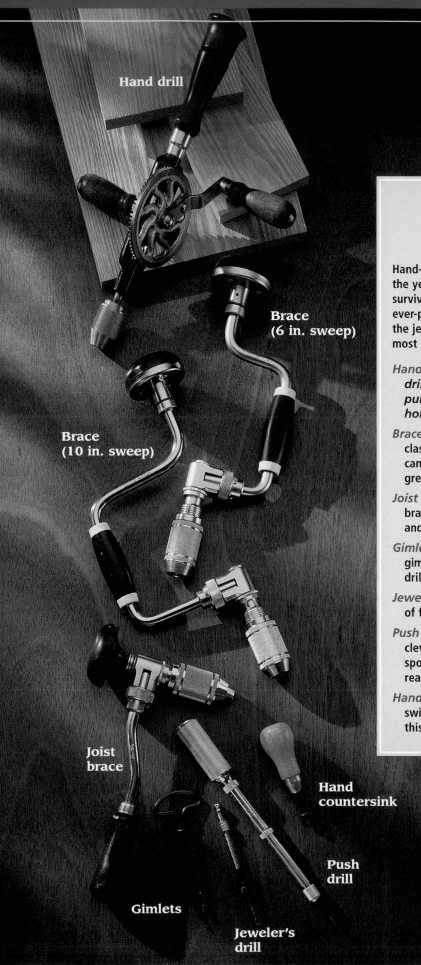

Hand drill

Brace
(6 in. sweep)

Brace
(10 in. sweep)

Joist
brace

Hand
countersink

Push
drill

Gimlets

Jeweler's
drill

Drills

Hand-powered drills have taken on many forms over the years. The examples shown to the left are the survivors of hand-powered drill evolution. From the ever-popular brace-and-bit to specialty tools such as the jeweler's drill, all of these drills can be found in most hand tools catalogs. They include:

Hand drills: **Sometimes called "eggbeater" drills, these clever devices are general-purpose drills that are built to drill small holes very quickly.**

Braces: The graceful sweep of a brace-style drill is a classic among hand tool profiles. Big or small, they can deliver surprising amounts of torque with a great deal of control.

Joist braces: These special-purpose, ratcheting braces are designed to fit into stud wall cavities and bore holes for wiring and plumbing.

Gimlets: Not well known, but extremely convenient, gimlets are simple twist drills that are sized to drill quick-and-easy pilot holes for wood screws.

Jeweler's drills: For exceptionally accurate boring of fine holes, you can't beat these precision tools.

Push drills: Also known as *Yankee drills,* these clever tools make quick work of drilling holes in spots your cordless drill couldn't dream of reaching.

Hand countersink: There's no need to stop and switch bits on your power drill when you've got this simple tool to countersink your pilot holes.

Anatomy of a brace

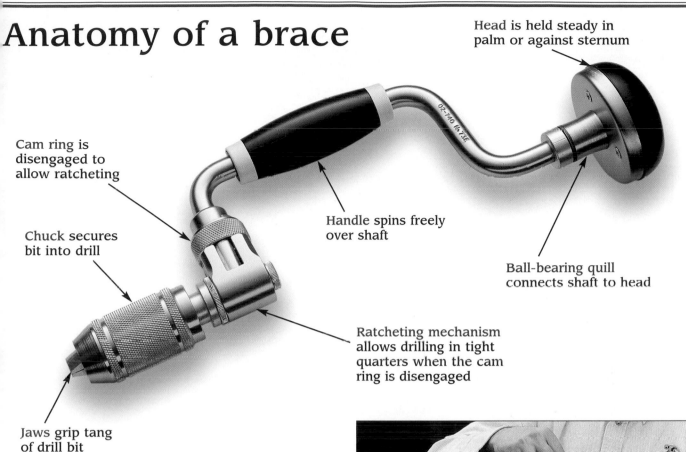

Head is held steady in palm or against sternum

Cam ring is disengaged to allow ratcheting

Chuck secures bit into drill

Handle spins freely over shaft

Ball-bearing quill connects shaft to head

Ratcheting mechanism allows drilling in tight quarters when the cam ring is disengaged

Jaws grip tang of drill bit

Braces

The brace-and-bit is the meat and potatoes of hand drilling. Boring large holes requires considerable leverage, and the powerful brace supplies it through its smooth, ball-bearing action crank. The power of the brace is dependent on its *sweep* (the diameter of a full swing of the handle). Braces are available with many sweep ranges. Drills with greater sweeps are capable of more torque, while smaller sweeps are better suited for cramped quarters. A brace with a 10-in. sweep is a good general-purpose tool. You may want to purchase a 6-in. model for working in tight areas and for quicker action when drilling smaller holes.

The drill bits used with a brace are called *auger bits,* and are sold in 1/16-in. increments starting at 1/4 in. dia. and increasing in thickness up to 1 in. An adjustable expansion bit can increase the drilling capacity to as much as 3 in. dia. As well as boring big holes, a brace can also be used to bore deep holes due to the length of the auger bits.

Some older braces will only accept auger bits with square-tapered tangs, but most modern braces are fitted with a chuck that will hold regular straight-shank twist bits up to 1/2 in. dia. Most braces made and sold today include a ratcheting mechanism that allows you to drill in awkward places where there is not enough

Brace-and-bit drilling technique. **When drilling with a brace-and-bit, keep the bit from wandering by maintaining constant pressure on the head, with the force directed evenly over the tip of the bit. Rotate the handle in a smooth, circular motion. Avoid pressing too hard on the head, as this can also cause the bit to wander and makes it more difficult to maintain a smooth sweeping motion. Be sure to secure the workpiece before drilling.**

clearance for the full sweep. The ratcheting mechanism is also useful in circumstances where more pull torque is required, such as when using a screwdriver bit to drive or extract screws. The ratchet can be engaged to operate in either a clockwise or counter-clockwise direction, and should be disengaged when operating the drill with a full, free-swing sweep.

In addition to the standard style, braces have been made in several specialized designs over the years for drilling in restricted spaces. One well-established style is the *joist brace,* which has a long handle set at a 90° angle to the bit, allowing you to operate the drill in a stud wall cavity *(See photo, right).*

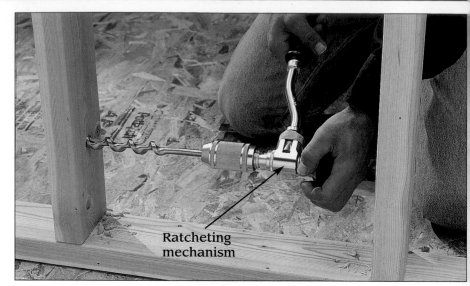

Joist brace: The hand-driven right angle drill. **The joist brace is a specialized version of a standard brace, designed to be used between studs in a wall cavity. Equipped with a ratcheting mechanism, it features a handle that's perpendicular to the drill bit.**

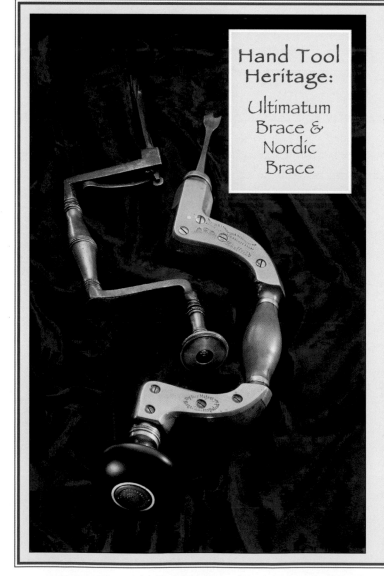

Hand Tool Heritage:

Ultimatum Brace & Nordic Brace

B etween 1829 and 1925, over 500 patents for braces were issued in the United States alone. With so much variety, antique braces have become highly sought-after collectibles. Among the better-known types of early braces are *framed braces* that feature solid metal, protective sideplates (usually brass) joined by a metal rod. A wooden brace handle rotates on the metal rod. The wooden infills were most commonly ebony, but rosewood and beech (shown) were also used. The 13-in.-long framed brace shown here, dubbed the *Ultimatum Framed Brace,* was manufactured by William Marples & Sons in Sheffield, England, between 1856 and 1860. The original patent for the *Ultimatum* was issued in 1849, and the tools were manufactured through the end of the 19th century. The ebony head is inlaid with an ivory ring and an inscribed brass screw-cap, which reads "Marples & Sons—Sheffield—Hibernia Works" and also includes the Marples Irish harp trademark.

Nordic Braces: The smaller, all metal brace shown to the left is an excellent example of the simple yet highly practical Nordic braces. At 10 in. long, it is a hand-forged, all-metal brace that is Norwegian in design. The chuck, forged as an integral part of the typically Nordic shaped frame, requires use of a specially designed flat-tanged bit held in place by a unique spring device. The handle, with its hammered beading, and the single-piece head are both fashioned from brass.

Hand drills

The hand drill is designed for rapid boring of small diameter holes in wood and lightweight metal. Able to spin a drill bit much faster than a brace can, a hand drill works in the same manner as an eggbeater, hence the tool's nickname: the eggbeater drill. Its speed, combined with its light weight and slim profile, makes the hand drill a convenient and efficient tool.

The quill that spins the chuck on a hand drill is powered by one or two small gears (called *pinions*) that are driven by a larger gear (called the *drive gear* or *speed gear*) that is connected to a hand crank. On better-quality hand drills, a pair of pinions (the *idler pinion* and the *drive pinion*) are mounted in a frame on opposite edges of the drive gear. The main purpose of the idler pinion is to track the drive gear as the drive pinion transmits the power to the quill. Cheaper hand drills have only a single-drive pinion mounted near the chuck.

Some hand drills have a two-position crank that works like high and low gears on a bicycle. For most jobs, the handle is fixed at the outer position on the drive gear to generate maximum torque. But if you are drilling small holes or boring through metal, glass, or very hard wood, set the handle at the inner position to increase the bit speed.

All hand drills have one handle at the end of the drill shaft and another mounted in the crank that is attached to the drive gear. Better-quality drills feature a third handle that's connected to the drill on the side opposite the crank handle. This handle is intended to provide increased pressure and control when you use your

Anatomy of a hand drill

Detachable side handle

Removable cap (for access to bit storage)

Frame

Top handle

Idler pinion

Crank handle

Quill

Drive pinion

Drive (speed) gear

Chuck

Jaws

body to apply pressure against the flat heel of the top handle. Side handles usually can be unscrewed and removed. Hand drill handles traditionally are made of wood, but high-impact plastic may be used on some newer models.

The three-jaw hand drill chuck is made to accept only non-tapered, round-shanked bits such as twist bits, brad-point bits and many common countersink and screwdriver bits made for power drills. The straight-flute drill points made for use with push drills also can be used. The jaw capacity of hand drill chucks generally is either ¼ or ⅜ in.

How to operate a hand drill

Vertical drilling

Horizontal drilling

Whether drilling vertically or horizontally, hold the hand drill straight and steady. Adopt a moderate, constant speed as you turn the crank handle. Apply light, even pressure against the top handle to impel the bit forward. When drilling on a vertical plane, use the palm of your hand to exert pressure on the top handle (left photo); on a horizontal plane, press your body against the flat of the top handle and grip the side handle to keep the drill steady as you crank (right photo). The crank is always turned in a clockwise direction (unless you're using a screwdriver bit to extract a screw). The chuck should be hand tightened; never use pliers or any other tool to grasp or turn the chuck.

Push drills

The push drill is commonly known by the Yankee trademark name registered to Stanley Tools, which first introduced the drill. With this simple tool, pushing downward on the handle causes an internal spiral shaft to rotate the chuck and the bit it is holding. Releasing the pressure on the handle allows the chuck to spring back to its starting position. The push drill is quick to set up, slips into a pocket or pouch, and can be used in tight spaces. Plus, the drill can be powered and positioned with only one hand, allowing you to hold onto other items, such as hinge plates or templates, while you drill.

Because pushing and releasing the handle imparts a back-and-forth rotary motion to the drill bit, a common spiral twist drill bit can't be used in a push drill. Instead, use special push drill bits with a single straight flute down the shaft that can cut in both directions. The special chuck on this drill dictates that the bits have a notch at the end of the shaft as well. Typically, the push drill has a hollow magazine handle that is equipped with eight bits by the manufacturer (from 1/16 in. to 11/64 in.). Powerful, small and versatile, the push drill is an excellent addition to emergency tool kits.

How to use a push drill

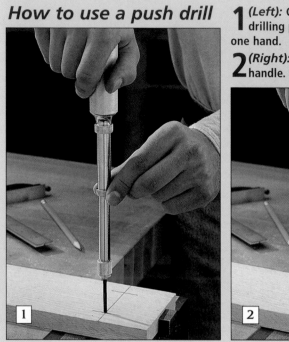

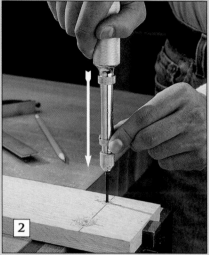

1 *(Left):* Center the bit over the drilling point; steady the drill with one hand.

2 *(Right):* Press down evenly on the handle. Repeat until hole is bored.

Specialty drilling tools

A hand (manual) countersink is used to widen the mouth of a hole to create a countersink for recessing screw heads. Among other advantages, this allows you to countersink without switching drill bits. The tool can also be used to deburr holes in soft metal.

A jeweler's drill is an Archimedean-style push drill used for boring holes as small as 1/74 in. The precise, controlled action works well for drilling any delicate object.

Gimlets are ring- or T-handled tools that look like miniature augers. They're used mainly for drilling screw pilot holes. Gimlets usually come in sets, sized to fit several screw sizes. They're also handy for drilling starter holes for larger drill bits.

Expansion bit

Auger bit

Spur

Threaded tip

Twist bit

Straight-flute bit

Spade bit

Brad-point bit

Drill Bits

Expansion bit: Brace bit with adjustable cutting diameter

Auger bit: Basic bit for boring larger holes with a brace

Straight-flute bit: Called "drill point," used with push drill

Brad-point bit: Used to drill smooth-sided holes; model shown (round tang) is used with a hand drill

Spade bit: For drilling larger holes with brace or hand drill

Twist bit: Used with hand drill; square-tang twist bits for braces can be found but are rare

Drill bits

Drill bits for hand-operated drills vary somewhat from the typical drill bits we're accustomed to using with power drills. The main point of departure is in the "tang" (the part of the drill shaft that's inserted into the jaws of the chuck). Most power drills accept bits with cylindrical tangs. These may be used with most hand (eggbeater) drills, but aren't designed for use with braces or push drills. The three-jaw configuration of most brace chucks requires a tapered, square-tanged bit. Push (*Yankee*) drills employ an oscillating action that requires a bit with a single vertical flute.

Auger bits are the bits used most frequently with braces. They're designed for slow, efficient wood boring. The threaded tip pulls the bit into the wood as it turns, whereupon the sharp spurs slice the out-

line of the hole, assuring clean entry (auger bits should never be used in a power drill). The cutting edges of the bit cut out waste as drilling progresses, and the twisted flutes draw the waste out of the hole. Auger bits can be purchased individually or in sets. Sizes range from ¼ to 1 in. by increments of ¹⁄₁₆ in. Auger bits are numbered according to the size of the bit in sixteenths of an inch: Thus, a bit marked 5 bores a ⁵⁄₁₆-in. dia. hole.

A "spin-off" of the typical auger bit, called an *expansion bit,* has two interchangeable and adjustable cutters that can be set to drill holes as large as 3 in. dia. or as small as ½ in. (See *photo, right*).

Twist bits. These are the common, straight-shank bits used in hand and power drills. Twist bits designed for wood have a longer

Use an expansion bit for big holes.
Standard auger bits for braces only come in sizes up to 1 in. dia. To drill larger holes, use and expansion auger bit with an adjustable cutter that can be micro-adjusted to cut holes up to 3 in. dia.

angle at the tip, giving them a sharper point than bits designed to drill metal. But since the wood bits aren't commonly available, almost everyone uses the all-purpose type designed for metal. Because these bits have a blunt-angled tip instead of a point, it's necessary to first make an indentation at the drilling point with an awl or center punch.

Twist bits are made of carbon steel or high-speed steel. While carbon steel is certainly hard enough to drill wood, high-speed steel bits are a better choice. They stay sharp much longer and don't burn the wood as readily. Twist bits also are made from special alloys or surface coatings for drilling stainless steel and other very hard materials.

The best way to buy twist bits is in a set that comes in a metal case, or *drill index*. The individual bits are cheaper this way, and a with a fairly complete set you should be prepared to drill just about any size hole you're likely to need. Standard kits are the 13-piece set (1⁄16 to 1⁄4 in. by 64ths) and the 29-piece set (1⁄16 to 1⁄2 in. by 64ths). If neither option provides enough selection

> When drilling a deep hole in hardwood, partially withdraw the bit occasionally to allow the chips to clear. The waste tends to compact and clog the flutes, reducing cutting efficiency and overheating the drill bit.

for your drilling needs, there are three other systems that fill in the gaps so you can drill precisely sized holes in the most infinitesimal increments: *Metric bits* progress by .05 mm; *Wire gauge* sizes start at No. 1 (.22 in.) and go down to No. 80 (.0135 in.); *Letter sizes* run from *A* (.234 in.) up to *Z* (.413 in.). Twist bits can also be obtained in extra-long lengths, up to about 18 in.

Brad-point bits are twist bits that are uniquely adapted for drilling crisp, accurately sized holes in wood. The tip is similar to an auger, but has a sharp brad point instead of the screw-threaded point. The brad point allows accurate positioning and prevents wandering, while the spurs score a clean hole perimeter with no tearout. Brad-point bits produce nearly flat-bottomed holes.

Single-fluted bits (Drill points) are designed for use with a push drill. Their single, straight flutes cut in both clockwise and counterclockwise directions, and a notch at the tip allows waste wood to exit the hole. Sizes run from 1⁄16 to 11⁄64 in. by 1⁄64-in. increments.

Drilling techniques

Traditional wisdom tells us there are two kinds of holes that can be bored in wood: straight and crooked. The former starts and ends where it's supposed to; the latter may start off well directed, but then wanders off indiscriminately. When drilling, always clamp the workpiece securely.

Drill speed. Drilling doesn't require excessive pressure or speed. With manual drilling you can feel when the drill bit is working at peak efficiency. Try to maintain that balance of feed pressure and cranking pace consistently throughout the operation.

Preventing tearout. If you're drilling clear through the workpiece, the wood fibers will tear out at the underside of the hole if precautions are not taken (See illustrations, right). One way to

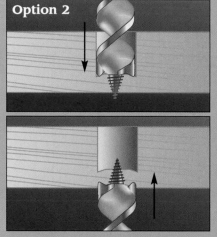

How to prevent tearout

Option 1

Work-piece

Backer board

Option 2

Use a backer board. A can't-miss trick for preventing drill tearout is to clamp a scrap board to the exit side of your workpiece. Drill until you're sure the spurs of the bit (or the bottoms of the flutes) have passed completely through the workpiece, then back the bit out of the hole.

Drill from both sides of board. In situations where using a backer board is awkward, drill through the workpiece until the point of the bit breaks through the exit side. Then, finish drilling the hole from the exit side, using the breakthrough hole as a drilling point.

prevent tearout is simply to clamp a backer board of scrap wood to the underside of the workpiece. If you're drilling with a spurred bit, like an auger or brad-point, you can use another method. As the drill bit

approaches the underside of the workpiece, slow down Check the underside and when the point pokes through, stop drilling and back the bit out of the hole. Flip the board over and, using the hole from the drill point as a centerpoint, carefully drill from the underside until the holes meet.

Drilling perpendicular holes. To bore a straight hole with a hand-powered drill, you need to sight the drill for plumb. First, get the drill started. After the bit has begun to bite into the wood, visually check the angle of the drill and the bit to the work. Sight from two points, roughly 90° apart, to get a correct reading, then check again after the hole is a little way along. When the tool is perpendicular to the work (either vertically or horizontally), you're all set. The eye is a very reliable guide, but you can use a try square just to be sure. When starting an auger bit or brad-point bit, you know you're square to the work if the spurs outline a complete circle of constant depth.

Drilling angled holes. To purposely drill an angled hole requires a little guidance. With a twist drill all you need is an angled piece of cardboard or a mark on the side of your wood to guide your eye. When using an auger at a severe angle, a guide block helps overcome the spurs digging in before the feed screw (See photos, lower right).

Drilling stopped holes. One way to drill a stopped hole to a given depth is simply to stop drilling periodically and check the depth of the hole with a small straightedge or calipers. But if you have more than one or two holes to drill to the same depth, it's easier if you use a *depth stop.* This can be as simple as a piece of masking tape wrapped around the bit at the proper point. A more accurate method is to bore a hole in a block of wood, then trim the block so the thickness equals the distance from the jaws of the chuck to the tip of the bit, minus the planned depth of the hole. Drill through the hole in the block until the chuck reaches the wood block. Many styles of manufactured gizmos are available as well to serve as depth stops and collars.

Guides for drilling perpendicular holes

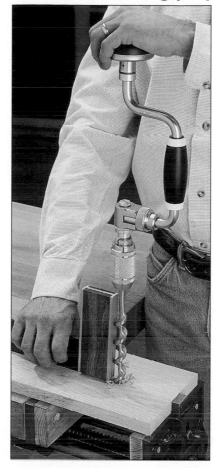

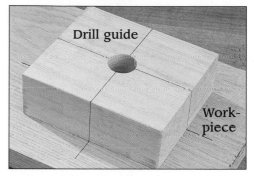

Make a drill guide (above). Mark a drilling point in the center of a piece of thick scrap wood, then draw intersecting lines through the drilling point. Extend the lines down the sides of the scrap. With the bit you'll be using, drill a hole through the drilling point, using a try square to make sure the hole is perpendicular. Mark the drilling point(s) on your workpiece, then draw intersecting lines through the point(s). Position the guide so the lines align, then clamp or tack the guide to the workpiece. Drill through the workpiece, keeping the bit centered in the hole in the guide.

Check with a try square (left). From at least two positions, use a try square to check the angle of the bit to the workpiece. Check as soon as the bit engages the wood, and periodically as you bore the hole.

How to make a guide for drilling angled holes

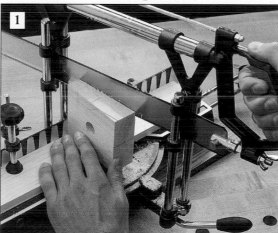

1 *(above):* Make a drill guide from a thick piece of scrap wood (See photo, top of page). Set the guide on-edge in a miter box and trim off the bottom at the desired angle of the hole.

2 *(right):* Clamp the guide to your workpiece with the trimmed side down so the bottom of the guide hole is centered over the drilling point for the angled hole. Drill the hole, keeping the bit perpendicular to the top surface of the drill guide.

Shaping & Smoothing

The first wood plane was created centuries ago to harness a chisel blade into a wooden frame, where it could be controlled and adjusted to produce smooth, even shavings rather than chips. The plane, along with other hand-operated shaping and smoothing tools (such as scrapers, drawknives and spokeshaves) quickly became essential to woodworking. With these tools, craftsmen could produce flat, smooth, square pieces of lumber from rough timber.

Up until just a few generations ago, wood arrived at the workshop directly from the sawmill, or even in the form of rough logs. It was the chore of the woodworker himself to hone the rough lumber into the finished stock he needed to complete his project. And this he did, using among other tools a host of hand planes.

Most professional furnituremakers today still buy their lumber in the rough but prefer to mill it to size using power jointers and power planers instead of hand planes. Woodworkers who lack these power tools purchase their stock already "dressed" to a flat, finished surface on two or four sides.

Despite these changes in the wood-planing landscape, hand skills are not in danger of becoming extinct. Many design colleges are now offering fine furniture programs focusing on hand shaping and smoothing. Fine woodworking with an emphasis on hand work has become one of the country's major hobbies. In response to this swelling demand, the manufacture of quality planes and other shaping tools is enjoying a rebirth. And even though you may not be able to find a good selection of hand planes at every corner hardware store or home center, mail-order woodworking tool catalogs abound, offering a varied selection of excellent shaping and smoothing tools.

Hand planes

Perhaps no tool, hand-operated or electrically powered, symbolizes the pursuit of woodworking more fully than the hand plane. Other tools can be employed (correctly or incorrectly) to perform a multitude of tasks that go far beyond the realm of woodworking. But the plane has one purpose and one purpose only: to shave thin curls of wood from woodworking and carpentry projects.

Even though most handymen and woodworkers don't do much of their own rough milling by hand these days, there are more than enough efficient and useful ways to use hand planes to ensure their continued presence as essential shop tools. A bench plane will straighten and square-up a board in a hurry—an important first step even when using dressed lumber. As anyone who has purchased dressed lumber can attest, the boards may have been planed to thickness, but they're often wavy, cupped, twisted or otherwise in need of some serious trueing.

Planes also are used to flatten and smooth uneven surfaces and joint transitions, as well as for chamfering, beveling, and shaping. They can remove a lot of material quickly or take translucently fine shavings. Since planes can remove very slight amounts of material from precisely targeted spots, they can be used to true-up joints for a perfect fit or to make very slight adjustments to drawers and doors that stick.

In addition to its excellence as a shaping tool, the hand plane works superbly for smoothing. In fact, when properly tuned and sharpened, the hand plane can produce a wood surface that rivals any power-sanded surface in smoothness.

For luster and sheen that cannot be duplicated any other way, many woodworkers finish their projects with a few swipes of a smoothing plane and a coat of oil or hand-buffed wax. A plane is also a very good tool for evening out and smoothing straight turnings on a lathe. And even if you own a power planer, there's always the glued-up tabletop that's too wide for the planer to contend with. And over the years, many planes have been

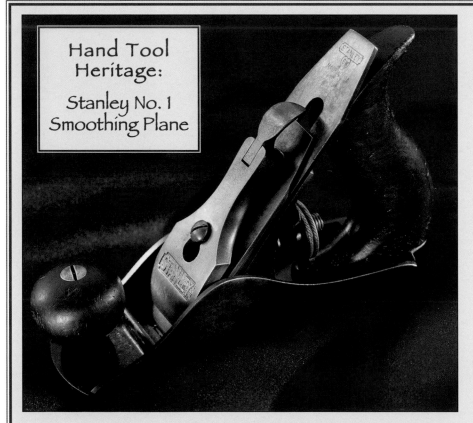

Hand Tool Heritage: Stanley No. 1 Smoothing Plane

The scarce *Stanley No. 1* smoothing plane, produced from 1867 to 1943, is the smallest of the Stanley smoothing planes at a mere 5²⁵⁄₃₂ in. long and 1¹⁷⁄₃₂ in. wide. A cabinet-maker or carpenter could easily carry it in an apron pocket, where it was always available to smooth small surfaces or do that final odd touch-up job. But despite its diminutive size it's considered one of the most desirable and collectible hand planes.

Many causes have been posited for the scarcity of the *Stanley No. 1:* Among them is the general reluctance of the woodworking community to accept such a small tool, which contributed to Stanley's decision in 1872 to produce the popular *No. 9* block plane, which featured an adjustable throat and more generous proportions than the *No. 1.*

Other smoothing planes produced by Stanley included *Nos. 2, 3* and *4.* The *No. 2* and *No. 4* had a lateral adjustment after 1885 so the cutter could be maintained parallel to the surface. The *No. 3* and the *No. 4* were large enough to be used for jointing work. All of the smoothing planes, except the *No.1,* were available with a corrugated sole.

The *No. 1* shown here is made of cast iron with a rosewood handle. It has the *AA* type *Sweet Heart* trade mark on its original cutter and the *KK* type notched rectangle on the lever cap, indicating it was probably produced between 1925 and 1928.

Hand Tool
Heritage:
Spiers
Smoothing
Plane

Although a number of British metalworkers made metal planes during the late 19th century, probably the most sought after metal planes, by user and collector alike, are the planes of Stewart Spiers of Ayr, Scotland, and Thomas Norris of London. The Thomas Norris firm later became *T. Norris & Son.* Their earlier metal bench planes, made of wrought iron or gun metal and, later, cast iron were not only efficient in use but were objects of beauty in design and material use as well. Core infills and handles were made of rosewood or ebony. In addition to bench planes they also made core infilled bull-nose, shoulder, chariot and other plane types.

The Stewart Spiers smoothing plane shown here resembles the Norris planes closely. It is 7 in. long and 2 in. wide, with a rosewood infill and handle. The brass lever cap and screw holds a two piece iron firmly in place. The iron cap is inscribed *"Stewart Spiers Ayr, Scotland, cast steel."* The 3/16-in.-thick cutter is inscribed *"Alex Mathieson & Son, warranted, cast steel."* Alexander Mathieson was a metal tool and iron producer in Glasgow, Scotland.

developed for specialized tasks like rabbeting and grooving.

Due to their close association with the craft of woodworking, old hand planes are extremely popular collectibles. The widespread practice of handcrafting beautiful wooden hand planes has added to their overall appeal.

In the mid-1800s, an American named Leonard Bailey developed a modern, metal-bodied bench plane with several new features that greatly improved its adjustability and ease of use. In 1869, *Stanley Rule and Level Co.* acquired Bailey's design and began manufacturing the Bailey bench plane. The tools became the most popular (and many believe the best) bench planes ever produced. Although more expensive than wooden-bodied planes, they were preferred for their durability and capacity for fine adjustments. The Bailey plane quickly became the standard for furnituremakers, carpenters, hobbyists, homeowners and schools.

Hand planes can be categorized in two groups: *bench planes,* and *specialty planes.* Within the bench planes group, you'll find subcategories: *smoothing planes, jack planes* and *jointer planes.* Specialty planes include *block planes, rabbeting planes, router planes* and *Japanese planes,* among many others.

Bench planes

The vast majority of planes in use today are members of the *bench plane* family. They are employed to perform the tasks most commonly associated with planing: flattening, squaring and smoothing wood stock. While most bench planes can be grouped into one of the categories noted above (smoothing, jack and jointer) some of the smaller models are simply called *bench planes.*

Mechanically, bench planes are all quite similar, except for the length of the sole. Most plane manufacturers use the original *Stanley* numbering system to denote standard sizes: Size numbers range from the very small *No. 1,* with its 5½-in.-long sole, to the 24-in.-long *No. 8* jointer planes.

Jack planes. The jack plane is a very popular general-purpose bench plane that includes the mid-sized *No. 5* and *No. 5½.* These are the planes to use for quick, coarse stock removal in preliminary planing of rough timber. Those who do a lot of this kind of work will often grind a blade to a slightly convex radius on its cutting edge so it can take deeper bites. A jack plane is also great for trueing moderately long edges and for general flattening and smoothing work. It's lightweight but still long enough to be accurate.

No. 2 bench plane

No. 4 smoothing plane

No. 5 jack plane

Wood-bodied smoothing plane

No. 7 jointer plane

Bench Planes

Bench planes are used for basic smoothing and jointing tasks. Typically, they're identified by a number (ranging from 2 to 7, with higher numbers assigned to larger tools), as well as by type. The three basic types of bench planes are jack planes, jointer planes and smoothing planes.

No. 4 smoothing plane is a very popular general-purpose plane. 9¾ in. long, 2-in.-wide blade.

No. 2 bench plane is the smallest bench plane to get frequent use. The high-end model shown is cast manganese bronze and cherry. 7 in. long, 1⅝-in.-wide blade.

No. 5 jack plane is sturdy and designed for heavy work. 14 in. long, 2-in.wide blade.

Wood-bodied smoothing plane is a versatile and very attractive wood-shop tool. Model shown is pearwood with a lignum vitae base. 8⅞ in. long, 1⅞-in.-wide blade.

No. 7 jointer plane has a long sole for edge-jointing boards. 22 in. long, 2⅜-in.-wide blade.

Jointer planes. As the name implies, these extra-long planes are used for trueing long edges for joining, as when gluing up tabletops. The 22-in.-long *No. 7* is the most common jointer plane today. The mammoth *No. 8* (24 in.) is increasingly hard to come by. The 18-in.-long *No. 6,* also called a *fore plane,* falls somewhere between the jack plane and the jointer plane.

Smoothing planes. The smoothing planes (*No. 2, No. 3, No. 4* and *No. 4½*) are the smallest bench planes. A favorite among woodworkers, these are easily handled and are great for young folks. Kept razor-sharp and set to produce an ultra-fine shaving, a smoothing plane is used to put the final finish on a surface that has already been leveled with a jack plane. Smoothing planes also are handy for cleaning up uneven joints after assembly, and all sorts of small work. Some people like to use a smoothing plane as an all-purpose tool, but keep in mind the fact that instead of leveling an undulating surface, a smaller bench plane can ride right up and down the hills and valleys like a roller coaster car.

Bench plane construction. At first glance, modern bench planes may seem complicated, but they really are ingeniously simple tools. Most bench planes have three basic components: the *blade;* the *lever cap* that holds the blade in position (on wood-bodied planes, the blade is secured with a wedge); and the *body,* which supports the blade assembly and controls the cutting (See *Photo,* next page).

Anatomy of a bench plane

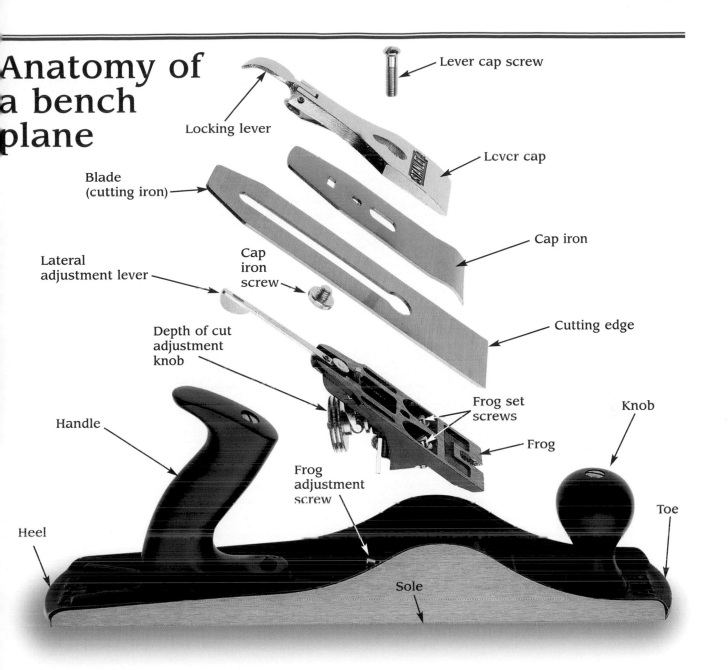

Lever cap screw

Locking lever

Lever cap

Blade (cutting iron)

Cap iron

Lateral adjustment lever

Cap iron screw

Cutting edge

Depth of cut adjustment knob

Frog set screws

Knob

Handle

Frog

Frog adjustment screw

Toe

Heel

Sole

The *blade assembly* does the work of the plane. It consists of a *cap iron* (also called a *chipbreaker*) and *blade (*also called a *cutting iron)* that are connected, then sandwiched between the *lever cap* and the *frog.* The body of the Bailey-style bench plane is usually made of cast iron, although some higher-end models use bronze alloys. The *sole* is the most important part of the plane body—it must be perfectly flat for the plane to be effective. An adjustable opening in the sole called the *mouth* or *throat* provides an exit slot for the blade. The front edge of the sole area is referred to as the *toe,* and the back is known as the *heel* of the plane. The *handle* and *knob* are mounted on the plane body.

Tuning a bench plane. A quality bench plane, properly tuned, is a versatile tool, capable of coarse, quick stock removal as well as fine, smooth finish work.

Flatten the sole. Start tuning with the sole of the

plane, which should be perfectly flat. Generally, the better the plane, the flatter the sole. Use a good steel straightedge to check it, sighting both lengthwise and sideways along the sole as you inspect for light passing under the straightedge.

If the sole of the plane is not perfectly flat, you have a couple of options. You could have it reground at a machine shop, but the cost might well exceed what you paid for the plane, and there's no guarantee it would be done right. Or, you can grind the sole back to flat yourself (a process called "lapping"). For this you'll need some sandpaper (aluminum oxide or silicon carbide, regular or wet/dry) and a dead-flat surface like a jointer table or a thick piece of plate glass. Use spray adhesive to attach 150-grit sandpaper to the flat surface. Butt the sheets end-to-end so you have a working area at least 1½ times the length of the plane sole. Remove the frog

Tips for lapping a plane

150-grit

Plate glass

320-grit

STANLEY

"Lap" the sole. Inspect the sole of the plane to make sure it's flat. If not, you can flatten it using a process called "lapping." Adhere a sheet or two of 150-grit sandpaper to a dead-flat surface (such as a piece of thick glass or a jointer table). Rub the plane back and forth across the paper to grind down any high spots. Smooth the surface by rubbing on 320-grit paper.

Seat the frog. To ensure that the lower surfaces of the frog fit cleanly against the mating surfaces cast into the body of the plane, dab some machinists' lapping compound (also called valve grinding compound) onto the frog, insert it into the body of the plane and move it back and forth in position. The abrasive action of the compound will grind away small surface irregularities.

and the blade assembly. Directing pressure over the center, push the plane back and forth across the sandpaper. Check your progress; you can identify high spots on the sole by the fresh abrasions. Ideally, you want to get the whole sole flat, but the most critical points are the toe, the heel and the area around the mouth. Chamfer the edges of the sole with a file to smooth any sharp edges that could gouge your work. Then progress up to about 320-grit paper so the sole is nice and smooth. (See photo, above left.)

Re-seat the frog. In order to keep the blade from chattering, the frog needs to be solidly seated against the body of the plane. Also, its upper surface must be smooth, flat, and provide support close to the cutting edge. On quality planes both the upper surface that the iron rests on and the lower mating surfaces of the frog and the body casting are machined flat. Any roughness on the upper surface can be easily lapped in the same manner as the sole. If you're unsure how well the lower surfaces mate, you can put some machinists' abrasive lapping paste (available at auto parts and machine supply stores) between them and rub the frog back and forth (See photo, above right). NOTE: *On some cheaper planes the frog simply rests on painted cast sur-*

faces, and sometimes is not supported at all at the critical lower points. These frogs often don't reach down far enough to support the entire blade. Inexpensive planes of this type perform best when the frog is set so the blade rests on the back edge of the mouth.

File the cap iron. The cap iron needs to contact the blade cleanly all along the mating edges to provide proper support and prevent shavings from getting wedged between the cap iron and the blade. Hold the cap iron and blade together in front of a light source and check to see if any light comes through the joint. If so, file the cap iron with a file or an oilstone until it's smooth and meets the iron properly.

General maintenance. A plane needs only minimal maintenance: Wipe or blow it clean, retract the blade and release the tension on the cap lever after every use; keep the sole smooth and rust-free by buffing it occasionally with paste wax; clean and lubricate the threads of the depth-adjustment knob once in a while; and keep the blade sharp and properly beveled (See pages 151 and 152). To prevent nicks and dulling of the blade, either retract it fully before setting the plane down, or make a habit of laying planes down with the side of the body on the worksurface.

Setting up for a cut

As with any tool, achieving good results from your bench planes depends on careful, accurate set-up work before applying the tool to the workpiece. The three basic set-up steps are: adjusting the cap iron, setting the frog, and setting the cutting depth.

Adjust and align the blade and cap iron. See *Step 1,* right. The blade is connected with a screw to the cap iron (often called a *chipbreaker* because it breaks and curls the wood shavings as you plane). The closer to the cutting edge of the blade the cap iron is set, the sooner the shaving is broken and the smoother the resulting wood surface. The position of the cap iron should be set according to the work being done. For general work, set it between 1/32 and 1/16 in. from the cutting edge; for rough work with thick shavings set it wider; for fine smoothing, particularly on figured grain, set the cap iron as close to the blade as you can. Make sure the blade and cap are aligned, with their front edges parallel, before you tighten the cap iron screw.

Set the frog. See *Step 2,* right. When the blade assembly is removed, you can adjust the width of the mouth opening in the sole of the plane by setting the frog. Set the mouth opening according to the type of work you're doing: wide for rough "hogging" and narrow for fine finish work.

Set the depth of cut. When the blade, cap iron and lever cap are back in position and secured, set the depth of cut—the amount the blade projects through the mouth and beyond the sole—as described in *Step 3,* right. If shavings choke in the mouth, the depth of cut is probably too great for a small mouth opening. Remove the lever cap and cap iron to release the clogged shaving, and readjust the frog setting (mouth opening) or the depth of cut setting.

How to tune a plane

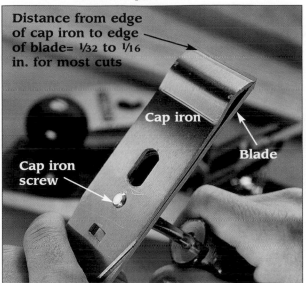

Distance from edge of cap iron to edge of blade= 1/32 to 1/16 in. for most cuts

Cap iron

Cap iron screw

Blade

Frog adjustment screw

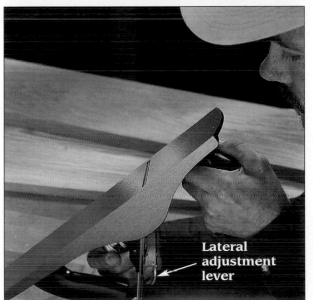

Lateral adjustment lever

1 Set the cap iron. Begin by lifting the locking lever to release the pressure on the lever cap. Remove the two-part blade assembly (the cap iron and the blade). Loosen the cap iron screw that holds the two pieces together. Adjust the iron and the blade so the distance from the front edge of the cap iron to the cutting edge of the blade is between 1/32 and 1/16 in. Make sure the edges of the parts are parallel and correctly aligned, then tighten the cap iron screw.

2 Set the frog. The frog is the "bed" that supports the blade assembly. Adjusting its position alters the distance from the cutting edge of the blade to the edge of the mouth (which affects the thickness of the wood shavings created—see text, left). To adjust the frog, loosen the two frog setscrews and turn the frog adjustment screw until the frog is at the desired position. Then retighten the set screws.

3 Set the cutting depth. Hold the plane upside down with the toe facing you and sight along the bottom. Turn the brass depth-adjustment knob until you can just see the blade projecting through. Push the lateral adjustment lever side-to-side if necessary until the blade projects evenly. Make a pass with the plane on the wood. You may have to modify the depth to produce the desired cut. Finish your adjustment with the knob engaged in a forward rotation so there is no slack in the setting.

Using a bench plane

Planing is a skill that relies on feel, and one that is easily developed with a little practice. It allows very precise control. For most work, set the plane to cut thin shavings; it's much easier to use and control this way, and you'll be able to create a smoother surface. For most planing tasks, the workpiece is clamped between bench dogs or stops on a workbench top or, for edge planing, in a vise mounted to the edge of the bench. If you're right-handed, stand alongside the bench with your right foot pointing toward the bench and your left foot forward, parallel with the bench.

Inspect your stock before you begin work to determine the grain direction. If it's difficult to tell which direction the grain runs, the first pass with the plane will let you know: If you're planing against the grain, you'll get small tearouts and the shavings won't curl well. Planing with the grain should allow smooth, easy passes that result in nicely curling shavings.

General planing tips:
• Effective planing requires a sharp blade with the correct bevel angle (See pages 151 and 152).

How to surface-plane with a bench plane

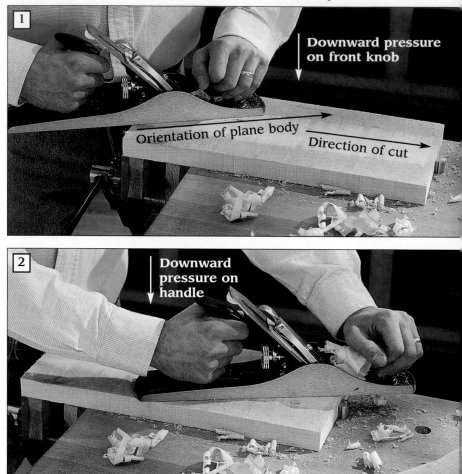

When surface planing a workpiece, angle the body of the plane so it's at a diagonal to the direction of the cut. Begin the cut with downward pressure exerted on the front handle of the plane. Then, as you near the end of the pass, lighten the pressure on the knob and exert heavier pressure on the handle at the back of the plane.

Don't let the chips fall where they may

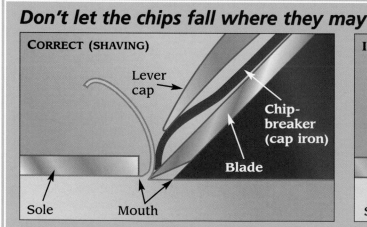

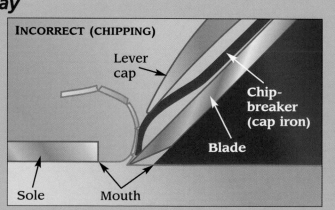

When used correctly, a bench plane should produce thin, smooth curled wood shavings that roll neatly off the cap iron (chipbreaker) that is mounted over the cutting blade. The keys to producing thin "apple-peel" shavings (left illustration), rather than rough chips (right illustration) are: set the frog so the mouth of the plane is not too wide; set the cap iron so its tip is between 1/16 and 1/32 in. above the cutting edge of the blade; do not attempt to remove too much material; and make sure the blade is very sharp.

- Always remove dried glue before planing.
- If you're starting with rough lumber from the mill, scrub it with a wire brush first to remove any grit embedded in the fibers.
- If you can avoid knots, do so; they can also dull or nick the cutting edge of the blade.

Surface planing (smoothing). Smoothing a rough surface is one of the fundamental tasks that can be accomplished with a bench plane. Generally, larger planes (jack planes, fore planes and jointer planes) are more effective for this job. Take up the plane with your lead hand on the knob and your back hand around the handle (you may want to point your forefinger at times for control). This should be a relaxed position that will allow your body to rock forward and get the free swing necessary for smooth, easy planing. As you begin to cut, press down on the front knob of the plane to keep the toe of the sole flat on the board. Orient the plane so the body is at a diagonal direction to the line of the cut, but make sure your hands move forward parallel to the line of the cut as you work. For curly- or swirly-grained wood, you may need to plane at right angles to the grain—called *cross planing*. Keep the pressure on the plane even throughout the stroke. Then, as you reach the end of the board, transfer pressure back to the handle to keep the heel from bouncing. This avoids the problem of rounding over the ends, allowing you to plane evenly all along the board. As you push the plane, rock your weight forward from your back foot to your front foot. If the board is long, step forward to finish the planing stroke–don't over-reach with your arms.

Start surface planing by leveling any noticeable high spots, but then focus on overall, even planing. Overlap your planing strokes. Check the surface periodically with a straightedge at several points across the board. Your goal should be a flat, smooth and tearout-free surface, but don't become overly finicky trying to create a glass-smooth surface: that's what scrapers and sandpaper were made for.

Edge planing. When jointing or squaring the edge of a board with a jointer plane, start and end the first pass with the blade a bit shy of each end. Continue planing the middle of the board until the plane stops cutting. At this point the edge will be slightly concave, but the high spots at the ends of the board will prevent the plane from cutting too deeply. To finish the edge-planing cuts, take a final shaving or two to knock the ends down to the level of the middle section of the board edge. This method is fairly trustworthy when using a long jointer plane on boards up to about 3 ft. long. But always check your edge-planed boards with a straightedge to make sure they're level and square. If you're having trouble holding the plane flat (which can cause the edges to be rounded over) stabilize the plane by letting your fingers curl under the sole of the plane and ride against the side of the wood as you plane.

Basic bench planing techniques

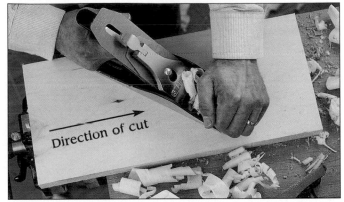

Direction of cut

Smoothing. Final smoothing of a surface is done using the same general techniques used for any kind of surface planing (See photos, previous page). For best results, use a *No. 4* or smaller smoothing plane. Make sure to work with the grain direction, keeping the body of the plane diagonal to the cutting direction.

Edge planing (jointing). Use a jointer plane to flatten and square the edges of boards in preparation for edge-gluing, or for making wood joints. Start planing in the center of the board, then strike off the ends so they're even with the rest of the edge. Use a straightedge to check your work.

Rabbeting. Large rabbet grooves can be cut with a special rabbeting plane (See pages 92 to 93) that features a blade that runs the full width of the sole of the plane. Clamp a stopblock to the workpiece at the shoulder of the rabbet and plane away stock until the correct depth is reached, using the block as a guide.

Planing end grain. To plane end grain effectively, the cutting blade of your plane must be very sharp. You can use just about any type of bench plane to smooth and square the end of a board, including specialty planes called block planes that resemble bench planes (See pages 90 to 91). It is critical that you make extremely

Planing end grain. Planing a smooth, flat surface onto end grain is one of the trickier planing tasks you'll face. You can use any type of bench plane for the job, as well as specialty planes with flat soles, like the block plane shown above. Clamp backer boards at the ends of the board edge to prevent tearout, and hold the plane at a 45° angle to the board as you take very shallow planing passes.

Preventing tearout on end grain

Do not cut straight across board: This can cause tearout at ends.

Plane from each end of the edge and toward the middle of the board.

Chamfer the end of the board before planing to prevent damage from tearout (then rip to width).

Clamp a backer board to the end of the workpiece before planing.

shallow cuts when planing end grain, and that you hold the plane at about a 45° angle to the board while pushing it straight ahead so the cutting direction follows the end of the board (See photo, below, left). This oblique planing technique in effect lowers the cutting angle, creating a smoother shear-cut. Avoid planing straight across end grain, as this can cause the side grain at the far end will splinter. To avoid side tearout, clamp a backer block made from scrap wood next to each end of the board edge. Alternately, you can plane partway toward the center from each end, then smooth out the middle of the board.

Making & using a shooting board

SHOOTING BOARD FOR MITERED WORKPIECES

A *shooting board* is a jig used to guide a plane and steady the workpiece when smoothing the end of a board (they also can be used to trim veneer or plane the edges of thin wood). To make a shooting board, cut two pieces of ¾ in. plywood to the same length (about 20 in.): one of the boards (the *guide board*) should be 3 to 4 in. narrower than the other (the *base*). Attach the boards face-to-face so the ends and one side are aligned. Attach a wood strip to the underside of the base at one end to form a *lip* that's butted up against your workbench to hold the shooting board in place. Then, cut a *stopblock* the same width as the guide board. For planing square workpieces, cut a square stopblock. For mitered workpieces, cut a stopblock that is mitered at a 45° angle on two opposite sides (like the stop block shown above). Attach the stopblock to the guide board. To use the shooting board, set the workpiece on the guide board with one edge butted flush against the stopblock. The end of the workpiece to be planed should overhang the edge of the guide board slightly. Lay a jack plane on its side and plane the end of the workpiece: the sole of the plane should follow the guide created by the edge of the guide board.

The term "Nordic" is used by collectors to describe tools that either originated in the Nordic nations of Europe, or were made by Nordic immigrants in America. As a class, Nordic tools are highly regarded for the quality of the craftsmanship with which they were made and the unique decorative features that make them highly recognizable.

The Nordic plane pictured above is beautifully hand-carved *double razee:* a wooden-bodied plane cut away in the rear, or in both the front and the rear, to lower the line of thrust in relation to the surface being planed. Located in northern Minnesota, it is 15½ in. long by 3⅛ in. wide. A ¹⁄₁₆-in.-thick steel plate is fastened to the rock maple plane body by 16 handmade screws. The closed handle is believed to be carved from hickory. The plane body is chamfered at front and rear and on both sides. The cast steel plane iron is held in place by a carved wooden lever cap. A large handmade screw passes through the lever cap, on the handle side of a forged pin, which goes through the body of the plane and the lever cap. When the screw is tightened against the iron, the lever cap pivots on the pin, forcing the lower end of the lever cap against the iron to hold it in place. Two triangular steel plates strengthen the cheeks of the throat and prevent the pin from damaging the plane body. The maple knob is fastened to the body of the plane with two small wooden dowels that extend from the bottom of the knob and fit into holes in the plane body. When the large handmade screw that goes through the knob is tightened the knob cannot be turned.

Unfortunately, makers of Nordic planes seldom marked their planes with their name, or the year in which the plane was made. However, the plane iron is marked *James Cam, warranted cast steel.* James Cam died in 1837, suggesting that the plane could be more than 160 years old.

Wood-bodied planes

Wooden-bodied plane devotees prefer the feel of wood in the hands over cold, hard iron, and contend that wood-against-wood results in less friction than metal-against-wood. Whether this latter is true or not, wooden-bodied planes (such as the Nordic plane above and the wood-bodied smoothing plane on page 84) are lighter and do have an undeniable charm for those of us who work with wood. But, historically, wooden-bodied planes have had one major drawback: adjustments are few, and those that are possible must be done by tapping with a hammer, which makes fine tuning difficult and eventually batters the wood. But tool evolution has done away with those few objections. A full line of fine German wood-bodied planes that incorporate all the easy adjustability of metal planes (even the width of the throat opening) are now available.

Some woodworkers prefer to make their own wood-bodied planes, either patterned after classical designs or created to satisfy their aesthetic and ergonomic sensibilities. There are also handsome, well-made reproductions of old planes currently being produced by several small tool companies.

Standard
No. 9½ block
plane

Low-angl[e]
No. 60½
block pla[ne]

Japanese plane

Circular plane

No. 271 router
plane

Specialty Planes

Circular plane: Flexible sole allows use of plane on concave and convex surfaces. 10 in. long, 1¾-in. blade.

Japanese plane: An excellent plane for working softwood, the solid oak body won't dent or mar wood and the 40° blade angle limits gouging. 11 in. long, 3⅛-in.-wide, 2¼-in. blade.

Block planes: Small, versatile bench-style planes can be operated easily with a single hand. Shown are a standard 6-in.-long plane with a 1⅝-in., 20° blade, and a low-angle block plane with a 12° blade (a good choice for planing end grain).

Side rabbet plane for trimming and widening rabbets and dadoes. 5 in. long.

Bench rabbet plane has a blade that runs the full width of the sole for cutting up to vertical surfaces, as when cutting rabbets or leveling drawer bottoms. 13 in. long, 2⅛-in. blade.

Rabbet & fillister plane has a "D"-shape steel handle and two blade positions for cutting rabbets or fillisters. Adjustable stop controls depth of cut. 10 in. long, 1½-in. blade

Trimming/chisel plane: "Shoulder" style plane designed for delicate trimming and rabbeting work. 5½ in. long, ¾ in. blade.

Router planes cut and smooth grooves and dadoes. Larger No. 71 has removable fence and can cut straight or curved grooves. Smaller *No. 271* is useful for cleaning out the bottoms of grooves, especially when cutting recesses for inlays.

No. 79
side rabbet plane

No. 10 bench
rabbet plane

No. 778 rabbet &
fillister plane

No. 92
trimming/chisel
plane

No. 71 router plane

Specialty planes

Over the years creative toolmakers have developed countless specialty planes that perform a multitude of unique functions. Woodworkers may choose to invest in specialty planes for a number of reasons: to accomplish specific tasks quickly or with very little set-up time; for greater accuracy than is afforded by power tools; or simply because they enjoy working with hand planes. Some specialty planes, such as the block plane, are quite similar to the more common bench planes discussed earlier in this chapter. These flat-bottomed tools are used mostly for smoothing wood stock. But more typically, specialty planes are used to make specific kinds of cuts that are often more akin to chiseling than smoothing. Rabbets, dadoes and grooves are perhaps the most common types of cuts made with specialty planes.

Anatomy of a block plane

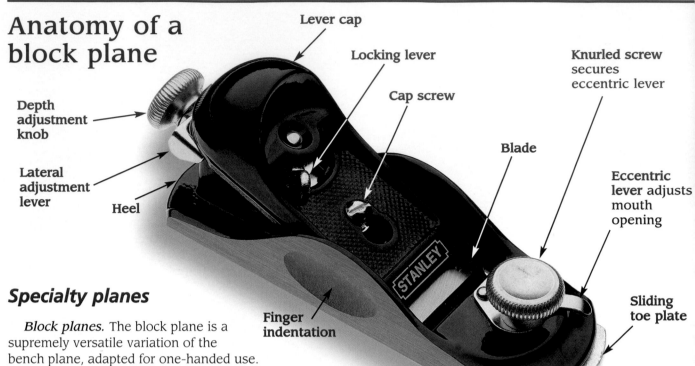

Lever cap

Locking lever

Cap screw

Knurled screw secures eccentric lever

Blade

Depth adjustment knob

Lateral adjustment lever

Heel

Eccentric lever adjusts mouth opening

Finger indentation

Sliding toe plate

Specialty planes

Block planes. The block plane is a supremely versatile variation of the bench plane, adapted for one-handed use. It is an essential item in any toolbox, even if your woodworking is limited to home maintenance tasks. It's small (usually about 6 in. long), lightweight and ergonomically designed. The characteristically bulbous lever cap fits comfortably into the palm. The index finger rests on a dished-out knob at the toe, and the side walls of the body casting are often scooped out as well, for easy gripping with the thumb and second finger. The body is generally cast iron, though some are brass or bronze.

The block plane's greatest assets are size and maneuverability. In awkward situations, working one-handed allows you to hold the workpiece with one hand and operate the plane with the other. And because it is small, a block plane can be slipped into a pocket or the pouch of a tool apron for on-site work.

The block plane has many uses. It's particularly good for small planing jobs, as it can even handle tiny pieces that would drop right into the gap behind the blade of a bench plane. It's excellent for all kinds of trimming and fitting work: fitting doors and drawers, trimming overhanging veneer or veneer edge tape, flushing-up small joints, fitting small miters, even easing or chamfering sharp edges. Finish carpenters find a block plane handy for fitting molding and for knocking down the end grain to shorten a board or a piece of trim by that critical millimeter. Its compact size and versatility also make the block plane a popular tool with modelmakers.

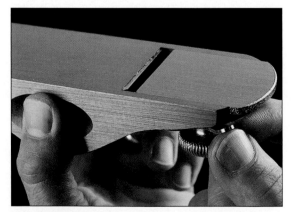

The sliding toe plate on block planes is adjusted with a lever (called an *eccentric lever*) that is held secure with a knurled knob. Adjusting the position of the toe plate widens and narrows the mouth through which the blade extends in the sole of the plane.

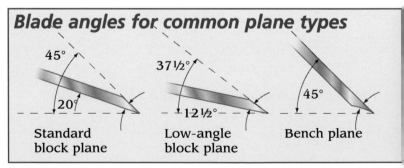

Blade angles for common plane types

45°

20°

Standard block plane

37½°

12½°

Low-angle block plane

45°

Bench plane

The angle of the cutting blade to the workpiece has a bearing on the type of cut you can make with a plane. Steep blade angles cut more aggressively, while shallow angles cut more cleanly. Keep in mind that the cutting angle is affected by the amount and direction of blade bevel. Even though it is set at a low 20° blade angle, the cutting angle of a standard block plane is the same as a bench plane (45°) because the bevel faces up. Low-angle block planes provide a shallower cutting angle (37½°), making them well suited for work where tearout is a concern, such as cutting end grain.

Specialty planes in use

Rabbet-and-fillister plane is a highly accurate rabbet-cutting plane that can be micro-adjusted for great precision. It features two blade positions: when the blade is installed in the forward position, the plane can be used to cut fillisters (recesses). Set the blade in the back slot to cut rabbets.

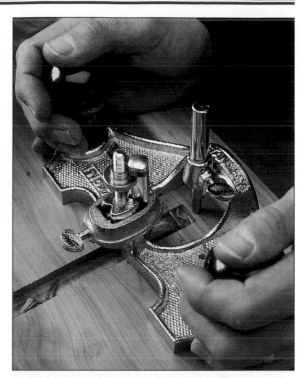

Router plane can be used with or without a fence to chisel dadoes and grooves by hand.

Trimming/chisel plane has precision-ground sides that are exactly square to the sole of the plane, making it an effective tool for chiseling rabbets or cutting tenon shoulders.

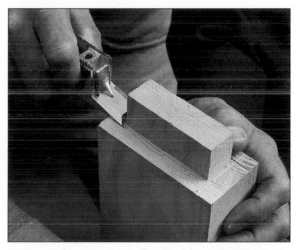

Remove the top piece of a shoulder-style trimming/chisel plane and it becomes a highly effective tool for refining wood joints.

Although there are many block plane models available, the *No. 9½* (standard) and *No. 60½* (low-angle) made by Stanley and Record can team up to meet just about any planing challenge. With a basic design that has remained virtually unchanged for more than one hundred years, these are the two most popular block planes in the world today. Among their better features are the easy-to-adjust mouth opening and cutting depth. The block plane differs significantly from the bench plane in that the blade is mounted with the bevel up rather than down. This configuration, along with the design of the blade mounting, has both pros and cons. The first thing to be aware of is the cutting angle. Many people think all block planes are better suited than bench planes for end-grain work, since their blades are set at a lower angle. While the blade in the standard block plane is mounted at 20° (as opposed to 45°

on a bench plane), the bevel points up so the 25° bevel angle becomes a part of the cutting angle, bringing it up to 45°, the same as most bench planes (see illustration, previous page). The *low-angle block plane's* blade is set at 12°, so it truly does cut at a lower angle, giving it a bit of an advantage, particularly for end-grain trimming.

The manner in which the blade is mounted and held in the plane also affects the plane's functioning. Block planes lack a frog to support the cutting blade and they don't have a cap iron to provide stiffness and break chips. As a result, the blade may chatter under stress. But this tendency is partially offset by the fact that the blade bevel faces up on a block plane, allowing it to be positioned closer to the edge of the throat and gain some stability.

Tuning a block plane. To get the most out of your block plane and minimize planing problems, a little bit of tuning goes a long way. First, check to see if the blade is flat. If not, lap it flat on a coarse diamond whetstone. Next, check the mating of the blade to the flat strip on the plane bed. To do this, coat the back of the blade with machinists' layout dye or artists' oil paint, and slide it into position in the plane body. Any colored areas left on the bed indicate high spots that need to be filed down. Finish by lapping and waxing the sole (See page 86).

Setting up for a cut. To set up a block plane, first mount the blade bevel-up and turn the depth knob so the cutting edge extends just to the mouth in the sole. Turn the lever cap handle to lock the blade. You should be able to push the blade sideways only if you push very hard. If it shifts too easily, unlock the lever cap and tighten the cap screw slightly. If your plane has no lateral adjustment lever, straighten the blade by forcing the lever cap and blade into square, moving them as a unit. Finally, adjust the mouth opening by loosening the knurled screw near the toe of the plane and using the eccentric lever to shift the sliding toe plate toward the blade. The gap between the blade and the edge of the mouth should be $1/32$ to $1/16$ in.

Rabbet planes. Although there are different types, all rabbet planes are made with a full-width blade that cuts flush with the square-milled sides of the plane body. *Bench-style rabbet planes* are designed to efficiently cut a rabbet (an L-shaped step recess or *rebate* along an edge or across the end of a board). *Shoulder planes*, are smaller tools designed to refine or correct existing joints.

The *Record No. 778* rabbet plane is a good example of the style sometimes called a *rabbet-and-fillister plane.* It has an adjustable fence so you can set a rabbet width that remains constant throughout a rabbeting cut and from one workpiece to the next. A finely adjustable depth stop controls the depth of the rabbet you cut, while a scoring spur slices the wood ahead of the blade when planing across the grain to avoid tearout. When the blade is installed in the forward cutting position, the tool can be used to cut fillisters (recesses in frames that accept panels, such as window glass).

The *bench rabbet plane* looks and works like a jack plane. It has no stops or fences, so the outlines of the rabbet need to be marked out on the stock and planing done to the lines. A strip of wood can be clamped to the workpiece to guide the plane until the rabbet is deep enough that the side of the plane body can be pressed against the shoulder of the rabbet for guidance.

While you may not need a bench rabbet plane if you're handy with a router, a *shoulder plane* is a useful tool for any serious craftsman. It trims end grain and cross grain to cut or fine-tune rabbets and grooves. It is very handy for making woodworking joints, including tenon shoulders and faces, rabbets, lap joints and

Circular planes

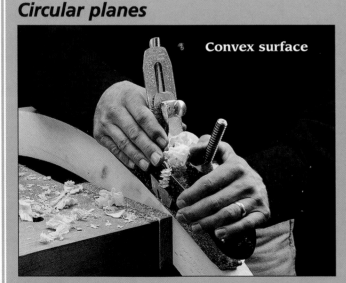

Convex surface

Concave surface

Circular planes, also called *compass planes,* are basically bench planes with a flexible sole designed to conform to concave or convex surfaces. Adjust and set up a circular plane as you would a bench plane, but don't hold the plane at an angle to the cutting direction when you plane. To take advantage of grain direction, work from the ends of the workpiece toward the middle when cutting concave shapes, and work from the middle toward the ends on convex shapes.

Replacement of wooden plane functions by metal *combination planes* started in earnest about the middle of the 19th century.

In 1883, *Stanley Rule & Level Co.* started producing its innovative and famous *No. 45 Combination Plane.* Promoted as "Seven Planes in One," the cast-iron plane had a rosewood tote, knob and fence. From 18 to 23 cutters were included, depending on the date of production.

Stanley first produced the *No. 55 Universal Combination Plane* in 1897. Billed as "A Planing Mill Within Itself," the cast-iron *No. 55* came with 55 cutters in four labeled boxes. It had the ability to duplicate almost all functions performed by planes other than bench planes, including rabbeting, chamfering, beading, ploughing and dadoing Production of the *No. 55* stopped in 1963.

The *No. 55* shown here is 11-in.-long, nickel-plated cast iron. The label on the original box and the "Sweet Heart" trademark on the skate indicate that production was between 1921 and 1925.

Hand Tool Heritage: Stanley No. 55

ladoes. While larger shoulder planes offer good reference on long cuts, the *bullnose plane* is a small, snub-nosed shoulder plane that is light and easy to handle, with a cutting edge very close to the front of the plane to enable it to fit into some pretty tight spots.

The *side rabbet plane* is a valuable tool that allows you to widen a rabbet or a dado groove that you've cut just a bit too narrow. It can be used in either direction n rabbets or grooves as narrow as ½ in. It has an adjustable depth stop and a nosepiece that can be removed to allow clearance for cutting into corners.

Router planes. Although the *router plane* was designed to cut grooves and dadoes (work now generally done with the electric router and table saw) it has other uses that make it a viable tool today. It can smooth the bottom of a roughly cut dado or shallow mortise, either with or across the grain, and can square up the end of a stop-dado cut made on the table saw. It has a depth stop and an adjustable fence for straight or curved cuts. The tiny version is great for narrow work such as inlays, and for cleaning up flat backgrounds in woodcarvings.

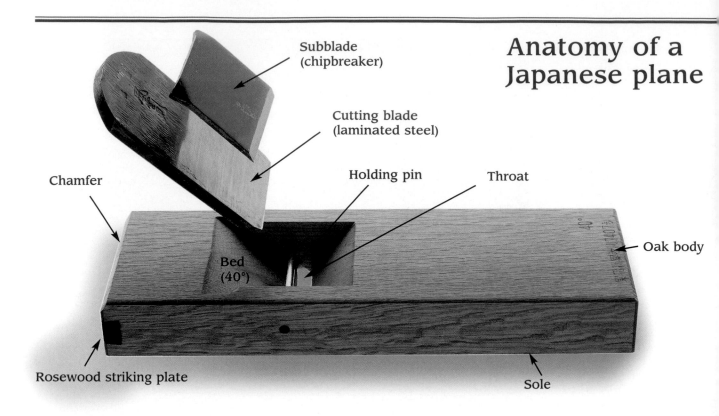

Subblade
(chipbreaker)

Cutting blade
(laminated steel)

Anatomy of a Japanese plane

Chamfer

Holding pin

Throat

Oak body

Bed
(40°)

Rosewood striking plate

Sole

Japanese planes

At first glance a Japanese bench plane looks deceptively simple compared to its Western, metal cousin. In reality, it's a highly evolved cutting machine that, though it requires more maintenance and skill from the user, can yield unparalleled control and flawless, polished surfaces.

Like Japanese saws, the Japanese plane is pulled, instead of pushed, across the wood. The plane body is invariably made of Japanese white or red oak. A notched slot accepts two blades that are inserted face-to-face and wedged between the bed and a metal holding pin. The blades are relatively short and thick, and are laminated of soft and hard steels in the traditional manner, the same as Japanese knives and chisels. The main cutting blade is mounted bevel-down, as in a Western plane. The smaller subblade functions as a chipbreaker.

Planes are very important in traditional Japanese woodworking, where sanding is rarely done. Instead, planes are used as finishing tools to create smooth, highly polished surfaces. In addition to the standard Japanese bench planes, there are countless specialized planes for specific tasks.

When new, Japanese planes need to be extensively tuned and reworked. The blades require specialized maintenance, the wooden bodies need ongoing upkeep and readjustment from wear and atmospheric changes. And the planing itself requires a high level of sensitivity and concentration. Thus, Japanese planes are not for

everyone, and their appeal and popularity here is not as widespread as that of Japanese saws and chisels.

However, Japanese planes have many devotees in the West, and if you're willing to negotiate the learning curve you can readily find informative articles and books on the subject. By all accounts, you may be rewarded with almost magically long, thin shavings, mirror-smooth finishes and a unique degree of sensitivity, adaptability, intimacy and control.

Using a Japanese plane. **All Japanese planes are designed to be pulled, not pushed, across your workpiece. Grasp the body of the plane with your dominant hand, and steady the blades between the thumb and forefinger of your other hand. Applying even pressure draw the plane toward your body.**

Drawknives & Spokeshaves

Inshave drawknife is designed for scooping or hollowing chair seats, bowls, etc.

Carpenter's drawknife can be used on flat or curved surfaces.

Carver's drawknife for shaping carving blanks and reducing stock.

Half-round spokeshave has a concave blade for smoothing and shaving round stock.

Radius spokeshave has a 2 in. radius convex blade for smoothing large flutes and other concave profiles.

Adjustable spokeshave can be set for smoothing profiles of varying radius. Flat-face version (shown) used for flat and convex surfaces; round face version is made for concave surfaces.

Inshave drawknife

10¼-in. carpenter's drawknife

4½-in. carver's drawknife

Half-round spokeshave

Radius spokeshave

Adjustable spokeshave

Drawknives

In days gone by, drawknives were designed for specific building trades, such as coopering, boat-building and timber framing. Their handles and blades were specially configured to accomplish a unique job done efficiently and comfortably. Before the emergence of the hand-held circular saw, every carpenter had a drawknife that he used for numerous tasks. It's faster and far less laborious, for instance, to cut down a panel that's an inch or so too wide using a drawknife than to rip it with a hand saw. Quite a few of these classic styles are still being made today and are available from most mail-order tool suppliers.

Contrary to the first impression a newcomer may have, drawknives are neither hard to learn to use nor particularly unsafe; they just require a little practice and some common-sense safety habits.

Drawknives are outstanding tools for rough and rapid shaping—for example, roughing out curved or tapered furniture legs—before finishing with finer tools. They can remove large amounts of material quickly, and yet when applied skillfully they can be quite precise, slicing off the thinnest of shavings.

Drawknives have long, open, single-beveled blades with a handle on each end. The basic all-purpose, or *carpenter's drawknife* has a straight, flat blade and large cylindrical handles perpendicular to, but in the same plane as, the blade. Other types have dropped or angled handles. Some have a flat blade that's curved forward when you view it from above, so it produces a smooth shearing cut. Drawknives with blades curved upward are used for hollowing. Some have a shallow curve for tasks like shaping a chair back rest. Others, such as the U-shaped *inshave,* have more pronounced curves for scooping out bowls and chair seats. Carvers and sculptors often use smaller drawknives with ball-shaped handles for more control on finer work.

The long, open blade on a drawknife permits cutting in many ways to suit different situations. A drawknife is generally pulled toward your body (hence the name), but it can cut on the push stroke The easiest way to use one is to hold it flat with the blade skewed at an angle to the workpiece to make a shearing cut with minimal tearout. A drawknife can be used bevel-up or bevel-down. Bevel-down may be easier for the beginner, as the knife is more likely to run up out of the wood than it is to run too deep. Bevel-down is a good blade position for concave shapes, whereas bevel-up is commonly used for convex rounded curves and flat work. Turn the handles up or down to adjust the depth of cut. As with any edging tool, check the wood and cut with the grain as much as possible.

Since a drawknife must be razor-sharp to work properly, it must be handled with care. Keep your body a reasonable distance from the workpiece when cutting. Protect the blade edge and your hands by storing the tool (preferably, hang it up away from other tools) as soon as you're finished using it. On small drawknives, the blade ends are closer to the handles; grinding or filing the corners of the blade until they're blunt will help avoid thumb cuts. And always brace your work securely.

How to cut with a drawknife. **With your workpiece secured, rest the blade of the drawknife on the workpiece. For better shearing action, skew the blade. Standing behind the workpiece, draw the drawknife toward your body in long strokes, following the grain of the wood.**

Bevel up or bevel down? **Orienting the blade bevel downward allows you to rest the blade on the workpiece and maintain a constant cutting angle more easily. It also prevents the blade from gouging too deeply into the wood, and may be a better practice for beginners. Cutting with the bevel up allow you to take more aggressive cuts.**

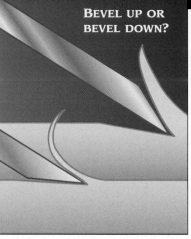

BEVEL UP OR BEVEL DOWN?

Protect your thumbs

File down the corners **of a drawknife blade to reduce the risk of cutting your thumbs on the blade. The corners are seldom involved in cutting a workpiece and, in fact, are likely to gouge the workpiece if they do contact it.**

Anatomy of an adjustable spokeshave

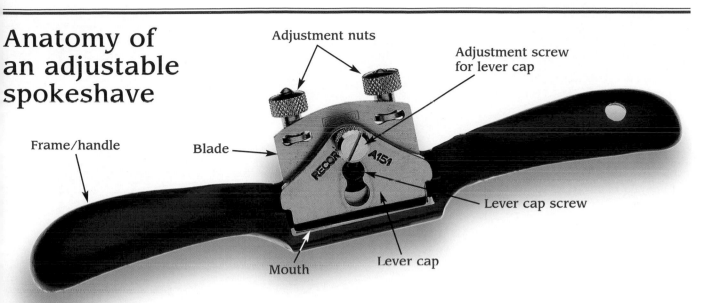

Adjustment nuts

Adjustment screw for lever cap

Frame/handle

Blade

Lever cap screw

Mouth

Lever cap

Spokeshaves

A spokeshave is to a drawknife as a plane is to a chisel. A drawknife, like a chisel, requires the operator to control the smoothness of the cut and keep the open blade from digging in. The more refined spokeshave, however, is actually a small plane with arms. The depth of cut can be set to produce an even, thin shaving every time. While it can't hog out wood like a drawknife, the spokeshave is much easier to learn to use. In fact it feels quite natural in the hands, and once you try one you may wonder how you got by without it.

The spokeshave is a brilliant tool for shaping all kinds of curved or irregularly shaped objects, and can quickly run a chamfer around the edge of a curved panel. It is truly a unique tool that serves a purpose that no other tool can. The spokeshave cuts quickly and leaves a much smoother surface than a file or rasp, and is easier to control than any power shaping tool. The name came from the tool's original use for shaping wooden wagon wheel spokes.

As with drawknives, spokeshaves have a history of specialization that has dwindled in recent years. Many different types are still available today, although the basic flat-bottomed model is the most versatile. The most useful have two adjusting screws that make blade depth adjusting easier and let you correct the blade angle. Spokeshaves are also available with concave or convex cutting edges and soles. The concave is especially good for such work as shaping chair spindles, while the convex can smooth scooped-out areas such as seats roughed out with a curved drawknife.

To use the spokeshave, take a handle in each hand, holding it lightly with the fingertips, not gripping it tightly in the palms. This way you can roll your wrists and pivot your fingers as you work up and down the contours of the workpiece. The spokeshave can be

pulled or pushed to suit the situation and, particularly, the grain direction. Because a spokeshave has a short sole, you can follow dips and bumps in the workpiece. Keep the shavings thin, and cut with a diagonal shearing cut whenever possible for clean results and to minimize chatter that can cause ridges.

Since the spokeshave is a plane, the blade is sharpened and set just like that of a plane. The spokeshave blade is quite short, however, and when honing, it may be helpful to grip it with locking pliers or make an extension out of a piece of scrap wood with a slot to accept the blade with a friction fit. And as with a plane, a waxed sole improves performance significantly.

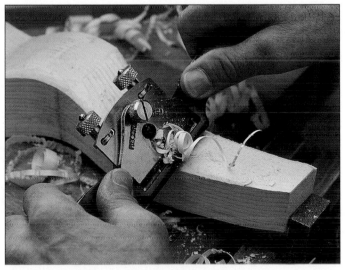

Not just for making spindles. **Although spokeshaves were devised to make spindles for wagon wheels, an adjustable spokeshave with a flat sole can be used for planing flat surfaces along tight curves that cannot be smoothed with a bench plane or block plane.**

Files, Rasps & Rifflers

A. **Rifflers** (7½ in. long)
B. **File card/brush** (for cleaning files)
C. **10 in. cabinet rasp**
D. **10 in. cabinet file**
E. **Perforated steel shaper** (*Surform*)
F. **Combination rasp** (4-in-1)
G. **Second-cut No. 49** (patternmaker's) rasp

H. **10 in. round file**
I. **10 in. round rasp**
J. **10 in. wood file** (coarse) with handle
K. **Needle files**
L. **Micro-plane rasp** (perforated steel shaper)

Almost anyone who works with his hands in any capacity, even performing the most minor tasks, has reason to use a file or rasp at some point. They can be used for smoothing as well as shaping on practically every workable material. Woodworkers and metalworkers rely on them, as do jewelers, watchmakers, plumbers, farmers, auto body shops, sculptors in any material and even farriers, who use them on horse hooves. There are literally hundreds of styles, offering a wonderful diversity, but leaving many of us lost in a murky sea of terminology. But deciphering the options is really not all that complex.

Files are classified according to: (1) kind of teeth, (2) coarseness, (3) shape or style and (4) length.

Anatomy of a file
(10 in., half-round, double-cut cabinet file shown)

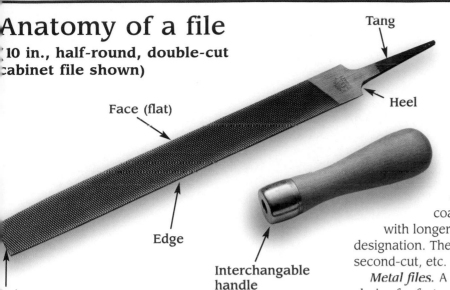

Tang

Heel

Face (flat)

Edge

Point

Interchangable handle

result of their intended use. The *mill file,* for example, is a flat, single-cut file made for sharpening sawmill blades and cutters, and used for general fine finish metalwork. The shape of the surface to be filed will determine the cross-section of file you choose for a particular situation.

Length. The length of a standard file is measured from point to heel, exclusive of the tang. The degree of coarseness is also related to the length, with longer files being coarser within a given cut designation. The relative differences between bastard, second-cut, etc. remain proportionate, though.

Metal files. A flat, double-cut bastard file is a good choice for fast, rough cutting on metal. For finer work, like smoothing a hack saw cut or cleaning up rough edges on hardware, go to a mill file (single cut). *"Home and garden" files* (slightly coarser than a smooth flat file) are specially made for sharpening garden tools like hoes, shovels and mower blades.

Round files and rasps are used for rounded or circular openings, and when working on tight concave curves. Tapered round files are often called *rattail files.* *Three-square files* are triangular in section and are handy for cleaning out square corners or filing internal angles greater than 90°. Single cut triangular files, called *taper files,* are made in a variety of sizes specifi-

Kinds of teeth. Files have rows of parallel chisel-like teeth running diagonally across their faces. Those with a single set of teeth running in one direction are called *single-cut files.* They are meant to be used with light pressure, and leave a smooth finish on metal. Single-cut files are typically used for sharpening tool blades. *Double-cut files* have a second set of diagonal teeth crossing the first, creating a series of points that yield a faster, somewhat rougher cut. Rasps have large, individually cut pointed teeth designed to chew through soft materials, particularly wood, for quick, coarse shaping. A rasp-worked surface will be deeply scored, and will need to be smoothed with a file, a spokeshave or sandpaper.

Coarseness of cut. Based on the number and size of the teeth, both files and rasps are designated as either *coarse, bastard, second-cut* or *smooth.* A less common system, known as *Swiss pattern,* is used to categorize finer cutting files. They are available in seven cuts, from *No. 00* (coarsest) to *No. 6* (finest). The Swiss pattern is used on precision files for tool-and-die makers, jewelers, modelmakers, as well as home craftsmen. The familiar tiny needle files and rifflers are cut in a Swiss pattern.

Shape and style. Files are generally named according to their shape: for example, *flat, round, half-round* and *three-square* (triangular). But some files received their names as a

Tooth cuts & file profiles

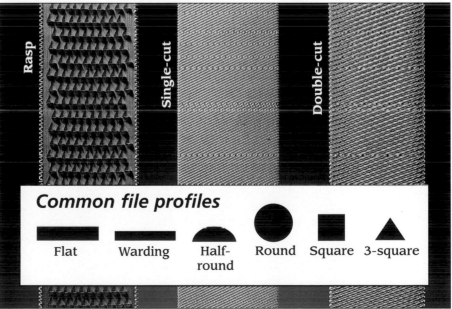

Rasp

Single-cut

Double-cut

Common file profiles

Flat   Warding   Half-round   Round   Square   3-square

File teeth are ground in two basic patterns: single-cut and double-cut. Single-cut teeth cut more aggressively, but do rougher work than double-cut teeth. Rasps employ rasp-cut teeth for fast stock removal. Files and rasps are produced in several different shapes, each with its own advantages and disadvantages. For general woodworking and carpentry, a half-round file profile is the most versatile.

cally for sharpening saw teeth angled at 60°.

Wood files. For woodworking and carving, the most desirable file shape is usually the *half-round.* The flat side can be used for flat and convex surfaces, while the rounded side is great for shaping concave contours. Fine files will clog easily when used on wood. A bastard double-cut will work well for smoothing out rasp marks, but better still are the files made exclusively for woodworking. The *wood file* has a coarse cut and is the next step down from a rasp; but where the rasp teeth make deep scraping cuts, the teeth of a wood file cut with a smooth shearing action. The *cabinet file* is slightly finer than a wood file and gives a smooth, clean cut.

Plastics files are designed to cut smoothly on a variety of plastics, such as acrylic and countertop laminate, with minimal clogging. *Warding files* are thin flat files, good for getting into narrow slots and recesses.

Rasps. Rasps cut much faster than files, and are good for roughing out a shape. *Wood rasps* and *cabinet rasps* can be purchased in several cuts: bastard, second and smooth. They can be used to file wood, plaster, soft stone and soft metal. The best rasps are called *patternmaker's rasps.* They have staggered teeth that produce a smooth cut and a fine finish on wood.

Needle files. In carving, shaping and sculpting, one often encounters fine details and intricate shapes that a normal-size file can't handle. That's where the tiny *needle files* and *rifflers* come into play. Needle files are simply miniature files in the usual selection of shapes. Rifflers are curved, and come in some rather unusual shapes. Both types are available in either file or rasp cut, and are best purchased in an assortment pack so you're ready for any detail that presents itself.

Combination files include two or more kinds of files and/or rasps on one blank for convenience.

NOTE: *Edges of files and rasps are specified as either single-cut, double-cut, or a safe edge, which means it has a smooth surface with no teeth.*

Using a file. Using a file is a two-handed operation. Hold the handle with one hand and the point with the other. File and rasp teeth face forward, so that's the direction in which they cut Combine a forward push with a slight rocking movement to the side. Strokes should be long, slow and full, applying just enough pressure to cut (too much pressure will just cause clogging). Lift the file (or at least release pressure) on the return stroke. Dragging a file backward will dull it quickly.

Drawfiling is a technique that gives an extra-smooth finish, and is often used in shaping long, narrow objects. Hold the file perpendicular to the length of the surface and use the file sideways. With a double-cut file you can draw the file back and

Progressively finer filing

When filing wood, as when sanding, you'll get the best results by using a series of progressively finer tools to shape, then smooth your workpiece. In the photos above, a coarse rasp is used to shape the tapered portion of this leg blank (top photo). Then, a wood file (bottom photo) is employed to smooth out the rasp marks. A cabinet file will be used to further smooth the surface.

forth, since one set of teeth cuts in each direction.

Maintaining files. File faces are all teeth, so they can clog fairly easily, rendering the tool useless. Rasps have more space around their teeth but they too can suffer from buildup, particularly when used on resinous wood. Periodic cleaning is a necessity for optimal cutting performance. A combination file card and brush has wire bristles on one side for the rough stuff and a brush on the other for finer cleaning. If choked with stubborn resinous sawdust, you can try gently heating the file just enough to scorch the impacted dust, which can be brushed out. Rubbing the file with chalk prevents clogging.

Protect the teeth from damage (or from damaging anything else) by hanging files up or storing them in a canvas tool roll. Files and rasps can be used on a variety of materials, some of which will dull them faster than others. If you work with abrasive materials like stone or (oddly enough) soft brass on a regular basis, you may want to keep a set of files just for that purpose. Eventually any file will wear out, but since files are made with good-quality, hardened, high-carbon steel, careful grinding can give them a second life as chisels or lathe scrapers.

Always fit a file with a handle before using it. The tang is sharp enough to be dangerous, and at the very least is quite uncomfortable to hold. The wooden handle fits over the tang, and is tightened by grasping it (with the file sticking up vertically) and rapping the base of the handle on the bench top. Universal handles have screw-tightened jaws.

Rifflers are tiny rasps with profiled ends for getting into just about any size or shape cranny you may encounter. They're generally sold in sets, and are used mostly in woodcarving.

Perforated-steel shapers

These are often called *Surform* tools, since Stanley's innovative line of shapers by that name popularized the style. Auto body shops quickly discovered they could shape half-hardened body filler easily and rapidly with these tools, avoiding the dust and noise of grinding the fully-hardened stuff. Woodworkers and carpenters were soon won over as well by the unprecedented efficiency these tools offered compared to standard rasps. Today several manufacturers market perforated shapers with their own variations and improvements.

The basic Surform-type has a thin steel blade that is perforated to create hundreds of razor-sharp raised cutting edges. A newer style, known as a *micro plane rasp,* has a cylindrical stainless steel blade whose teeth are shaped like tiny scrub plane blades (with a slightly rounded front) and have three sharp edges, making this type even faster and smoother cutting.

Perforated steel shapers are held and used like the other filing tools their shapes are patterned after. Work at an angle to the grain and gradually lighten your pressure as you finish the shaping.

Cleaning files & rasps

A combination file card/brush is equipped with stiff wire bristles on one side for removing clogs between the teeth of the file. The brush on the other side has stiff bristles that can handle most file cleaning without scratching the tool surface.

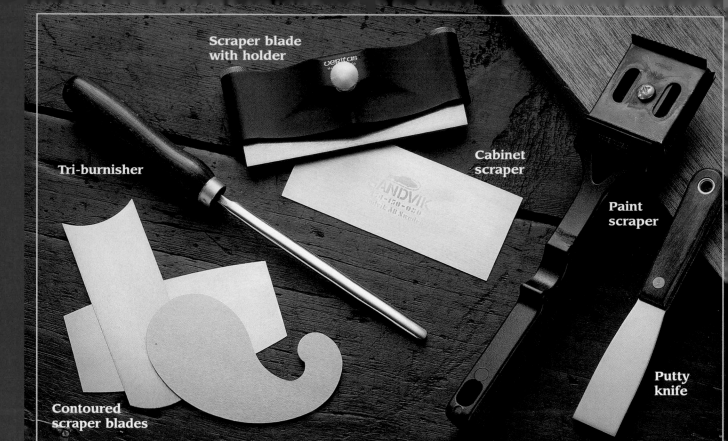

Scraper blade
with holder

Cabinet
scraper

Tri-burnisher

Paint
scraper

Putty
knife

Contoured
scraper blades

Scrapers

Cabinet scraper: Rectangular steel blades with polished edges for imparting a glass-smooth surface on wood prior to finish application. 6 in. long, 2½ in. high, .030 in. thick.

Scraper blade with holder: Cabinet scrapers are inserted into this ergonomic holder to protect your hand from fatigue and insulate your fingers from heat build-up.

Contoured scraper blades: Provide a wide variety of profiles for scraping concave and convex surfaces.

Paint scraper: Best known as a tool for removing paint, can also be used in the shop to scrape dried glue.

Putty knife: Can be used for scraping chores where a sharp edge is not desired, and to apply putty and filler to your woodworking projects.

Tri-burnisher: Combining the burnishing functions of round and triangular burnishers, tri-burnishers can be used to burnish a hook on just about any type of scraper.

Cabinet scrapers

Cabinet scrapers are common finishing tools in fine wood shops, but given their utility and ease of use, they should be more widely known than they are. For smoothing wood surfaces, they simply can't be beat. A plane always runs the risk of tearout, especially on irregular grain, and can leave tiny ridges. Sandpaper is slow, messy and leaves fine scratches. A cabinet scraper, when sharpened and used correctly, takes shavings like a plane, but thinner and across a wider surface. And, it won't cause tearout—even on a burl. Unlike sandpaper, which requires you to work through numerous grits to progress from rapid stock removal to a fine surface finish, a scraper cuts quickly and leaves a finished surface.

Scrapers are comfortable doing everything from crude work to the very finest woodcrafting. A few tasks they're often used for include smoothing a surface before fine sanding, scraping off dried glue, and even smoothing and dressing a lacquer or varnish finish. The scraper also excels at flushing up inlays and leveling high spots. Overhanging edgebanding that has been brought nearly flush to the surface with a plane or router can be quickly trimmed with a scraper. A scraper is also the best tool for removing saw, planer or plane

Pushing a cabinet scraper. Hold the scraper at an angle of about 75° to the surface being scraped. Press the back face with your thumbs to cause a slight flex in the blade, then push forward slowly and evenly. Angle the scraper so one corner leads.

Pulling a cabinet scraper. Flex the scraper with your fingers and draw the tool toward your body at about a 75° angle.

marks, and for smoothing tearout. Scrapers tend to work better on hardwoods than softwoods.

Cabinet scrapers are simply small sheets of spring steel. They come in several sizes and shapes. The standard 2½ × 5 or 6 in. rectangular scraper is for general flat work. To scrape moldings and concave curves, use contoured scraper blades in paisley-shaped, gooseneck and other assorted shapes.

Sharpening cabinet scrapers. The scraper's cutting edge is a sharp hook, or *burr,* that's created by bending over the square edges of the steel. For instructions on sharpening a cabinet scraper, see pages 156 to 157.

Using cabinet scrapers. Hold the scraper with both hands, with your thumbs against the near face and your fingers on the other face. Since there's a burr on all faces, you can push or pull the scraper as you please— you'll find each handy at different times. Flex the blade into a slight arc and drag it along with the top edge slightly ahead of the bottom, but not at too low an angle. The scraper cuts better if held askew to the direction of the grain, but keep the movement of the scraper parallel to the grain whenever possible. Reversing the skew angle with each stroke helps assure even cutting as you overlap strokes. Be careful when pushing the scraper with the thumbs, as it's easy to bow it too much so it scoops out a trough in the wood.

Turn the scraper to expose a new edge, or stop and refurbish the edges as often as necessary to maintain sharp, efficient cutting. If you're only raising dust, not shavings, it's a sure sign the edge is dull. It just takes a minute with the burnisher to flatten the burr out again across the face and turn it again along the edge. You can do this several times before the burr begins to get ragged and you need to go back to the file and stone.

A good scraper can get uncomfortably hot on the thumbs and fingers after awhile. You can try switching scrapers to allow it to cool down. Some people pad their thumbs with surgical tape or leather finger protectors available in many catalogs.

Other alternatives are available in the form of holding devices that shield the fingers from the blade. Several types of blade holders in wood or metal and plastic accept standard scrapers, and have the added advantage of a screw to set the desired amount of bow in the scraper. Some people prefer to use a frame-type cabinet scraper, often called a *scraper plane.* The blade is rather narrow, but it is held firmly in a cast-iron body with wing handles similar to a spokeshave. This requires that the blade be beveled to a 45° angle, however, so maintenance is a bit trickier.

Paint scrapers

Paint scrapers have replaceable blades bent over at an angle (usually forming a U, with an edge on either end) to allow them to be mounted in a handle. These are used for removing paint and varnish, and are indispensable for scraping off the old loose paint flakes on a house exterior before painting. With one hand holding the handle, you can use the other hand to press down on the head to give a better bite.

Putty knives

These are not technically scraping tools, but scraping is certainly one of their many uses. Putty knives come in a range of blade widths, and you have a choice of flexible or stiff blades. Stiff-bladed tools are used for scraping, and do a great job of stripping wallpaper or prying up peeling paint on the side of a house. Flexible putty knives are used to apply pasty or dough-like materials, such as putty, wood filler and spackle.

½-in. sanding stick

Synthetic steel wool (abrasive pads)

2-in. sanding stick

Abrasive foam sponges

Sanding cord

Steel wool

Sanding block

Contour sanders

Adhesive and hook-and-loop sanding pads

Sanding Tools & Materials

The universe of sanding tools and materials has expanded in recent years, for hand sanding and power sanding alike. A little research and comparison shopping before your next sanding project could turn a tiresome chore into a simple and easy undertaking.

Sanding sticks: Available in several sizes, accept coarse, medium or fine "belts."

Synthetic steel wool: Abrasive pads perform tasks of steel wool with less mess.

Sanding cord: Can reach hard-to-reach areas.

Steel wool: Useful for general cleaning around the house.

Contour sanders: Soft sanding blocks shaped to fit common contours and profiles.

Sanding pads: Made for power sanders, but can be used with sanding blocks.

Sanding blocks: Most prefab models accept quarter-sheets of sandpaper.

Abrasive sponges: Disposable products with surprisingly strong bite.

Hand sanding

Power sanders have so completely taken over the task of sanding wood that, in many ways, it's made us a lazy. And perhaps more than any other power tool (possibly excepting the router), sanders have led directly to the decline in our hand tool skills. Because we now use sanders for so many activities that were once the responsibility of planes, chisels and scrapers, our idea of what sanding is really for has changed greatly. If you're feeling a little troubled by this shift, you need only consider the subject of hand-sanding for a refresher course.

Sanding, in its traditional sense, is more like polishing than planing. It's a final refinement of a wood surface that prepares it to accept a wood finish. Far from being an afterthought, sanding is the critical last step in the woodworking process. It can make or break the look of your work, as the quality of the finish is only as good as the quality of the sanding. You can spend a long time carefully working on a project only to ruin it with a sloppy sanding job. Don't hurry into it; sanding should be left until all work with cutting tools is done, as sandpaper canno do the job of a cutting edge and residual grit left in the grain will quickly dull steel tools used subsequently. Proper sanding does take some time and yes, it's rather tedious; but it is a worthwhile investment in your project.

Sandpaper. The particles on modern sandpapers (no longer actually sand) are highly faceted mineral crystals bonded to a paper or cloth backing. The quality of a particular sandpaper depends on the inherent sharpness of the given mineral's facets, and their ability to stay sharp. Most modern materials are *friable;* that is, they are not only very hard and sharp, but also brittle, and break off to expose new sharp edges. Quality also depends on a proper adhesive bond and good paper or cloth backing. Buying cheap "no-name" sandpaper may seem like a bargain at first, but if the sheets wear out prematurely, you'll find the savings don't hold up either.

Older, softer, natural abrasives like flint and glass have given way to much harder, longer-lasting synthetic materials. The most common are *aluminum oxide* and *silicon carbide.* Aluminum oxide is derived from bauxite (aluminum ore) and is an impure form of what occurs naturally as sapphires and rubies. It is tough and durable, and is a great, all purpose abrasive, performing well on metals and plastics as well as wood. Silicon carbide, also called carborundum, is almost as hard as diamond. Its sharp, even crystals will cut very hard substances, like stone and steel. The most common use of silicon carbide is on the black wet/dry sandpaper used for polishing.

Garnet has been around a long time as an abrasive particle, and though it is relatively soft, it is favored by some for just that reason. Garnet is not so brittle and doesn't fracture, it simply dulls. This quality, often combined with a hide glue adhesive that has more give than the newer resin bond papers, can give a very smooth finish to wood and actually glazes end grain pores so they accept stain more evenly. *Emery,* a natural abrasive, is softer than the synthetics but is a traditional favorite for polishing metal.

The terms *open coat* and *closed coat* refer to the distribution of the abrasive grains on the backer.

Grading information is printed on the back face of most sandpaper sheets. The key information to know is the grit and the type of mineral used. Aluminum oxide paper (shown in 150 and 220 grit above) is a good, general-purpose sandpaper.

Closed coat abrasives are tightly packed all over the surface, and are only used for metal or where clogging is not an issue. More common, open coat only has 40 to 70% coverage and is therefore more suitable for wood. Special sandpaper is available coated with zinc stearate, a dry lubricant, to further prevent loading when fine-sanding paint, lacquer and varnish finishes, or resinous woods.

The backing sheet on sandpaper is either paper (graded by weight from *A* to *F*) or fabric (*J, X* or *Y* weight). Only the lightest, most flexible sheets (*A* and *B* weight in paper, *J* weight in cloth) are suitable for hand-sanding. Cloth is more flexible for contour work and lasts longer, but is much more expensive. *A* and *B* weight aluminum oxide is good all-purpose paper for general wood and light metal work. The waterproof paper and adhesive on wet/dry sandpaper allows it to be well lubricated with water or other liquids to minimize loading. This type of paper is typically used for sanding between coats of finish on wood, and should be soaked.

Sandpaper is graded according to the size of the abrasive grains, or grits, on its surface, and its cutting power is directly related to the coarseness of these grits. The finer the abrasive, the less apparent are the scratches it leaves in the surface of the wood. The range runs from 16 grit to 1200 grit (with 16 resembling gravel and 1200 a baby's bottom), but typical woodworking usually doesn't require more than 100, 150, 220, and 320 (occasionally, 80-grit may be needed for rough work and 400-grit for sanding between coats of fine finishes). Anything coarser than 80 grit is usually only used in machine sanding, and grits finer than 400 are for polishing.

For most sanding operations, particularly hand-sanding, 9 × 11-in. sheets are the standard. They can be purchased either individually, in packs of a few sheets or (more economically and with a greater selection) in packs of 50 or 100.

Sanding blocks. Occasional contour work can be done with a folded sheet in the bare hand, but hand-sanding is generally done

DIY sanding block made from a 1½ × 2½ × 4½ in. piece of scrap wood is a perfect fit for quarter-sheets of sandpaper. A piece of ⅛-in.-thick cork glued to the bottom provides cushion and helps preserve the life of the sandpaper sheet.

Sanding cords can smooth or remove finish from grooves that are inaccessible for any other sanding tool. They're especially useful when sanding round or cylindrical objects.

with some kind of sanding block or pad. There are all sorts of fancy sanding block contraptions out there, but a simple wood or cork block is the easiest to use, cheapest, and most comfortable. The common rounded-top solid cork block is fine, or you can make one up from a block of wood, 4½ × 2½ × 1½ in. high, with a ⅛-in.-thick cork sheet glued to the bottom, and all top corners rounded over. A half-sheet sander, made twice as long and used sideways, is even better for leveling imperfections when you're applying a reflective finish that will magnify any distortions. Wood alone can be used for a block, but it tends to wear the paper more quickly. Hard felt, cork or rubber on the bottom works better. To tear sandpaper to size, fold it, then tear along the sharp edge of a tabletop or a hack saw blade.

Contour sanding. For sanding contours, flexible foam pads work well. One popular style is a thin circular pad with an elastic hand strap to hold it on. It accepts standard 5- or 6-in.-dia. adhesive or hook-and-loop sandpaper disks. Contour sanding grip sets include a variety of foam rubber shapes (convex, concave and angles) that you can wrap a piece of sandpaper around. You can also make up your own shaped sanding block to fit a particular shape or molding. Make it out of a solid cork block or a soft wood like pine, and if dimensions are critical, remember to take into account the thickness of the sandpaper.

There are even sandpaper devices made just to ease sanding tiny grooves, beads and routed surfaces. Abrasive cords and tapes will get into narrow scroll saw

> When the sanding power is supplied by your arm, not a motor, you gain a new appreciation for the virtues of doing clean, careful work during the building phase of your project.

kerfs and fine details on wood or metal. Sanding sticks are miniature manual belt sanders with pointed noses to get them into tight situations.

Sanding techniques. When sanding wood, keep the block flat and sand parallel to the grain. Take long, even strokes, overlapping as you progress across the surface. Avoid concentrating on localized defects unless you feather the surrounding area in well. Be particularly careful sanding around edges, corners, and facets, as details and crispness can be lost easily, making the whole work look kind of shaggy. Sanding should be done with a firm touch, but too much pressure or excess speed will not allow the abrasive particles to cut properly.

The general procedure is to work through progressively finer grits of paper until the wood looks and feels smooth enough for the chosen finish. Painted projects require only minimal sanding. When applying lacquer and varnish on most woods, anything finer than 150- or 220-grit is overkill. Oil finishes don't fill up the pores and sit on the surface, so they benefit from finer sanding. Harder, denser woods (especially exotics like rosewood) often need to be finish-sanded to a finer grit than softer wood species, and very dark woods like ebony show sanding scratches (and any other flaw in the finish) even more.

To avoid unnecessary sanding, start with the finest grit possible given the condition of the wood. Sand well enough with each grit to completely remove the coarser scratches of the previous paper. Tap the block sharply on the bench or against your palm periodically

A low light illuminates defects. **Position a portable light next to your project after sanding to cast a low-angle light across the surface of the wood. The shadows from the low light will spotlight potential problems, such as dents and scratches.**

Make a tack cloth. **Many inferior sanding jobs occur because the residual grit was not wiped away completely. Avoid this problem by wiping with a tack cloth between sanding sequences and before applying a finish. Cheesecloth moistened in a 1:1 solution of linseed oil and varnish yields a good, homemade tack cloth.**

as you sand to loosen impacted wood dust from the sandpaper. And always brush off the surface of the work before moving to a finer grit, so all the larger grit particles are removed.

It's hard to see minor unevenness, defects and scratches when sanding, but when you get that clear finish on, they'll all shout out to you loud and clear. To detect problems before the finish is applied, aim an adjustable light at a low angle across the surface. This helps illuminate any potential problems.

When you're done sanding, "break" or ease all sharp corners and edges lightly with sandpaper, just enough so they're not dangerous or too delicate.

When sanding very small workpieces, sometimes the best way is to mount the paper face up on a flat surface and bring the workpiece to paper. For bigger jobs, you can stick the sheet down with spray adhesive.

Other abrasives

Steel wool is a venerable smoothing material. It comes in four grades: from *0* (coarsest) for removing rust and scouring metal to *0000* (finest) for buffing a smooth, satin finish on everything from metals to varnish and lacquer.

Steel wool has some inherent drawbacks. It can rust, it crumbles easily, and it can leave hard-to-remove steel fibers lodged in wood grain. Naturally, alternatives have been developed. *Nylon abrasive pads* consist of a flexible mesh, permanently impregnated with abrasive minerals. The 6 × 9-in. pads come in a variety of colors that each represent a given coarseness (the green is what you probably already use in the kitchen to scrub pots and pans). They can be cut to size, they can be

used dry or with any liquid or solvent, they resist shredding, and they can be rinsed clean. They're good for furniture stripping, for surfacing metals, plastics, and finishes, for smoothing and polishing turnings on the lathe, and for cleaning and rust removal.

Abrasive foam sponges come in thin, flexible pads for contour sanding or regular one-handed sanding block size. The soft sponge pads are coated with abrasive on the outside, whereas the stiffer, semi-flexible blocks have grits impregnated throughout. The softer style works well on wood, while the harder is for cleaning and de-rusting metal tools and machine surfaces.

Steel wool (synthetic & natural)

Coarse

Medium

Fine

#0

#000

#0000

Striking & Fastening

The hammer and the mallet are perhaps the simplest tools found in any workshop. Although they take many forms and are crafted in numerous sizes from widely varying materials they are, in essence, just handles with heavy heads for striking. And yet, every carpenter, every woodworker and every experienced do-it-yourselfer always seems to have his favorite: that one single hammer that just feels right some how, and never seems to miss its target.

In truth, there isn't really a lot to be said about hammers. As with any tool, you should make sure the one you're using is appropriate for the job at hand. You don't want to try and drive a 16d nail with a tack hammer, after all. Mallets are a little riper for discussion, mostly because few of us own more than one or two of the old, crumbly rubber-headed ones. But if you do much furniture work (making it or fixing it) you should look into the subject of mallets with some interest. Mallets have changed a lot over the years, and some of the new special-purpose ones are quite impressive. Fastening is the crux of woodworking and carpentry. In joining board to board, things are built. How well you choose and use fasteners and fastening tools has an enormous impact on any project. So it certainly doesn't hurt to browse through the following pages and take a quick refresher course on fastening fundamentals. Screwdrivers, wrenches and pliers all are discussed in detail, and you'll even find some good pointers on "unfastening" tools as well.

Hammers

Tack hammer with magnetic, split peen is used to drive upholstery tacks and other small nails or brads.
Claw hammer is the basic all-purpose hammer type, suitable for driving and pulling nails.
Framing hammer is heavier than claw hammers for driving larger nails, like those used in frame carpentry. Ripping claw is typical.
Cross-peen hammer, also called a Warrington hammer or a cabinetmaker's hammer, has a thin head for starting small nails and round head for driving them.

Hammers

The current range of familiar hammer shapes, each developed to serve a specific task, has been around for a very long time. Even though we can now choose from "space-age" handle materials, the basic designs of the claw hammer, the ball peen, and all the rest have never met a serious challenge.

Hammers are not one-size-fits-all tools. Don't expect to be able to drive wire brads, framing nails and splitting wedges with the same tool.

Generally, it's easy to distinguish a quality hammer from a poor one. A good, name-brand hammer obtained from a reputable tool or hardware dealer has a smooth, well-finished, forged head mounted solidly on a sturdy handle and balanced for comfort and efficiency. Cheap, discount store or flea market hammers often have weak handles and rough, misshapen heads marred by casting blobs. An improperly hardened, cast (rather than forged) head can chip and lose its shape, and a poorly ground face is good only for bending nails and hammering fingers.

Some safety concerns should be considered when working with hammers. Never strike one hammer against another, and don't strike with the cheek (side) of the tool. Only the face is properly tempered and ground for pounding. Don't use a tool with a loose or damaged handle, or a chipped or mushroomed face. And there is always the danger of flying shards and particles, so you should wear safety glasses or goggles any time you use a striking tool.

Claw hammers. The most practical type of hammer for general woodworking, carpentry, and household use is the *claw hammer.* One end of its head has a face for driving nails and the other end boasts a two-pronged claw for prying nails out. Most reliable manufacturers have dropped the perfectly

Anatomy of a claw hammer

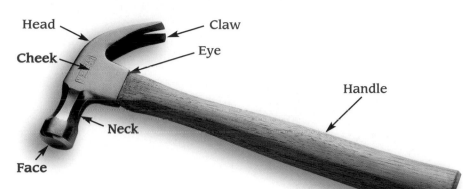

flat face in favor of one with a slightly convex dome, known as a *bell face.* This design is less likely to bend a nail that's not struck squarely, and it permits you to drive nailheads flush with or slightly below the surface without leaving a hammer dent. Some larger framing hammers are available with a

checkered pattern milled into the face. When hammering forcefully, this helps the face grip the nailhead, reducing the occurrence of glancing blows that cause flying nails. The checkered face is not for finish work, however, as it can leave a

Hammer handles & heads

Handles. Hammer handles are made from many materials these days, each with its own pro's and cons. The traditional choice of material for a striking tool handle is straight-grained American hickory, still considered by many professionals and amateurs to be the best. This extremely strong, resilient wood has two important benefits. It provides the spring necessary to minimize impact shock and strain on the muscles, and gives the user good control by transmitting the feel of the nail's progress. Occasionally, ash is used as well. The one drawback to wood is that it can be damaged or broken if abused. However, a wooden handle is easy to replace.

Steel hammer handles are used frequently on larger hammers. A steel handle is strong and won't crack or splinter. But it can be jarring on the arm, as it doesn't absorb shock well. Some manufacturers have tried to overcome these drawbacks by jacketing the steel in plastic. Fiberglass was introduced as a handle material to try and marry the toughness of

steel with the shock-damping characteristics of wood. While durable, a fiberglass handle that sees a lot of overstrikes can fray and eventually break. The most recent introduction in handle design is graphite. Stronger and stiffer than fiberglass, it can better withstand the extreme stresses involved in heavy nail pulling. Steel, fiberglass, and graphite handles all generally come with cushioned grips.

Heads. Hammers are classified by the weight of the head. A 16 oz. claw hammer is a good mid-weight tool for home and shop use. It'll handle medium-sized finishing and casing nails and brads. For driving large nails into building lumber, a framing hammer in the 20 oz. range has more power. Framing hammers range up to 28 oz., with handles as long as 18 in. Framing hammers often have a *ripping claw.* While the curved claw has more leverage for pulling nails, the straighter ripping claw can also do minor demolition work like prying apart boards and removing siding.

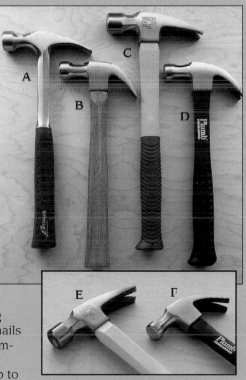

A. 20 oz. steel framing hammer
B. 16 oz. wood claw hammer
C. 24 oz. graphite framing hammer
D. 16 oz. jacketed fiberglass claw hammer
E. framing head with ripping claw
F. standard claw head

Correct nailing technique

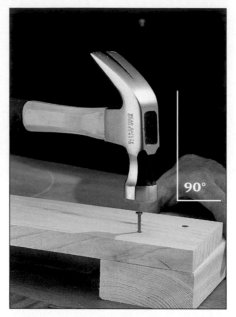

1 *Set the nail.* Hold the nail in a vertical position and rap it lightly until it is fully seated in the wood.

2 *Drive the nail.* Strike the head of the nail with a series of blows, making sure the head of the hammer is square to the nail head at impact.

Recommended nailing patterns

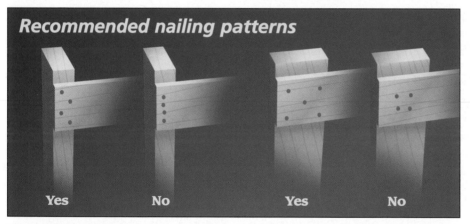

Yes   No   Yes   No

When nailing a wood joint, the most important factors are spacing and pattern. Keep the nails well away from the end or edge of the board, and avoid patterns where adjacent nails are aligned.

Two toe-nailing techniques

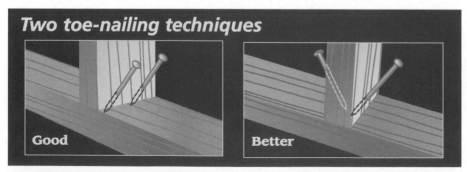

Good   Better

Toe-nailing is an effective technique for attaching a vertical member to a horizontal member. Whenever access allows, drive nails on opposing faces of the vertical member. Clamping or tacking a stopblock on the side opposite the nail prevents the vertical member from shifting as you drive the nail.

waffle pattern in the wood.

Except for checkered-face framing hammers, a good hammer should have a smooth striking face with an even chamfer to prevent chipping. The slot between the claws should be beveled so it can grip a nail shank by biting into it.

Claw hammers are made in a range of sizes and styles, and personal preference plays a major role in which one is best for you. When choosing a claw hammer, take a few practice swings at the store with your prospective purchase, and choose the one that feels best in your hand. A hammer needs to suit not only the work being done, but your own strength and ability as well. Although a heavy hammer exerts considerable force, striking with it for extended periods of time can be very tiresome.

The weight and balance of the hammer, along with the length, shape and handle material, should combine to transmit the maximum amount of power with the least amount of energy or strain.

Using a claw hammer. While pounding with a heavy, blunt object may seem like an instinctual motion, specific hammering techniques can give you the best results with the least frustration: Grasp the hammer firmly, but not tightly, near the butt of the handle—handles usually are shaped so your hand will conform most comfortably near the butt. In this position, you get maximum leverage from the handle and the full striking power of the head, along with the benefit of the proper, controllable balance. You also create a more direct angle of descent and impact on the nail.

Hold the nail upright and perpendicular to the wood surface. Center the face of the hammer on the nailhead to set up your stroke, then raise the hammer and tap the nail lightly a couple of times until it's started and will stand on its own. Then, get your hand out of the way and drive the nail with firm, positive blows. You don't need to club

Over the centuries, specialty hammers have been designed for just about every imaginable use and trade. For example, for tasks where sparking creates a hazard, brass-headed hammers were devised. For delicate jobs, like glazing windows and modelmaking, very precise hammers with task-specific heads were created. Silversmiths and goldsmiths have long use dedicated smithing hammers.

Among the more unusual, and interesting, special-purpose hammers is the bill-posting hammer. This unique striking device truly proves the old idiom that necessity is the mother of invention.

Back in the latter part of the 19th century, entertainment was founded on the traveling show in greater America. Circuses, medicine shows, Wild West shows, religious revivals and even political rallies toured the land, moving from town to town in search of a crowd. With modern mass communications still a generation in the future, spreading the word through advertising was a challenge. The dominant publicizing medium selected by the organizers of these events became the hand bill. Just prior to its appearance in a town, advance men arrived to drum up interest by blanketing the area with colorful posters trumpeting the impending arrival of their fabulous show of shows. It was an effective practice, except for one glitch: the exotic, colorful posters and handbills proved to be tempting targets for the townfolk, who often ripped them down almost as soon as they were posted. To discourage this practice, the bill-poster hammer was developed and enlisted.

With its long, spindly handle, the bill-poster hammer allowed the advance men to tack their posters well out of the reach of most of the would-be poster thieves—and because it could be unscrewed like a pool cue, it fit neatly into his valise or briefcase. The rare 30-in.-long bill-poster hammer shown here, with its elegantly shaped hickory handle, was made around 1886 by the *A. R. Robertson Co.* of Boston, Massachusetts.

Hand Tool Heritage: The Bill-poster Hammer

Drilling pilot holes

Pilot holes prevent cracking and assure that nails will enter wood joints cleanly. They also prevent the nail from wandering and breaking through the surface of the wood. A twist drill is a very handy tool for drilling quick, accurately positioned pilot holes.

Setting nail heads

Use a nailset to drive finish nailheads below the wood surface. Make sure the nailset is centered on the nail head and in a vertical position. A single well-placed blow on the butt of the nailhead should be enough to set any nailhead. Nailsets are made in three common sizes for accurate matching to any nailhead.

the nail to death, nor do you want to baby it along with soft, polite taps. When driving small nails, simple wrist action should supply sufficient power. If more power is needed, combine the wrist action with a pivot at the elbow, bringing the forearm into play. For heavy blows, use your entire arm, flexing at the wrist, the elbow, and the shoulder. Even when taking powerful swings with the hammer, maintain a light grip on the hammer, or too much of the impact will be transmitted to your hand and arm, resulting in discomfort, inefficiency and possible injury.

Try to keep the hammer face perpendicular to, and centered on, the nailhead with each stroke. When you

strike the nail squarely you avoid glancing blows, lessening the chance of bending the nail or sending it flying. If the nail does bend, and the bend is slight, you can often straighten it by gently tapping it upright. If the bend is substantial, you're better off pulling out the nail and starting over with a new nail. If the second one bends, you may be hitting a knot and you should consider relocating to a new spot on the board. If you continue to have problems with nails bending, or any time you're nailing into hardwood, drill pilot holes for the nails first.

Splitting your workpiece is always a concern when driving nails, especially when working with harder

Tips for pulling nails

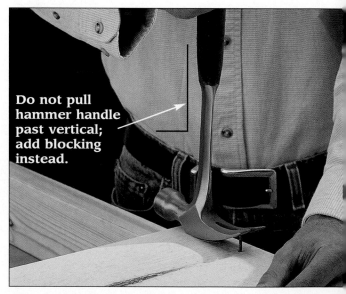

Do not pull hammer handle past vertical; add blocking instead.

Increase your leverage. Before attempting to pull longer nails, set a block of wood beneath the hammer head. This increases leverage and usually prevents you from pulling the hammer han-

dle past vertical (which reduces leverage and can cause the nail shank to damage the workpiece). The block also protects the wood surface from the hammer head.

A *brad pusher* is an effective alternative to hammering in tight spots where delicate fillisters and rabbets are easily damaged. Attaching retainer strips is an example of a job that's a perfect fit for a brad pusher.

A *split, magnetized peen* is a common feature on tack hammers. With a little dexterity and practice, you can pick up an upholstery tack by the head, using only the peen, and drive it into a seat board with a one-handed blow. This allows you to hold the upholstery fabric in position with your other hand. In case you're curious, the reason for the split peen is that one side is polarized north, and the other south.

Maintaining hammers

Keep the hammer's striking face clean and free of oil so it can strike squarely without slipping. Inspect wooden handles for splits. and check the head to make sure it isn't loose. With a wooden handle, you can usually drive the wedges further into the handle end to tighten the head. A handle of any other material must be either replaced with a wooden one, or the whole tool discarded. Replacement wood handles are available to fit any hammerhead. A handle comes as a kit, complete with all necessary wedges and instructions.

woods or when nailing near the end of a board. The nail point can work like a wedge, separating the wood fibers as it goes in, thus increasing the splitting hazard. Here's a trick for reducing the likelihood of splitting your workpiece with a nail: because a blunt tip will crush its way through the wood (rather than separating the fibers), strike the point of the nail a couple of times before driving it into the board.

Setting nails. When nailing into a surface that will be exposed, as in cabinetry or finish carpentry, use a nail with a brad-style head that can be driven well below the surface with a nailset. The tiny exposed nail hole is then filled with wood putty or spackle. When setting a nail, ease up on the force of your blows as the nailhead nears the wood surface. This will keep you from accidentally denting the wood surface with the face of the hammer. Stop nailing while the nailhead is still protruding a bit, then finish the job with the point of the nailset held firmly against the nailhead. Sink the nail about 1/16 in. Nailsets are available in a few sizes—buy yourself a set of nailsets so you'll always have a well-matched nailset for any nailhead.

Cross-peen hammers

Cross-peen hammer. Also called a *cabinetmaker's* or *Warrington* hammer, this style has a wedge-shaped tapered peen ending in a narrow, flat surface. (The peen is the rear end of a hammerhead, opposite the face). This cross-peen makes it easy to start small nails and brads without your fingers getting in the way. After the nails are started, the head is flipped around and the flat, circular face is used to drive the nails or tacks home in the usual way. The cross-peen hammer is popular in furnituremaking and cabinetmaking, where any nails tend to be small and a claw-end is not a necessity. The size and weight of the head is selected to correspond with the nails used. An average weight would be about 10 or 12 oz.

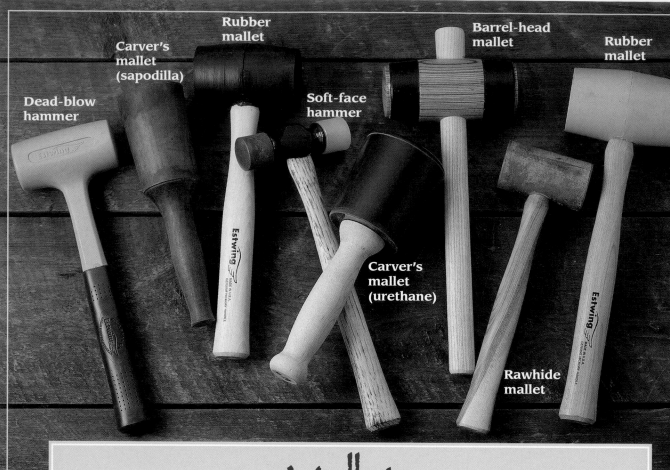

Dead-blow
hammer

Carver's
mallet
(sapodilla)

Rubber
mallet

Soft-face
hammer

Barrel-head
mallet

Rubber
mallet

Carver's
mallet
(urethane)

Rawhide
mallet

Mallets

Rubber mallets are used in the shop mostly for knocking wood joints apart. Black rubber is more common, but white rubber won't streak.

Carver's mallets drive woodcarving chisels and gouges. Sapodilla and urethane heads shown.

Dead-blow hammers are filled with buckshot for enhanced striking power.

Soft-face hammer has rubber and urethane faces for metalworking and driving steel tools.

Barrel-head mallet is a general-purpose mallet with head made from laminated beech impregnated with resins for greater strength.

Rawhide mallet is the precursor to rubber mallets. No longer commonly used.

A mallet is simply a hammer whose head is made of a material softer than steel. It can be used for driving another tool, such as a chisel, or for striking a surface without marring it. With heads made of diverse materials, from the common wooden carpenter's mallet to the fine metalworker's horn mallet, mallets are used in many disciplines.

Wooden mallets

Wooden mallets are traditional woodworker's tools.

Carpenter's mallet. The classic woden mallet, known as the *carpenter's mallet,* actually gets more use in the shop these days than at the construction site. It's the standard mallet for driving wood chisels in furniture and cabinet work. The broad, flat striking face allows you to keep your eyes on the cutting edge of the chisel,

without worrying about aiming your blows. The faces are angled relative to the handle to accommodate a natural, comfortable swing that strikes its target squarely. Another style of wooden mallet sometimes used for driving chisels has a barrel-shaped head.

The top of the carpenter's mallet handle is wider than the hole in the mallet head to prevent the head from flying off. Normal usage keeps the head wedged tightly on the shaft, but if it should ever loosen, simply tap the butt end of the handle on your bench to drive the head back on tightly. Close-grained, hard-wearing European beech was, and still is, the most common mallet wood. More recent introductions include resin-impregnated beech for increased durability, and dense tropical hardwoods for extra weight. A mallet with a 5-in.-long head is well sized for most general tasks.

Carver's mallet. The head of a carver's mallet is a graduated cylinder that's often lathe-turned, together with the handle, from a single piece of wood. The shape makes sense for a woodcarver, who often must strike a gouge from many different angles in quick succession. A round-headed (and round-handled) mallet doesn't need to be adjusted constantly in thc hand to align the face, as a flat-faced mallet would. Traditional woods are beech (which is often impregnated for greater hardness and density) and *lignum vitae,* a heavy, rock-hard exotic wood that has been over harvested and has thus become scarce. Lesser-known tropical hardwoods such as *sapodilla* frequently are used instead of lignum vitae. Carver's mallets are also made with hard urethane heads, which some people prefer, since the better shock absorption makes them easier on the elbows.

Soft mallets

In addition to wood, mallet heads are made from a number of soft materials that provide greater shock absorption or are able to knock woodworking joints together or apart without damaging the wood surfaces.

Rawhide & rubber mallets. The old-fashioned rawhide mallet has a cylindrical head fashioned from coiled leather. They're still available today, but the rubber mallet has supplanted them in most shops. A rubber

Reset mallet heads on wooden handles by rapping the butt of the handle on a hard surface.

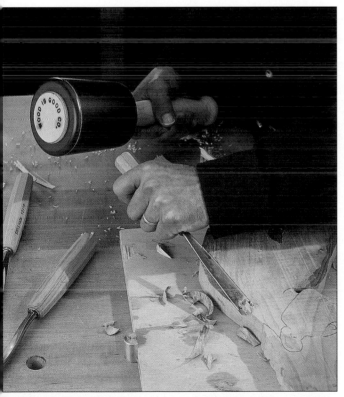

The head of a carver's mallet is a graduated cylinder, which allows the woodcarver to strike tools from different angles and positions without repositioning the mallet in his hand. The head of the mallet shown here is made of urethane.

The classic carpenter's mallet is really more of a woodworker's tool. Its primary purpose is striking wood chisels. The large carpenter's mallet shown here has faces that are angled to the handle so it can deliver a square blow with a short swing arc.

Sapodilla is a fairly obscure tropical hardwood that is often substituted for lignum vitae (traditionally, the preferred species for making carver's mallets). While sapodilla rivals lignum vitae in density and hardness, it is much more susceptible to checking and cracking. To help prevent drying out and checking, store sapodilla mallets in airtight plastic bags.

mallet is valuable around the shop for tapping together (or knocking apart) stubborn furniture joints and cabinet carcase parts. Because black rubber can leave black marks on your workpiece, a white-rubber mallet is a better choice. Carver's mallets are also made with hard rubber heads, which some people find easier on the elbow.

Dead-blow hammers. A dead-blow hammer serves the same purposes as a rubber mallet, but its soft, plastic-covered head is partially filled with metal buckshot. As the head strikes the work, the shot follows through to sustain the impact and increase the power of the blow, while eliminating rebound and deadening vibration. These relatively new striking tools are especially well suited for knocking apart furniture joints. Available in a wide range of weights, an 18- or 21-oz. model is suitable for most work.

Soft-face hammers. Soft-faced hammers have replaceable cylindrical faces, or tips. The hammer is chosen according to the weight of the central portion of the head. Tips generally screw on to both ends of the head, and are available in a great variety of plastic densities, from extra soft to extra hard, as well as in copper, brass and lead. Soft-faced hammers are typically used by auto-body shops for pounding out dents, or for any thin metal work. Choose a face that's slightly softer than the material you're striking. Not limited to metalworking, these mallets are useful any time you want to have good control over the impact and minimize surface damage.

A soft-face mallet is used primarily in metalworking, especially in the auto body trade. But in the shop it's a handy tool to have around for striking other metal tools, as when you're driving the ripping claws of a hammer into a wood joint.

Pound for pound, a dead-blow hammer packs an amazing amount of punch. The rubber head is filled with buckshot. As you strike a blow, the inertia of the shot gives an extra boost to the mallet head, allowing you to strike forcefully in confined areas.

Screwdrivers

A. Slotted, square shaft
B. Slotted, round shaft
C. Cabinetmaker's
D. Magnetic, ratcheting
E. Spiral ratcheting (Yankee)
F. Square drive
G. Torx
H. Phillips
I. Jeweler's
J. Driver bits
K. Offset ratcheting
L. Offset

A screwdriver is a simple tool, consisting of a thin shank with a blade or tip at one end and a handle on the other. Traditional cabinetmaker's screwdrivers have oval wood handles, but most modern screwdrivers have fluted plastic handles molded onto the shank. Both styles are designed to be easier to grip and turn than a smooth round handle (and also to prevent the tool from rolling off the table).

There is no such thing as an all-purpose screwdriver; the tool you select is based on the type and size of screw being used, and the amount of clear access area around the spot where the screw will be driven. Trying to force an over- or undersized screwdriver into service will either strip out the slot or pattern in the screwhead, making it unusable; or it will cause the screwdriver to slip off the screw and mar the work (or both).

The conventional straight-bladed tool that's come to be known as the *slotted screwdriver* is manufactured in a wide array of tip sizes to match different sized slotted screws. Slotted screws vary in diameters and slot thicknesses, constituting 18 screw sizes. They also vary by head shape—flat-head, round-head, hex-head and others. Because of the great variation in slotted screws, you can never have too many sizes of slotted screw-

Anatomy of a screwdriver

Handle

Square shaft

Blade

Face

square-drive) have taken over in most trades, including woodworking. The reason for the change is quite simple: screwdrivers are less likely to slip out of the positive, strip-resistant shapes of these more complex head patterns. As a result, you can apply more torque than you can to a slotted screw. A good indication of the change in screw types can be found in prepackaged screwdriver sets. It wasn't too long ago that these sets included a full selection of slotted screwdrivers, with only a couple phillips-head screwdrivers. Now, a typical set has at least an even mix of slotted and phillips, with a few Torx and square-drive tools thrown in to boot.

drivers on hand, although a basic set of the four most common sizes can handle the majority of the screws you'll encounter.

The length of a screwdriver shank usually varies in accordance with the size of the tip: the larger the tip, the longer the shank. But for just about every tip size, you can find extra-long or extra-short (known as *stubby*) screwdrivers for sale.

Because slotted screws historically have been the most prevalent, slotted screwdrivers are still the most common. But in recent years, the phillips-head screw and other, newer variations (such as Torx-head and

No tool category would be complete without its specialty members. And in the screwdriver category, there are plenty. *S-shaped offset screwdrivers* permit access to very tight spots. Many screwdrivers have square or flattened rectangular shanks to permit an adjustable wrench to be applied to the shaft if additional torque is needed. The tiny *optician's* and *watchmaker's* screwdrivers, available in sets, are sized to fit miniature machine screws and are handy for repairing eyeglasses and the like.

There are many gizmos on the market to assist in the hand-driving of screws without a heavy, awkward power drill or driver. Several types of *ratcheting screwdrivers* are made, most accepting standard hex-shank driver bits (See below). The ratcheting action minimizes wrist-twisting, which eases one-handed screwdriving since you're not constantly readjusting your hand position. Offset ratcheting models work at a 90° angle so you can get at seemingly inaccessible screws.

The *Yankee* spiral ratcheting screwdriver works similarly to the *Yankee* push drill (See page 76). Pushing down on the tool handle creates a turning action at the tip for rapid, light-duty screwdriving. These drivers are reversible: they can be set to either drive or retract screws. They are also spring-loaded to maintain constant pressure in the screw slot, automatically returning to the driving position after each stroke. The Yankee driver uses specially-designed bits.

Driver bits. With the advent of electric-, air-, and battery-operated power drivers has come the inter-

Screw/screwdriver head types

		Phillips-head screws are standardized such that across the entire range of screw sizes and styles there are only five slot pattern sizes, numbered 0, 1, 2, 3, and 4.
		Torx screws have a star-shaped slot pattern that forms a strong union with the torx driver. For tamper-resistance, used often in automotive accessories and electronic equipment.
		Square-drive screws eliminate slippage and provide a measure of tamper resistance. Used most frequently with power drivers.
		Slotted screws are the traditional wood screw head types but are becoming less common as newer head types with less slippage are developed. No. 2 (¼ in.) through No. 20 (3 in.) gauges are sold at most hardware stores.
		Hex-socket (slotted) are used mostly in machinery on sheet metal, but are becoming more popular for woodworking and carpentry because they can be driven with a hex driver attachment. Hex shapes available with non-slotted screwheads.

changeable driver bit. This brilliant invention makes it possible to own a screwdriver for every screw known to man, and to keep them all in a pocket-size candy tin. But driver bits are not just for power drivers. Driver bits are just the tips of screwdrivers, with the ends of their shafts having a hexagonal cross-section. Most can be fitted into a magnetic screwdriver for hand-driving. The magnetic screwdriver is a plastic-handled tool with an open sleeve that accepts interchangeable driver bits. In addition, using driver bits has another advantage: they all have a cabinet tip (See photo, right) so you can run them into counterbore holes without scarring the wood. Small bit sets include the most commonly used sizes and types.

The right way to drive a screw

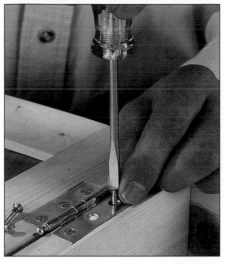

1 *Get started on course.* After drilling a pilot hole (and counterbore or countersink hole, if needed), press the screw tip lightly into the hole. Center the screwdriver in the slot or recess and start the screw, supporting the shaft of the screwdriver with your free hand.

2 *Drive the screw.* Steady the tip of the screwdriver blade with your free hand, and turn the handle in smooth, even rotations. Apply slight downward pressure on the butt of the screwdriver handle. Support the blade so it doesn't cause damage if it slips out of the screwhead.

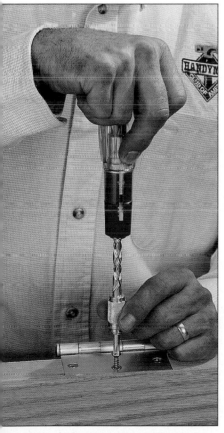

A spiral, ratcheting screwdriver (also known as a Yankee screwdriver) converts downward hand pressure into a twisting motion for light screwdriving tasks.

Cabinetmaker's screwdrivers

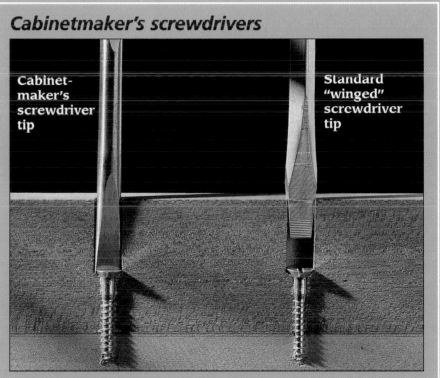

Cabinetmaker's screwdriver tip

Standard "winged" screwdriver tip

When driving screws into countersink or counterbore holes, do not use a screwdriver with a blade that's wider than the screwhead, or the surrounding wood surface will be marred. Instead, use a cabinetmaker's screwdriver with its tip parallel to the sides and the same width as the round shafts. Cabinetmaker's screwdrivers are also popular for electrical and electronics work, and are available with typical plastic-handle styles.

Screwdriving techniques

Pilot holes. When screwing into hardwood or near the ends of a softwood board, the material must be predrilled to accept the core of the screw. The threads will then cut their own path into the wood beyond, resulting in maximum holding power. Without this entry (pilot) hole the wood is likely to be damaged or split, and it would be difficult, if not impossible, to drive the screw—the stress can even wrench the head right off the screw.

Fully-threaded screws (sheet metal or drywall-type) require a pilot hole the size of the core, or slightly smaller. Wood screws need two holes: a short clearance hole the same diameter as the shank, or unthreaded portion, and the smaller pilot hole (a calipers is a good tool for measuring and comparing screw and drill bit diameters). In most cases, the pilot hole should be nearly as long as the screw, but with softwood and medium-to-small steel screws it can be about half as deep as the screw will go.

When fastening two pieces of wood together, the top board should be drilled with a clearance hole clear through. (With fully-threaded screws, make the hole the same diameter as the crest of the threads.) The lower board gets a pilot hole. This way, the threads only bite into the bottom piece, forcing the two pieces to draw together tightly. (If the screw threads bite into both boards the screw can actually force the boards apart.)

Countersink and counterbore holes. Flat-head screws are meant to sit flush with the surface of the wood, so the hole must be countersunk before the screw is driven. Special countersink/counterbore drill bits are the best tools for drilling these holes (See page 77). Drill slowly—when the screw is driven correctly into as

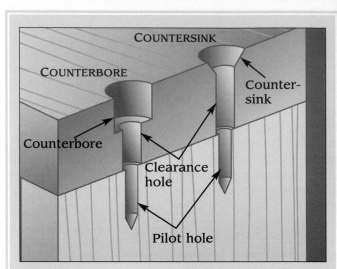

Counterbores & countersinks are driven for flat-head wood screws so the screw head will be recessed below the wood surface. A countersink hole has a beveled top to allow the screw to be driven flush or just below the surface. Counterbore holes are intended to be filled with a wood plug after the screw is driven.

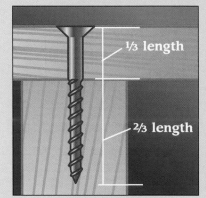

Follow the two-thirds rule: Screws should be driven through the thinner workpiece first, whenever possible. The lower two-thirds of the screw should end up in the lower board after the screw has been driven.

Tips for driving screws

Use a steel screw as a pilot for brass screws. Brass screws are quite soft and their heads can twist off with the slightest resistance. It's a good idea to run a steel screw of the same size in first, stopping just shy of fully tight. Then, back out the steel screw and drive the brass screw home.

Let a wrench lend a hand. In times where you need a little extra torque, but can't quite seem to generate it with your hand, grasp the shaft of a square-shafted screwdriver with the jaws of an adjustable wrench.

countersink hole, it should sit perfectly flush or slightly below the surface. Counterboring can be done to hide a screw, or to allow you to screw through a thick workpiece with a shorter screw. A hole is bored to the desired depth with a drill bit slightly larger than the screwhead diameter. For anything but a flat or oval head screw the hole must be flat-bottomed, and so is drilled with an auger or brad-point. It is best to drill the counterbore hole first, and then use the centerpoint of the counterbore as a guide to drill the screw hole(s). If you want to hide the screw, cut (or purchase) a wood plug of the same wood species. Glue and tap the plug into the counterbore, with the grain oriented the same as the surrounding wood. After the glue has dried, carefully pare the plug flush.

Driving. To drive a screw, start by selecting a screwdriver of the proper size and type for the screw. Never use a bent driver or one with a damaged tip. Place the workpiece on a solid surface or clamp it in a vise. Never try to hold it in your hand; if the blade (remember, it is a blade) should slip, you could get a nasty cut or puncture. Set the screwdriver blade firmly and solidly into the slot or recess of the screw and turn the driver while maintaining downward pressure to keep it locked into the recess pattern (See photos, page 125). It helps (and with slotted screws it's necessary) to use your free hand to guide and steady the shaft of the screwdriver while you twist the handle. Rubbing the screw threads across a block of beeswax will make the screw easier to drive (don't use soap, as it absorbs water and can rust the screw). A drop of oil does the same thing for a machine screw, and will also help prevent rust.

If you strip out or chew up the recess pattern in the screwhead, withdraw the screw while there's still some purchase left in the head. Re-drill and try again with a new screw.

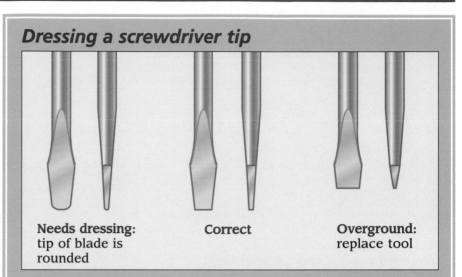

Dressing a screwdriver tip

Needs dressing: tip of blade is rounded

Correct

Overground: replace tool

A slotted screwdriver can be dressed, or reground, to repair a damaged or worn blade. This can be done on a grinding wheel (take care not to overheat the blade and draw the temper) or with a flat file. The faces should not have a sharp, wedge-like angle (as in the right illustration) but should be nearly parallel (as in the middle illustration). The tip should be straight across and square to the shaft so it fits snugly in the screw slot (not rounded, as in the left illustration).

Dress the face. The two faces of the screwdriver blade should be smooth and nearly parallel. Use a grinding stone on your bench grinder to grind the blade back to shape on worn slotted screwdrivers.

Dress the edge. The edge of a slotted screwdriver should be flat and square so it mates cleanly with the screw. Use the tool rest on your bench grinder to set a perpendicular contact angle between the blade and wheel.

Wrenches

A. Ratcheting closed-end wrench
B. Box-end wrench
C. Nut driver;
D. Adjustable wrench

E. Allen wrench set
F. Open-end wrench
G. Ratcheting socket driver
H. Combination wrench

Wrenches

Wrenches can be divided into three types: *fixed wrenches*, *adjustable wrenches* and *socket wrenches*.

Fixed wrenches. Fixed wrenches fall into three general categories: *open-end wrenches, box-end* (sometimes called *closed-end*) wrenches and *combination wrenches* (which have one open end and one closed end). Because each gauge of nut and bolt has a different sized head, there is a fixed wrench made to fit each size, progressing in 1/16-in. increments up to about 1 1/2-in. diameter. As the size of the wrench head increases, so does the length and bulk of the tool. This allows enough torque to be applied to the fastener.

Using fixed wrenches. Here are a few tips for using fixed wrenches:

• When selecting a wrench for a nut or bolt, it's important to use the proper size. If the wrench is too big, it can slip, which will wear down and round over the corners of the bolt head. The usual result is bruised knuckles and a bolt that is very difficult to turn. If you can't find a fixed wrench that fits the nut you're working on, don't try to make another size fit; either use an adjustable wrench or go out and get the right size.

• With a wrench of the right size you should have ample leverage to tighten and loosen any nut or bolt. But overtightening fasteners can cause the fastener to break or overstress and damage the workpiece.

• When loosening a tight bolt, don't beat on the wrench with a hammer or try to extend the handle, as his can break the wrench.

• If the nut is rust-frozen and impossible to move, apply a penetrating lubricant (such as *WD-40*) and allow it to sink in a for few minutes before trying again. If it still won't budge, cut off the nut with a hacksaw or cold chisel.

• Snug the wrench down onto and around the nut or bolt all the way so the grip is secure.

• Screws, bolts, and nuts are almost always threaded so a clockwise motion tightens them. But the action of the motors in some machinery requires a reverse threading, so if a nut seems tight, test it in the other direction before giving it all the power you've got.

• Whenever possible, pull on a wrench rather than pushing it. This is a good way to prevent skinned knuckles when a tight nut suddenly breaks loose or the wrench slips.

Open-end wrenches. This type of fixed wrench has an open mouth that slides onto the nut or bolt from the side. The mouth is offset slightly in relation to the shank of the wrench to accommodate use where the sweep of the wrench is restricted. In a cramped space where only a small portion of a turn is possible, flipping the wrench over will present a new angle and allow it to seat again on the fastener head for another turn.

Offset head increases turning radius

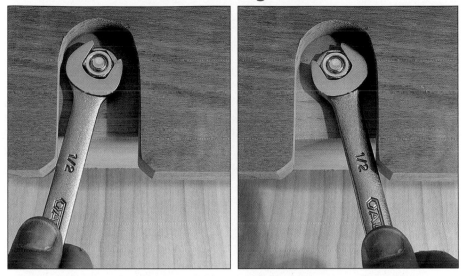

Increase your cranking power in confined areas by flipping your open-end wrench over after each turn of the nut or bolt. This is the primary reason why open-end wrenches have offset heads

Box-end wrench. This style has a circular, enclosed wrench end with 6 or 12 points that grab the hexagonal fastener's corners (12 points permit use on a square nut or bolt). The ends are offset from the horizontal plane of the shank to allow finger clearance when the wrench is being used. The fully-enclosed design with multiple contact points gives this tool a more secure grip than an open-end wrench.

Combination wrench. With a box end and an open end on the same tool, this is the most versatile fixed wrench. The only drawback to combination wrenches is that you'll need more of them to complete a set—open-end and box-end wrenches have ends of different sizes, whereas both ends of a combination wrench fit the same size nut or bolt.

Allen wrenches

Also called *Allen keys,* these are L-shaped, six-sided rods that fit into the hex (or Allen) recess pattern in a screwhead. Allen wrenches come in many sizes from very small to quite hefty, designated in fractions of an inch or in millimeters. The common L-shaped key can be used from either end, but you have best leverage when the long end is used as a handle. Allen wrenches are sold individually and in sets: some sets are linked together into a single Swiss-army-style tool that fits into a pocket.

Adjustable wrenches. The adjustable wrench, also called a *crescent wrench* owing to the shape of its jaws, is a very practical tool to own. A single adjustable wrench performs the work of many sizes of fixed wrenches (including metric). It has one fixed jaw, and one adjustable jaw that is opened and closed by turning a knurled screw. For occasional use, a small and a large crescent wrench will serve, but if you do quite a bit of fix-it work you'll find a small set of combination wrenches to be worthwhile. An adjustable wrench is a handy and versatile tool, but it doesn't grip as securely or with as much strength as a fixed wrench.

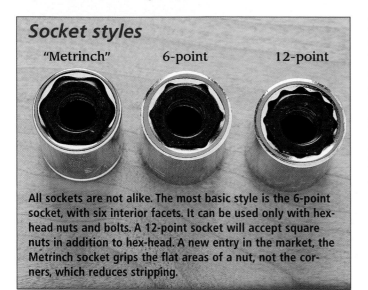

Socket styles

"Metrinch"   6-point   12-point

All sockets are not alike. The most basic style is the 6-point socket, with six interior facets. It can be used only with hex-head nuts and bolts. A 12-point socket will accept square nuts in addition to hex-head. A new entry in the market, the Metrinch socket grips the flat areas of a nut, not the corners, which reduces stripping.

When gripping a nut or bolt head with an adjustable wrench, wrap the head of the wrench around the fastener so the fastener strikes the angled faces at the back of the wrench throat. The wrench has greatest strength when it is pulled in the direction of the open end, so the pressure is applied against the the fixed jaw. As the tool is used, the movable jaw can loosen, so check it periodically.

Socket wrenches. A set of socket wrenches offers another alternative for turning nuts and bolts. They speed the work immensely, provide a firm grip that won't slip off, and they're capable of great leverage.

A socket is a hollow cylinder (available in several lengths depending on the depth of reach required) with a series of pointed facets around the inside, similar to the inside dimension of a box-end wrench. The rear end has a square opening that fits onto the shaft of a ratchet driver. Driver shafts come in several sizes (much like drill chucks), with ¼, ⅜ and ½ in. being the most common.

Most socket sets are sold along with a ratchet driver handle. The ratchet can be set to work in either direction, for tightening or for loosening. Driver handles are also available with other mechanisms, configurations and extensions to suit almost any situation. Socket sets are made in standard or metric sizes.

Smaller ¼ in. drive sockets can also be snapped into an adapter shaft for power driving with a drill or driver. Small nuts can be turned with a nut driver (a tool that looks like a screwdriver, but has a socket end).

Pliers

Pliers are gripping tools with serrated jaws that open as the long handles are separated and close as they're squeezed together. The closed jaws form what's called the *nose.* Pliers are operated one-handed and are valuable for all sorts of fixing and repair work around the

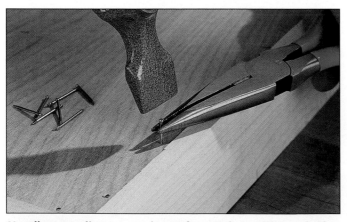

Needlenose pliers are used most frequently in wiring and other detailed work involving small workpieces. They can also be used to hold brads and small nails when starting.

house and shop. They're used for electrical wiring, for bending or straightening hardware and small metal pieces, for cutting thin wire or brads, and for many tightening, loosening, turning, pulling, twisting, holding, clamping and cutting tasks.

Pliers should not be used on nuts and bolts, except as a last resort if the corners have been so rounded off that a wrench won't work. A wrench is designed to mate with these fasteners, where the serrated jaws of pliers can mangle the head.

Pliers come in a great variety of specialized designs for specific work: Some have bent or angled jaws for reaching over and around obstructions; some have smooth, flat faces for working with delicate materials; some have rounded jaws for bending thin metal rods and looping fine wire in jewelry and small metalwork; some types have jaws that move parallel to one another; and some have flat, cushioned jaws for working with glass.

Needle-nose pliers. Long-nose and needle-nose pliers have long, narrow jaws that taper to a point. They are used for electrical and other work in tight, narrow

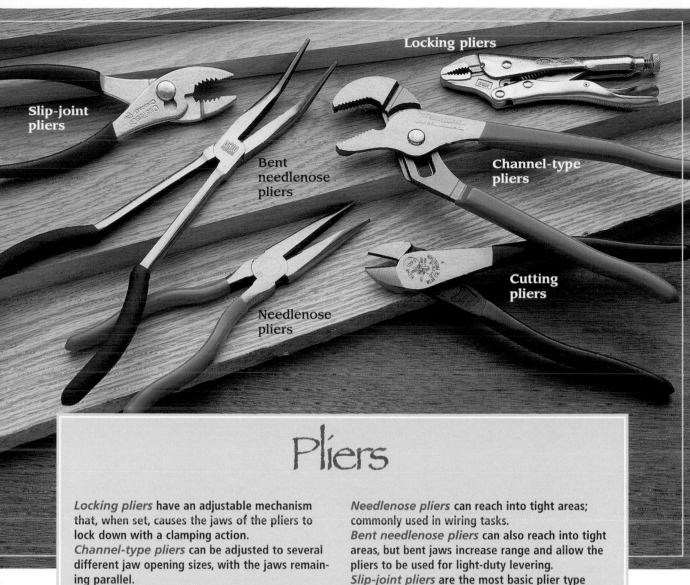

Pliers

Locking pliers have an adjustable mechanism that, when set, causes the jaws of the pliers to lock down with a clamping action.
Channel-type pliers can be adjusted to several different jaw opening sizes, with the jaws remaining parallel.
Cutting pliers is another term for wire cutters.

Needlenose pliers can reach into tight areas; commonly used in wiring tasks.
Bent needlenose pliers can also reach into tight areas, but bent jaws increase range and allow the pliers to be used for light-duty levering.
Slip-joint pliers are the most basic plier type used for general grasping tasks.

areas. They're also superior to tweezers for retrieving or for precisely placing tiny parts in hard-to-reach places. Needle-nose pliers are light-duty tools and should not be severely stressed—the jaws can bend.

Slip-joint pliers. This versatile tool has found its ways into more homes than any other type of pliers. It has an adjustable pivot point so the jaws have two positions to allow for greater opening capacity. The jaws are curved at the back so they can grip round objects such as rods and pipes. A 6 or 8 in. size will do most work, although a 4 in. model is handy for small jobs.

Channel-type pliers. There are several variations on these pliers, but they all have sliding adjustable jaws that allow a much greater opening capacity than slip-joint pliers. They can grip round pipes or objects of many shapes.

Locking pliers. Commonly known by the proprietary name *Vise-Grips,* these are a unique combination of pliers, wrench, and clamp. They grip like pliers, but a knurled screw in one handle can be adjusted so the handles, when pressed together fully, create a compound action that locks the jaws against the object with tremendous force. The grip is easily released by pressing outward against the locked handle. This locking action prevents slipping and will hold securely while leaving the operator's hands free. The basic locking pliers is available from 5 to 10 in. in length with curved or straight jaws. It can be used as a pipe wrench, pliers or a clamp to hold parts in process, and it is the best tool for removing a rounded-over nut. Locking pliers are also available in other designs, including those with extra-wide jaws; a long or bent nose; C-clamp-style jaws; or with wide, flat jaws for clamping sheet metal.

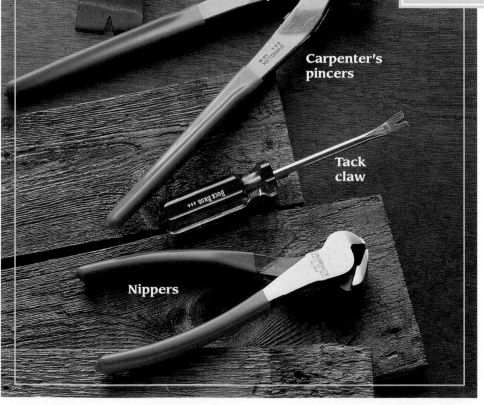

Flat bar

Cat's
paw

Carpenter's
pincers

Tack
claw

Nippers

"Unfastening" Tools

Cat's paw is designed exclusively for pulling nails. The back of the head can be struck with a mallet to drive the claw into wood and underneath an embedded nailhead.

Carpenter's pincers can pull or cut nails and even wire.

Tack claw is a small version of a cat's paw used to pull tacks and brads.

Nippers can cut nails or wires flush to the wood surface.

Flat bar is a multi-purpose tool that can be used for demolition or to pull nails.

There are times when you must *undo* construction or woodworking work. Even the best of us make mistakes that need to be redone. Remodeling a space to suit different needs is a common *undoing* undertaking. But whether you're replacing a section of siding or restoring an entire house, there are tools available to simplify the task. Since most wooden building construction is done using nails, most "unfastening" tools are designed for prying and nail pulling. Some tools can provide great leverage for heavy structural gutting, while others specialize in separating boards without damage so they can be salvaged and reused.

Cat's paw. A cat's paw, some-

The carpenter's pincer is a highly aggressive nail-pulling tool. Its thin-profile jaws can reach beneath a nailhead that's nearly flush to the surface. By rocking back on the rounded jaws, great pulling pressure can be applied to the nail. If all else fails, the hardened cutting edges can bite through even the thickest nails.

The flat bar is an indispensable demolition tool. With its slim profile it can be slipped between boards easily. The angled handle provides extra leverage for prying. Although its primary purpose is not to pull nails, the claw end and the nail pulling slot allow it to wrench out a nail or two as needed.

times called a *nail puller,* is a tool made purely for extracting nails—particularly stubborn nails with heads close to or below the surface of the wood. There are many designs, but each has some sort of straight bar with an angled, scooped-out claw on the end. The claw is shaped so it can be driven into the wood beneath the nailhead to pry up embedded nails or brads. Some cat's paws have another claw or a ripping and prying chisel on the straight end of the bar. The most common size is about 10 or 11 in. long, although shorter ones are also available for use with smaller nails. A *tack claw* is a light-duty variation of the cat's paw that looks like a screwdriver with a claw instead of a driver tip. It's a handy tool for pulling tiny wire brads, tacks and nails.

Flat bar. Also called a *pry bar* or *Wonderbar,* this tool is made of flat steel with nail slots at both ends for nail pulling. But what the flat bar truly excels at is prying apart nailed elements. The beveled ends are set at dissimilar angles to provide leverage in different ways. These ends can be slipped (or driven) in between parts (for example, siding or baseboard against a wall). If you work carefully, all the pieces can usually be removed with little damage. This is particularly desirable when doing renovation work on old houses with valuable millwork and detailing.

Wrecking bar. The wrecking bar, or *ripping bar,* is a hexagonal steel rod with a flattened, angled chisel on one end and a hook that terminates in a claw on the other end. A *crowbar* has only the wedge-shaped end

for levering and prying, with no hook. Wrecking bars are brawny tools and are available up to several feet long for extremely heavy work. Either end can be driven between wooden parts, and the long, straight bar then delivers enormous leverage to pry them apart. The claw will pull large nails much more easily than a claw hammer can. A large wrecking bar or crowbar also works as a lever to move heavy objects like machinery in the shop or large stones in the garden.

Pincers & nippers. Pincers and nippers are end-gripping pliers that are very similar visually but have slightly different purposes. *Carpenter's pincers* are used for gripping and pulling nails, and are ideal in tight spaces where there's no room for a claw hammer. The outer faces are flat, so they won't dent the wood as easily as a rounded cat's paw. A 7- or 8-in. tool is a good average size. To use pincers hold them upright, perpendicular to the work, and grab the nail shank right at the surface. Withdraw the nail by pushing the tool down to the side, levering against the wood. For a long nail, you can get a second bite anywhere along the nail's shank or place a block beneath the jaw. When using pincers on delicate or show-quality work, protect the surface with a shim or scrap of wood.

If you simply can't remove a nail or don't want to risk damaging a finished surface, you may need a pair of end-cutting nippers. On this tool, the mating jaws are hardened and sharpened for cutting off nails and wire almost flush with flat surfaces.

Clamps
& Vises

Clamps and vises are easy hand tools to overlook, but what they lack in glamour they more than make up for in sheer utility. In fact, they are the tools that hold every workshop together.

Because clamps are made in so many styles and sizes, each with its own particular purpose, it's fair to say that a quick examination of a handyman's clamp collection is the quickest way to discover what kind of work he likes to do. If he has a wall full of 6- and 8-ft.-long pipe clamps, his interests probably run toward cabinetmaking. If C-clamps are the most populous type of clamp you see, it's a pretty good bet that he has a penchant for metalworking. Miter and frame clamps suggest he enjoys picture framing. Miniature clamps are the hallmark of a model-maker. And if quick-action clamps dominate, he's probably a devotee of frame carpentry or even landscape construction.

In the same way, the presence of vises can tell you a lot about their owner: whether the main work-bench is fitted with a bench vise or a woodworking vise is the first clue to look for.

While it may be interesting to try to take a furtive peek into other people's interests, the best reason to get to know more about clamps and vises is to evaluate your own needs and your own shop. Does your collection match your interests?

Clamps

Like an extra set of strong hands, clamps are handy devices for innumerable tasks in practically any workshop project. But particularly in woodworking, clamping plays an essential role. After all the surfaces have been cut, squared, prepared and shaped; after all the joints are cut and fit; comes the moment of truth: assembly. Clamps make it possible to "dry-fit" an assembly together before you apply a single drop of glue to see how well things fit together. Once you are satisfied with the fit, clamps hold parts in place while you fasten them with nails, screws or glue.

In addition to assembly tasks, clamps have other woodworking uses. They can be used as temporary fence setups on drill presses, table saws and other shop machinery. Clamps can hold a variety of jigs, templates and fixtures onto workpieces and workbenches for layout and machining. Toggle clamps even become permanent working parts on some jigs, so the same jig can handle workpieces of different sizes.

Some clamps, such as the quick-action variety and pipe clamps, are so versatile that most woodworkers use them all the time. Other clamp types, like the four-corner picture frame clamp or the three-way C-clamp, are specialized for more particular uses, but they are indispensable when the need arises.

Clamping glue joints. Clamps have the gripping strength of Hercules, but don't use this as an excuse for building sloppy joints. Ill-fitting joints will always be just that; clamps can't perfect their fit without crushing the parts together. At worst, your workpieces will bow or twist and mar, and the clamps can bend or pop off. Too much clamping pressure can even force all the

Tips for successful clamping

• Clean wet glue off clamps right away, using a damp rag. Alternately, chip off dried glue with a paint scraper as soon as it dries. Few experiences are more frustrating than being in the middle of a tense, critical glue-up and reaching for a glue-encrusted clamp that won't slide.

• Wipe screw threads on clamps clean from time to time. Apply a bit of light oil to the threads as needed to prevent rust and keep the mechanisms turning smoothly.

• Whenever iron or steel clamps are used near glue squeeze-out (as, for example, when spanning edge-glued boards with bar clamps), keep the metal bars away from the glue or cover them with strips of wood or waxed paper. Otherwise, the bars can get stuck to the workpiece, or the glue can even react with the metal and stain the wood.

• Protect workpiece surfaces from clamp jaws by keeping plenty of clamp pads close by during glue-ups. Scrap ¼-in. plywood or hardboard work well.

Wood cauls

Alternate clamping pressure. **When edge-gluing boards for panels, alternate your clamps above and below the workpiece to distribute clamping pressure evenly along all the joints. It's a good idea to clamp wood cauls across the joints as well when you are not reinforcing the panel with wood biscuits. Cauls keep the boards aligned.**

Glue up in stages. **When assembling cabinetry and furniture, plan out the procedure step-by-step before you start. For complex glue-ups involving a number of parts, break the assembly into stages. Glue parts into subassemblies and allow them to dry. Then, glue the subassemblies together. Doing so reduces the number of wet glue joints to contend with.**

glue out of a joint, leaving it weak. Clamping a too-tight mortise-and-tenon joint will probably result in it jamming partway closed, with the glue seizing up so you can neither get it together nor apart. Or equally disheartening, the tenon breaks off. On the other hand, you can clamp a too-loose joint till it looks like the mating surfaces have changed places, but it's still a loose joint and will eventually open up.

Dry-fit a joint at least partway before gluing up. It should slide together snugly but not bind. Once the glue hits, the wood will expand a bit, and you need to account for the small amount of space the glue will take up in the joint. When clamping wood, tighten just enough to bring the mating surfaces into snug contact. Applying greater force is unnecessary, especially if you've taken the time and care to refine joints and mating surfaces so they fit tightly when you dry-fit the parts.

On long glue joints, clamp first in the center of the workpiece, then add clamps outward to the ends, tightening all the clamps evenly but not to final tension. This way, you'll avoid trapping the glue or allowing excess glue to migrate out of the joint. A couple of minutes is sufficient for this migration process to occur and for the wood to absorb some of the glue. Then, adjust the clamps to final tightness.

Building a clamp collection. A woodworking truism claims that you can never have enough clamps. Like most truisms it's valid—to a point. Choose clamps appropriate for the work you do. If you build on a small scale you may only need quick-action or C-clamps. Most woodworkers end up with a variety of clamp styles on hand, adding to the collection as projects dictate. Spend some time before you begin a glue-up to determine the number of clamps you'll need. A long cabinet assembly or edge-banding requires a pipe clamp about every 8 in., so one large project can turn

Protect your clamps and keep them accessible by devising a simple wall-mounted storage rack. A few lengths of scrap lumber and some ingenuity are all it takes to bring order to a jumble of clamps. Use notches to hold heavier bar and pipe clamps. Smaller clamps can simply be tightened onto your rack or hung from a loop of cord.

"plenty" of clamps into "not enough." Better to overestimate and return a few unused clamps than to end up midway through a glue-up and run short. Start off with a basic array and add to your clamp collection as needed.

Clamp storage. A good collection of clamps can add up to quite an investment, and a pile tossed on the floor or in a drawer is a poor way to store such valuable shop tools. You also want to keep your clamps accessible when you need them.

The best way to store clamps is to build a rack. A thick, narrow shelf with slots makes the perfect support for pipe and bar clamps, but these heavier clamps can also be hung from a scrap 2 × 2 screwed firmly to the wall. Quick-action clamps need something a little deeper: try shimming the 2 × 2 away from the wall with blocks to

allow a space for the jaws. C- and spring clamps are small enough to clamp or hang nearly anywhere—from an overhanging pipe, window sill or even a loop of rope attached to your larger clamp rack.

Since clamp supports can take up a lot of wall space, free-standing clamp racks with clamps hanging on both sides are also a great space-saving idea. Place the rack in a central location in the shop, or mount the rack on casters so you can roll it close to wherever you are working.

Headpiece

Slip clutch

Movable jaw

Handscrew

Tailpiece

Pipe Clamps

A woodworker's favorite, pipe clamps are the versatile, economical choice for large glue-ups. Best of all, pipe clamps can be sized to any length by simply installing a longer piece of pipe.

Pipe clamps are a mainstay for assembling edge-glued panels, frames and carcases for all sorts of furniture, doors and windows and cabinetry. A pipe clamp works like a small, elongated vise. It consists of a length of black or galvanized metal pipe with a fixed headpiece threaded onto one end and an adjustable tailpiece that slides along the pipe on the other end. A movable jaw in the headpiece adjusts in or out by way of a handscrew bored through the end cap on the headpiece. The tailpiece is outfitted with a "slip clutch" made of several metal plates that wedge against the pipe and fix the tailpiece in position. To reposition the tailpiece, simply squeeze the clutch against the back of the tailpiece jaw, and they will release their grip.

Pipe clamps are sold without the pipe included, so you can make up clamps in any length you need. Pipe is commonly sold in hardware stores and home centers in convenient lengths with pre-threaded ends. Head and tailpiece fixtures are available for ½- or ¾-in.-dia. pipe. Most woodworkers prefer to use ¾-in.-dia. pipe for their clamps, because it is sturdier and less likely to distort under pressure. However, ¾-in. pipe is heavier to handle than ½-in. pipe and creates clamps that are heavier overall than most other clamp styles. Because of their weight, pipe clamps can make smaller assemblies cumbersome and a bit unwieldy, especially if a long pipe clamp is used for a short application. As a rule of thumb, reserve pipe clamps for larger glue-ups, and use lighter-weight bar or quick-action clamps for smaller assemblies.

Applying pipe clamps. To use a pipe clamp, back the headpiece screw out nearly all the way so the jaw on the headpiece has plenty of "travel" before the screw is fully extended. This way you won't find yourself still needing a few more screw turns in the middle of installing the clamp. Set your workpiece between the clamp jaws and slide the tailpiece up against one end. Then, crank the headpiece jaw until it contacts the workpiece and slowly apply more pressure. Do not overdo it. The tension you feel on the handscrew is far less than the amount of force you are applying against the workpiece. One additional screw turn, or less, should provide all the clamping force you need.

Whenever possible, align workpieces in the clamp so the screw's line of trajectory runs through the center of the glue joint rather than outside of it (See *Illustration, below*). Otherwise, the clamping pressure will be uneven, which tends to "bow" the work away from the clamp. It can even cause the workpiece to pop out of the clamp.

Also, keep pipe clamps that are performing the same clamping function parallel to one another and square to the ends of the workpiece when arranging a glue up. This is especially important when gluing up panels or squaring a carcase. If clamps are skewed across a workpiece, they can cause the glue-up to distort so that it is no longer square or flat. You can also minimize distortion by alternating clamps above and below the workpiece (See page 136).

(See page 136).

Pipe clamp accessories

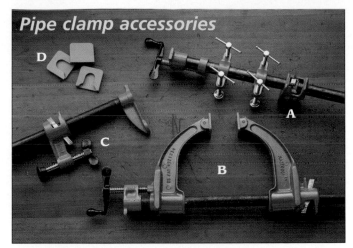

Accessory head and tailpieces can expand the capability of pipe clamps. *"Veneering" fixtures (A)* outfitted with thumbscrews slide along the pipe and apply downward pressure anywhere along the face of a panel, which is useful for pressing bubbled veneer flat or installing inlays. *Jaw extenders (B)* convert a pipe clamp into an 8- to 10-in. "deep reach" clamp, for clamping inset sections of a workpiece. You can even purchase head and tailpieces that act as *"spreaders" (C)* for exerting outward, rather than inward, pressure on a workpiece. Some manufacturers sell *rubber clamp jaw pads (D)* that slip over the jaw faces to keep them from marring wood. Or you can make your own from scrap.

Bar clamps

Bar clamps are essentially the same tools as pipe clamps, with a thin metal bar substituted for the pipe. Bar clamps generally are more expensive than pipe clamps, and the head and tailpieces cannot be removed from the bar. Light-duty bar clamps often have aluminum bars, but bars on better-quality clamps generally are made of high-carbon steel. I-beam style bars are the stiffest. Like their pipe clamp cousins, bar clamp headpieces have a sturdy steel handscrew and a movable jaw. Tailpieces lock into position on the bar either with a slip clutch or by way of a removable pin that fits into holes drilled along the length of the bar. Bar clamps range in length from 2 to 8 ft. Typical jaw depth from tip to bar is 2 in.

Clamping pressure

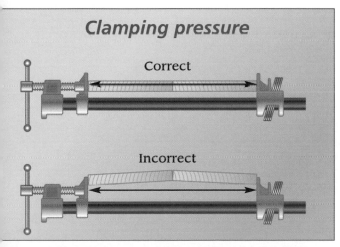

Correct

Incorrect

When possible, position your workpieces between the clamp jaws so that the center of the glue joint lines up with the handscrew in the headpiece. When workpieces, especially edge-glued panels, do not line up with the handscrew, the jaws can force the workpiece to bow away from the clamp.

Handclamps

A. Three-way edging C-clamp
B. Square-jawed deep-throat C-clamp
C. "Miter-style" spring clamp with pivoting jaws
D. Handscrew
E. Elongated C-clamp
F. Standard spring clamp with rubber jaw protectors

Handscrews

A woodworkers' favorite for generations, the hand-screw is much more than a sentimental relic; it's a powerful clamp with many features not found on its metal cousins. Outfitted with wide wooden jaws (some-times called "chops"), the handscrew can provide even, parallel pressure over a broad area. The jaws can also be skewed inward or outward to fit irregular work and odd shapes, and they have a relatively deep reach. Plus, the hard maple or beech jaws will not mar wood sur-faces, so handscrews do not require clamp pads and

are great for repairs on finished furniture. Handscrews are also a good choice for clamping plastic and metal. They are commonly used for face-gluing boards, press-ing blistered veneer flat and can serve as battens to align edge-glued boards. Handscrews are also good clamps for holding stops and jigs on machines near spinning blades where you wouldn't want to use a metal clamp.

Vintage handscrews were made completely of wood, including the threaded *hornbeam* screws (now called

Handscrew technique

Open or close a handscrew by gripping both handles and spinning the clamp hand over hand, like pedaling a bicycle. Rotating the jaws counterclockwise closes the clamp; rotate clockwise to open the jaws.

Align edge-glued panels by clamping a handscrew to each end of the panel so they cross all the glue joints like battens. Tighten by twisting the handles in opposite directions. Protect the clamp from glue squeeze-out by lining the edges with wax paper.

spindles). Wooden spindles were replaced by steel many years ago. Otherwise, handscrew design has remained virtually unchanged for more than a century.

Handscrews are sized according to jaw length. As jaw length increases, so does the maximum opening capacity of the clamp. Jaw lengths range from 4 in. up to 24 in., and the usable throat depth is roughly half the total jaw length.

Handscrew technique. Once you get the knack, handscrews are quick and easy to operate. Grasp the two handles and rotate them hand-over-hand in "bicycle-pedal" style to spin the jaws around the spindles. Rotate the jaws counterclockwise to close the clamp jaws and clockwise to open them. Open the handscrew so the jaws are slightly wider than the object being clamped, keeping the jaws parallel (rotating one spindle more than the other will skew the jaws). Place the workpiece between the jaws and twist the handles in opposite directions to tighten.

Spring clamps

A spring clamp works on the same coiled-spring principle as a clothespin, exerting focused pressure at the clamp tips without needing to tighten a screw. To open the clamp, simply squeeze the handles together.

Spring clamps are sized by the amount the jaw opens, and sizes range from 1 to 4 in. The 2-in. size is particularly handy and comfortable to open with one hand. The gauge and power of the spring increases with the size of the clamp—larger clamps require two hands to operate. Most spring clamps are made of

steel, though some are now being made of a strong plastic resin. Most manufacturers outfit the handles and jaw tips with soft rubber or plastic sleeves to keep them from slipping or marring workpiece surfaces.

Spring clamps are the clamps to reach for when you need quick, easy on-and-off holding power, as when

Notched handscrew

Get a grip on round objects by cutting opposing, triangular-shaped notches into the jaw faces of a wood handscrew. Be sure to apply enough clamping pressure in situations where a round workpiece is held in place for drilling to keep it from spinning in the clamp.

'Miter-style' spring clamps take the place of other shop-built jigs for holding miter joints tight during assembly. The jaw ends pivot and are outfitted with tiny teeth that hold workpieces securely.

C-clamps

No toolbox, "catch-all" drawer or workshop should be without a few trusty C-clamps, (also called *carriage clamps*). The commonness of these metal-bodied clamps is a testament to their range of usefulness as clamps and hold-downs in applications ranging from modelbuilding and light-duty household repairs to heavy-duty styles used for industrial metalworking.

C-clamps find their way into woodworking for attaching jigs, fixtures, and stops to woodworking machinery. C-clamps provide much greater clamping power than spring clamps, which makes them a better choice for gripping templates that must not shift during drilling, routing or sawing. Larger C-clamps are handy for face-gluing boards into blanks that become furniture legs or spindles.

The name "C-clamp" comes from the one-piece "C" shape of the jaw. Clamp bodies are made of aluminum or various grades of iron and steel, depending largely on the quality and size of the clamp. Frame styles range from round to elongated or square. Like woodscrews, C-clamps are sized by throat depth, which varies from ½ in. to about 18 in.

The clamping mechanism on C-clamps is a threaded screw that runs through one end of the clamp jaw. Most C-clamps tighten by way of a sliding pin handle on the end of the screw, though smaller versions may have a flat thumbscrew instead or simply a knurled end on the screw. A swiveling metal button on the other end of the screw presses the workpiece inside the jaw against a flat anvil on the other end of the clamp body. Since all C-clamps are made of metal, one drawback to woodworking with C-clamps is that these clamps will mar workpiece surfaces unless the button and anvil are

using temporary fence setups or quick hold-down devices. The jaw depth is relatively shallow, and spring clamps apply moderate pressure at best. Since spring clamps are convenient and relatively inexpensive compared to other clamp styles, keep at least a half dozen in various sizes on hand. You'll almost always need more than one for any clamping situation.

A unique innovation in spring clamps are those outfitted with pivoting jaws and tiny teeth that grab into wood and plastic. This "miter-style" spring clamp is used for holding angled and odd-shaped pieces, and is great for clamping the corners of mitered frames, boxes or even cabinets. It provides clamping pressure at the proper angle for miters—right across the center of the joint and perpendicular to the mating surfaces.

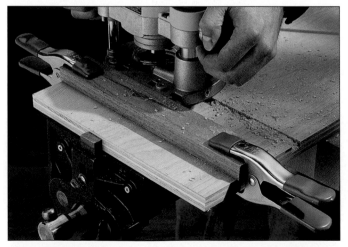

Spring clamps serve as quick set-up tools for holding temporary guide fences. When using a fence for a power tool, like this router, be sure to select spring clamps large enough to hold the fence securely so it doesn't shift during the machining process. Keep the clamps clear of spinning bits and blades.

Face-gluing blanks. Larger C-clamps installed side-by-side provide plenty of clamping pressure for face-gluing (laminating) strips of wood. Protect the outer surfaces of the blank from marring by installing scrap clamp pads between the workpieces and the clamp jaws.

Two-jawed clamps have taken innumerable shapes and sizes over the years to suit different specialized trades—not just carpentry, woodworking or metalsmithing. For example, this massive, two-jawed bookbinder's clamp was used in the days before mass-production publishing to press and flatten stacks of pages together before trimming, gluing and stitching. The clamp, made entirely of wood, has two large, 2-in.-wide, 24-in.-long wooden jaws. Two 1-in.-dia. threaded rods are fixed in place to the outer jaw and pass through holes in the other movable jaw. Two large 8-in.-long "nuts" provide clamping pressure by tightening against the movable jaw. Notice the curved profiles on the nuts, added no doubt to make tightening easier to do by hand.

covered with clamp pads.

The *three-way edging clamp* is a C-clamp fitted with a screw on each end of the clamp body, and a third screw centered midway between and perpendicular to the other two screws. This hybrid clamp is used for repairing edging of all types on wood panels, molding and plastic laminate. On finished furniture and antiques, where it isn't feasible to lay a long clamp across an entire surface, a three-way clamp can attach to an edge only and provide a third lateral screw for pressing a chip or separated veneer back into place. The most common size has a 2½-in. jaw opening and a 2½-in. throat depth.

Quick-action Clamps

A. Handscrew-style, slip-clutch head, quick-action clamp with cast-iron jaws
B. Handscrew-style, friction-fit head, quick-action clamp with cast-iron jaws
C. Pistol-grip quick-action clamp with trigger release mechanism and high-impact plastic jaws. Jaw faces outfitted with rubber pads.
D. Pistol-grip, quick-action "spreader" style clamp with plastic jaws and clamp pads
E. Modified handscrew quick-action clamp applies even pressure along full clamp face. Steel jaws are clad with high-impact plastic.

Quick-action clamps, which incorporate the tightening mechanism of a C-clamp and the spine of a bar clamp, have revolutionized smaller clamping tasks. A C-clamp can be frustratingly slow when you have to turn the screw a long way to fit around a workpiece. Quick-action clamps resolve this setup hassle by allowing the head (the jaw with the screw or pistol-grip) to slide quickly to any position along the bar. This way, you can exert clamping pressure as soon as the head contacts the workpiece. The tailpiece is fixed at the end of the bar. This configuration is the reverse of pipe and bar clamps, which have a sliding tailpiece and a fixed head.

Manufacturers have designed a number of mechanisms to lock the sliding head into position against the bar. Some quick-action clamps use a slip-clutch that can be finger-operated like a pipe clamp. Others employ tiny gear-like teeth on both the headpiece and the bar that engage each other when you apply screw pressure. Still others simply use the angled force of the jaw against both edges of the bar to hold the head fast. Regardless of the mechanism, all clamp heads should hold tightly without slipping.

Good quality quick-action bar clamps feature high-carbon steel bars and cast-iron jaws. Screws are adjusted by means of a hardwood handle, wing nut or C-clamp-style sliding pin handle. A recent variation on the quick-action clamp is the pistol grip style. To tighten these clamps, simply slide the head into position and squeeze the handle repeatedly. To loosen the clamp, pull the trigger located just in front of the grip. Spreader-style pistol grip models are also available.

Well-made, sturdy quick-action clamps are true professional-quality woodworking tools and should give you years of dependable service. Don't be tempted by lighter-duty versions with ⅛-in.-thick bars that are a few dollars cheaper to buy. Select clamps with ³⁄₁₆- or ¼-in.-thick bars, which are far less likely to deflect under pressure.

Quick-action clamps are classified by jaw depth (also called "reach"), measured from the bar to the center of the clamp face. Jaw depth ranges from 2 to 12 in. Quick-action clamps also come in many lengths, from a 4-in. opening capacity between the jaws, up to 5 ft. Generally the heft of the bar, head and tailpiece castings and the screw diameter increase based on jaw depth, not on clamp length.

What to buy. The most useful quick-action clamps for furnituremaking or carpentry are 12-in.-long clamps with 2½- and 4-in. jaw depths. Next, add several 2½-in. clamps in the 18- or 24-in. lengths. These are a great alternative to heavy pipe or bar clamps for gluing up boxes, drawers, and smaller edge-glued panels. For furniture or cabinetry, 4-in. jaw depth quick-actions in 3- or 4-ft. lengths are helpful for those times when you need a little deeper reach than pipe or bar clamp jaws can handle. Quick actions are also available in 7-, 9- and 12-in. jaw sizes for deeply inset clamping tasks.

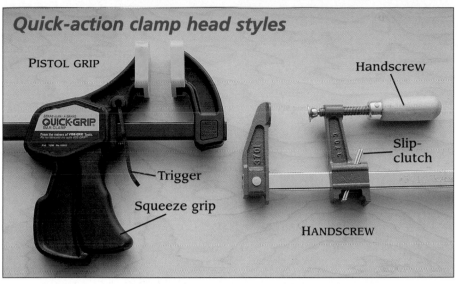

Quick-action clamp head styles

PISTOL GRIP

Handscrew

Trigger

Slip-clutch

Squeeze grip

HANDSCREW

Squeeze or twist. Head styles vary among manufacturers, but all quick-action clamps have heads that slide along the bar for quick setup. To provide final clamping pressure, squeeze the handle repeatedly on pistol grip styles or twist the *handscrew.* To loosen the clamp, squeeze the trigger or the slip-clutch.

Quick-action spreaders. Some quick-action clamp jaws apply outward force as you tighten the head. Called *spreader clamps,* they are particularly helpful for restoration and refinishing work, where parts must be disassembled by breaking glue joints. Spreaders apply *gradual,* rather than *impact,* force, which is far less damaging to parts and finishes.

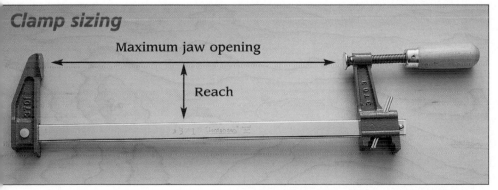

Clamp sizing

Maximum jaw opening

Reach

Quick-action clamps are classified by jaw depth (also called "reach"), measured from the bar to the center of the clamp face. Jaw depth ranges from 2 to 12 in. Clamp length is measured in terms of the maximum jaw opening, from 4 in. to 5 ft.

Specialty Clamps

A. Frame clamps hold four-cornered glue-ups (like picture frames) steady so assembly can occur in one clamping step.

B. Miter clamps secure a single miter or butt joint in place by way of two adjustable handscrews outfitted in a right-angle jig.

C. Band clamps use a ratcheting mechanism and a nylon or canvas belt to apply even clamping pressure around round or multisided glue-ups.

D. Toggle clamps come in assorted configurations and sizes, but all apply clamping pressure by means of a lever-activated adjustable shaft.

Miter clamps

Miter clamps, also called *corner clamps,* hold two workpieces up to 3 in. wide at a 90° angle to form a miter or butt joint. Unlike the "miter-style" spring clamp (See page 142) however, the miter clamp does not pull the joint together. It simply holds both pieces firmly with the corner exposed so you can nail or screw the joint together. This type of clamp is often used for building picture frames in conjunction with countersunk brads or corrugated fasteners. Some clamp models are adjustable for angles from 0° to 180°.

Frame clamps

Miter clamps hold one corner together at a time. *Frame clamps,* on the other hand, exert equal pressure on all four corners of a frame or box at the same time. This design keeps the joints closed and the whole assembly square. A sysem of threaded metal rods fits through small holding fixtures at each corner of the frame. To adjust the fit of the parts, simply turn the knurled nuts that hold each clamp corner together.

Band clamps

Band clamps, also known as *web* or *strap* clamps, work on a similar principle to a car's seat belt: A flexible band wraps around multi-sided or curved glue-up assemblies, providing even but diffused clamping pressure all around the object. For some curved work, coopering and chair assemblies, band clamps are the only clamp style that will work.

Band clamps have either 1-in.-wide nylon webbing or a 2-in. heavy-duty canvas or nylon band. Bands are tightened with a ratchet- or screw-operated mechanism that locks securely but is easily released for removing or repositioning the clamp. Some clamps come with corner blocks for clamping rectangular work, which also protects the strap from abrading against sharp workpiece corners.

Make sure you clean any glue from the band. A dried lump of glue will make a deep dent in wood with 1500 lbs. of pressure behind it!

In addition to their woodworking applications, band clamps are useful for strapping up bundles or crates. And for securing loads on a hand truck, in a wheelbarrow, or in a pickup truck bed, they can't be beat. Best of all, there are no knots to tie or untie.

How to tighten & release a band clamp

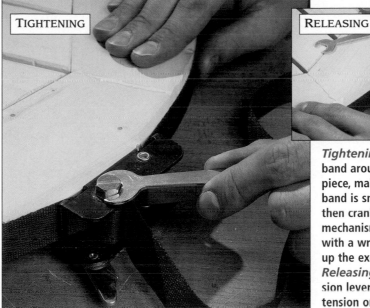

TIGHTENING

RELEASING

Tightening: wrap the band around a workpiece, making sure the band is smooth and flat, then crank the ratcheting mechanism (by hand or with a wrench) to draw up the excess band. *Releasing:* Flip the tension lever back to release tension on the band.

Toggle clamps

Toggles are fast-action lever-style clamps used for all sorts of hold-down situations, especially shop jigs. Most screw in place. Clamp pressure is adjusted by threading the clamp head and rubber bumper in or out before locking the lever.

Frame clamps allow you to glue up an entire four-corner frame assembly at one time. Adjust the glue-up for square by tightening or loosening the knurled nuts that hold the clamp assembly together. Since the clamp rods are threaded along their full length, the clamp can be resized to fit a multitude of frames.

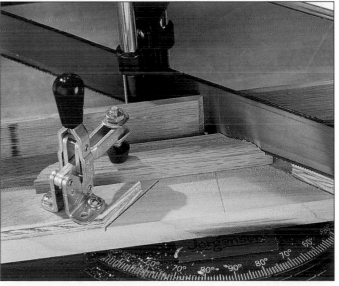

Toggle clamps can be screwed into any just about any position. They apply clamping force in one direction by way of a simple locking lever. This toggle clamp is serving as a hold-down for cutting short workpieces on a miter saw.

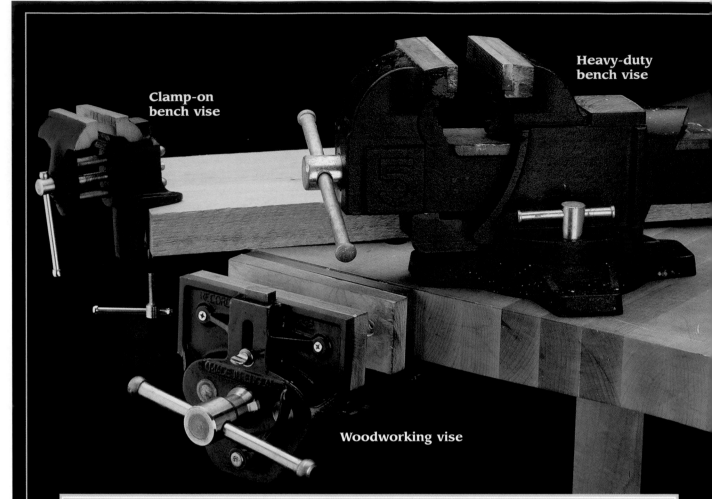

Clamp-on
bench vise

Heavy-duty
bench vise

Woodworking vise

Vises

A workbench isn't complete without adding some form of vise to hold and steady your workpieces. Depending upon the nature of your tasks, you have two basic styles from which to pick:

Woodworking vises feature broad jaws that are made to be lined with wood. Their large jaw proportions can handle all sizes and shapes of wooden parts,

including longer or wider boards. No serious woodworker should be without one.

Bench vises migrated long ago from metal shops into general-purpose home improvement. Outfitted with narrower jaw faces, swivelling bases and even anvils, bench vises adequately clamp everything from pipe to plywood.

Woodworking vises

Woodworking vises are meant to be permanently mounted into or against the edge of a workbench, where they hold workpieces in a convenient position while you work. The jaws have large, flat metal faces with a couple of holes in each for attaching protective wooden pads that keep the jaws from marring wood parts. (Make sure you countersink the screw heads in the pads so the screws won't gouge your work.)

Installing a vise. For typical woodworking vise installations, you'll need to notch out a recess in the edge of your benchtop to inset the fixed jaw of the vise. Mount the vise near a corner or on the end of your bench.

Position the vise so the top edges of the jaws are flush with the benchtop. If the vise bolts beneath the bench rather than into the side, you may need to add shims to lower the jaws to the right height. You'll need to modify the installation process based on the thickness of your benchtop and overall configuration of your workbench.

Buying tips. Buy the best cast-iron woodworking vise you can afford and you'll likely never need to replace it. For general-purpose woodworking, look for a vise with 7-in.-long jaws and a maximum open capacity of 8 in. Many vises have a pop-up steel dog in the top edge of the movable jaw to be used with bench dogs fitted into holes in the bench for clamping oversized work. Another time-saving feature worth having is a quick-release mechanism on the movable jaw that allows you to slide the jaw in or out without turning the handscrew.

Bench vises

Cast-iron or steel bench vises (also called *machinist's vises*) are common fixtures on most workbenches. Bench vises are really designed for rough metalwork, where marring isn't a big concern. Concave recesses beneath the jaw faces on some vises are made to hold pipe for drilling, cutting and threading. In a pinch, a bench vise can double as a woodworker's vise, but the narrower jaw faces don't provide the same broad support for clamping longer or wider workpieces, nor are the jaw faces drilled for installing wooden clamp pads. You'll need to line the jaws with scraps of wood, cardboard, leather or plastic to keep them from marring softer workpieces made of wood, non-ferrous metal or plastic. Clamp pads are especially important for jaw faces cast with gripping teeth.

Bench vises are available in different sizes and forms, but a 4-in. jaw opening is adequate for most home-improvement and metalworking tasks. A light-duty clamp-on style bench vise is handy to keep in your toolbox for quick setups on a sawhorse or collapsible

Anatomy of a bench vise

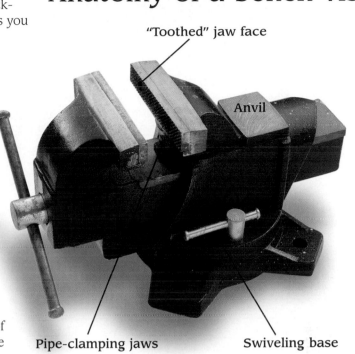

"Toothed" jaw face

Anvil

Pipe-clamping jaws

Swiveling base

workbench at the job site. Heavier bench vises bolt onto the benchtop with lag screws or carriage bolts and generally feature a swiveling base and a small anvil for forming metal. As with woodworking vises, position bench vises near a corner or on the end of your bench.

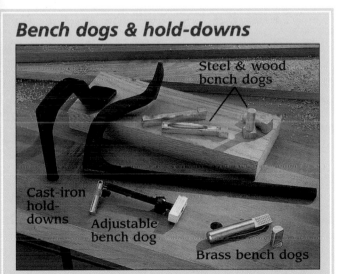

Bench dogs & hold-downs

Steel & wood bench dogs

Cast-iron hold-downs

Adjustable bench dog

Brass bench dogs

Most woodworkers outfit their benchtops with a row of holes intended to house bench dogs and hold-downs. These devices make it possible to secure workpieces flat to the bench without additional clamps. Hold-downs typically friction-fit into bench dog holes and are tapped into place and against a workpiece with a mallet. Bench dogs are used in conjunction with a pop-up dog on the vise or with another clamp to secure longer workpieces.

Wood shims

Installing a vise. **Woodworking vises bolt either to the edge or beneath a benchtop. You'll almost always have to modify the installation, unless you build your bench specifically to house a particular vise. Add shims between the vise and the bench to position the tops of the jaws even with the benchtop.**

Sharpening

A. Slipstones
B. Hard black Arkansas stone
C. 800/4000-grit combination Japanese waterstone
D. Medium-grit diamond stone
E. Soft Arkansas stone
F. Nagura natural honing stone (for waterstones)
G. Honing block
H. Coarse/fine synthetic oilstone

Sharpening hand tools

Chisels, plane irons, gouges, knives, cabinet scrapers and saws need to be sharp and well-tuned in order to perform the tasks you demand of them. If you're one of those woodworkers who cringes at the thought of sharpening blades—and there are many— put your mind at ease. Sharpening most hand tools is not complex; with practice and proper techniques, it's really quite easy to keep your blades in top working order.

Blade sharpness cannot be overemphasized when it comes to tool performance and safety. Bevel-edged blades on chisels, gouges and plane irons, as well as carving tools and knives, should be honed to near razor-sharpness and periodically touched-up on a sharpening stone or strop.

Rip and crosscut saw teeth need occasional sharpening, too. A few specialized but relatively inexpensive tools are available to make the task manageable. You can also have hand saws sharpened professionally at a reasonable cost by a saw sharpener in your area or by sending the tool back to the factory. Hire a professional to sharpen intricate or complex saw teeth, such as those on backsaws or Japanese cross-cut saws.

Chisels and plane irons

Sharpening a chisel is very much the same task as sharpening a plane iron; the only notable difference is in the bevel angle each blade type requires. The sharpening technique involves three steps: *grinding* (when necessary), *honing* and *stropping*.

Grinding must be done to correct an improper bevel angle or to restore a badly chipped cutting edge. The common method of grinding chisels and plane irons is with a motorized bench grinder outfitted with an 80- or 120-grit white aluminum oxide grinding wheel. The advantage to this type of grinding is primarily speed. However, "dry" grinding must be done with great care, as it is easy to overheat the steel of the blade. Once the edge turns a bluish color, its temper (or hardness) is lost and the edge will need to be reground to remove all of the burned steel.

To grind a blade on a bench grinder, start by grinding the cutting edge square to the sides of the blade, with the blade held perpendicular to the grinding wheel. Once the blade edge is square, adjust the grinder's tool rest to the proper bevel angle and grind the bevel. Angle the blade upward and into the direction of wheel rotation with the bevel facing the wheel. Advance the blade edge gently onto the wheel, then move the blade from side to side across the wheel in several light passes to create an even bevel across the width of the blade. Don't grind to a feathered edge, or you'll overheat the steel. Stop just shy, leaving a bit of the blunt edge, and finish off by sharpening the edge by hand on a flat stone.

It's also possible to grind with a sharpening stone instead of a grinder, following the same two-step grinding procedure. The process is slower but you don't run the risk of overheating and damaging the blade. You can use a Japanese waterstone or a natural or synthetic oilstone; a coarse diamond-coated stone cuts rapidly and can be used wet or dry.

Honing, also called whetting, is the process of sharpening the bevel to a keen edge using sharpening stones. Most stones must be lubricated, or else the pores in the stone will clog with fine steel particles, rendering them useless. Reapply oil or water as necessary while honing to keep the surface well saturated.

To hone an edge, start with a medium-grit stone. Steady the blade by holding it with both hands. Stroke the blade carefully back and forth along the length of the stone with the bevel facing down. Make long, steady strokes, taking care to keep the full bevel angle flat against the stone. Try to wear the stone evenly by using the whole surface, rather than concentrating on a narrow section in the middle. Otherwise you'll wear a trough in the stone that will need to be ground flat.

Hone the bevel until a tiny, thin flap of metal (called the *burr)* forms along the back edge of the blade.

A glossary of sharpening stones

Synthetic oilstones made of silicon carbide or aluminum oxide are available as general-purpose combination stones, with a coarse side and a finer side laminated together. Synthetic stones are too coarse for fine honing and are better suited for rough sharpening tasks (like sharpening an axe) or for grinding bevel angles and cutting edges.

Natural oilstones are intended for finer honing. *Washita* oilstones are the coarsest variety, followed by soft Arkansas, hard Arkansas, and hard black Arkansas. The latter is extremely hard and can produce a final polish. For routine honing, buy a soft and hard black Arkansas.

Japanese waterstones use water as a lubricating wash and are graded like sandpaper, with grit designations ranging from 80 (coarse) to 8000 (polishing). They are porous, particularly the coarser grits, and should be soaked in water for a half hour or so before use. Waterstones cut steel quickly and produce a fine polished edge without messy oil. However, they are softer than oilstones, so the surface needs to be periodically flattened.

Diamond stones are steel or plastic plates covered with a layer of black diamond particles imbedded in nickel. Diamond stones will sharpen all varieties of steel, including carbide, without a lubricant. They also provide a good grinding abrasive for flattening Japanese waterstones.

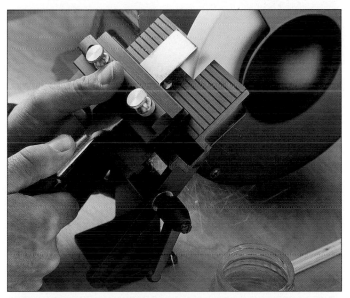

Grind chisels and plane irons to remove large nicks from the cutting edge. First, grind the edge square with the blade sides, then tilt the grinder's tool rest up to match the appropriate blade bevel and grind the bevel. Immerse the blade in water occasionally to keep it cool.

How to sharpen chisels & plane irons

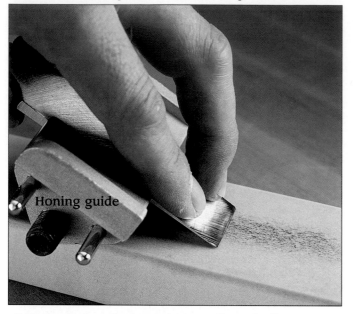

1 *Hone the bevel edge* against a medium-grit oil or water-stone to sharpen the cutting edge. Hold the bevel flat against the stone as you stroke it back and forth. A honing guide makes this task easier by holding the blade at the proper angle as you roll it along the stone.

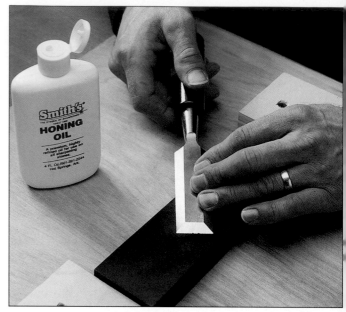

2 *Remove the burr* that develops from honing the blade bevel by stroking the back of the blade against a fine-grit sharpening stone. A hard black Arkansas stone, shown here, also polishes out scratches left by the machining process or by efforts made to flatten the blade back with coarser sharpening stones.

3 *Strop the blade bevel* by stroking it back and forth over a flat leather strop charged with honing compound. As when honing, be sure the full bevel contacts the strop. Stropping polishes the bevel and hones it to razor sharpness. You can also strop the back of the blade by holding it flat against the strop.

Remove the burr by turning the blade over and rubbing the back of the blade several times in a figure-8 pattern until the burr breaks free.

Switch to a fine-grit stone and repeat the honing process, polishing the bevel first then the blade back. Many woodworkers add an additional microbevel at this point. A microbevel is a tiny secondary bevel honed along the cutting edge at a steeper angle (usually about 5° higher) that adds a bit of edge durability. It also reduces the amount of overall honing required to replenish a sharp cutting edge. To create a microbevel, raise the blade slightly and give the bevel a few light strokes on your finest stone.

Stropping. For fine work like carving, hand chiseling and finish planing, where a super-sharp edge is needed, finish the sharpening process by *stropping*. A strop is a piece of leather charged with polishing compound containing fine abrasives. Honing compound is available in liquid, block or natural Nagura stone forms. Strops are made of leather or composition material. For stability, the material sometimes is glued to a block of wood about the size of a bench stone.

To strop a blade, apply an even coat of the honing compound to the leather. Stroke the blade over the strop, bevel side first and then on the cutting side of the blade. A slurry of metal particles will appear on the strop as you work. Continue stropping the blade until all fine scratches disappear on the blade face and a mirror-like finish develops.

How to sharpen a gouge

1 *Sharpen the bevel.* Hold the gouge perpendicular to the long axis of the sharpening stone, with the bevel flat against the stone. Starting at one corner of the curved bevel, stroke the gouge along the stone as you rotate it in your hands.

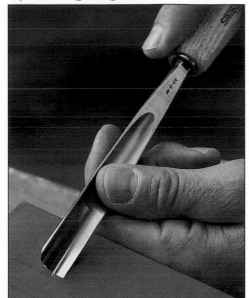

2 *Hone the blade edge.* By the end of the stroke, every part of the bevel should have made contact with the stone. Rock the blade back and forth along the bevel until a burr develops along the blade edge.

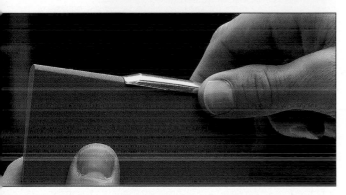

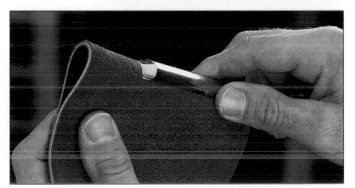

3 *Hone the concave blade back.* Use a slipstone to remove the burr along the blade edge. Stroke the blade over the stone, making sure the radius of the slipstone is smaller than the curvature of the gouge, to keep from damaging the cutting edge.

4 *Strop the blade back.* Polish the blade back using leather charged with honing compound. Flex the leather, rough side up, so it conforms to the shape of the blade. Use a flat leather strop and rocking strokes to polish the blade bevel.

Sharpening gouges

Sharpening gouges is a different process than sharpening straight-bladed tools. Refining the blade edge involves two steps: honing the outer blade bevel, then honing the inner curved edge to remove the burr.

When honing an *outcannel gouge,* hold the tool perpendicular to the long axis of the sharpening stone with the bevel facing the stone. Starting at one corner of the curved bevel, stroke the gouge along the stone as you rotate it in your hands, so that by the end of the stroke every part of the bevel has been rubbed across the stone. Rock the blade back and forth along the bevel, keeping the bevel in constant contact with the stone throughout the stroke. Stop each stroke as soon as you reach the opposite corner of the bevel to avoid rounding over the corner of the blade. Hone the bevel until you raise a burr along the cutting edge.

Next, hone the concave side of the gouge with a *slip stone*. A slipstone is a small honing stone shaped to match the inside curvature of the blade. Slipstones are available in a variety of shapes and also as "multiform" stones that combine a tapered round edge and a tapered angled edge for honing V-parting tools. Choose a slipstone that matches or has a slightly tighter radius than the gouge; never use one with a broader curve. If you are using a tapered slipstone, be careful not to use the portion that is wider than the blade or you'll spoil the cutting edge. Hone the inside of the blade until the burr wears away. Polish the blade bevel on a flat strop charged with honing compound. Rock the blade back and forth as you did when honing the bevel. Use a piece of leather, flexed so the rough side faces out, to strop the inside of the blade. Apply honing compound here as well. Once a gouge is sharpened, the edge can be renewed over and over by stropping.

Sharpening knives

Knife blades require sharpening of two beveled edges that come together to form the cutting edge of the blade. The process for sharpening each bevel is quite similar to sharpening blades with single bevels. You'll hone the sides of the blade flat, raise a burr along the cutting edge, remove the burr, and strop the cutting edge until it is razor sharp.

The sharpening angle of the the blade, formed by each bevel, is similar in function to a microbevel on a chisel or plane iron. Effectively, it reduces the overall amount of honing that needs to be done to refresh the cutting edge. Sharpening angles vary for different knives, from 8° to 10° for carving knives and 10° to 20° for general-purpose jack knives. The steeper the cutting angle, the more rigid and durable the edge.

Flatten the blade sides. To sharpen a knife blade, you may need to first flatten the sides of the blade to remove any nicks along the cutting edge. Lay the blade flat against a medium-grit sharpening stone and stroke back and forth along the stone lengthwise. Flip the blade and repeat on the other side. Grind the sides of the blade equally until the cutting edge disappears.

Sharpen and strop the cutting edge. Sharpen the cutting edge by raising the blade to the proper sharpening angle. For most knives, lay a quarter on a medium-grit sharpening stone to serve as a quick reference guide for setting the sharpening angle (about 10°). Stack two quarters for sharpening general-purpose jack knives to form a steeper 20° cutting edge. Hone the sharpening angle on one side of the blade (usually in 10 to 20 strokes), then flip the blade and repeat on the other side. Use a sweeping motion against the stone to sharpen cutting edges on blades with curved profiles. Watch for a burr to develop along the cutting edge. Switch to your finest stone or a leather strop to remove the burr. Polish the blade sides and cutting edge on a flat strop charged with honing compound.

Knife blade angles

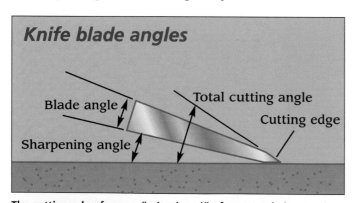

The cutting edge forms a "microbevel" of sorts on knives, so it needs to be sharpened by raising the blade to a steeper sharpening angle than the blade angle (10 to 20°). You'll need to hone each side of the blade at a consistent angle to form the twin-beveled cutting edge.

How to sharpen a knife

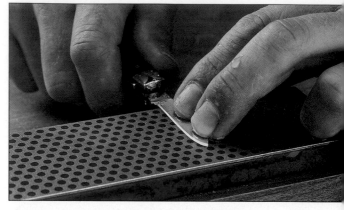

1 *Flatten the blade sides* by laying the blade against a medium-grit sharpening stone, like the diamond stone shown here, and stroking the blade back and forth. Since flattening the blade also reduces blade thickness, do this only when you need to remove nicks along the cutting edge. Flatten both sides of the blade until the cutting edge wears away.

2 *Sharpen the cutting edge* by raising the back of the blade 10° to 20° off of a fine-grit stone. Set the back edge of the blade against a quarter to serve as a reference for setting the sharpening angle. Lubricate water and oilstones first. Stroke the blade in a slicing motion on each side, 10 to 20 times.

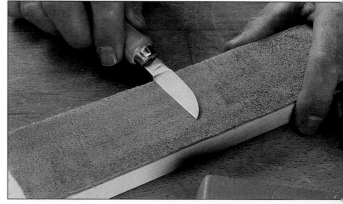

3 *Deburr and polish the blade* on a leather strop charged with honing compound. Polish both blade sides and the cutting edge. Stropping smooths away scratches left from flattening and hones the cutting edge to razor sharpness.

Tools for sharpening saws

Jointing jig

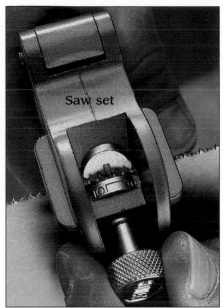

Saw set

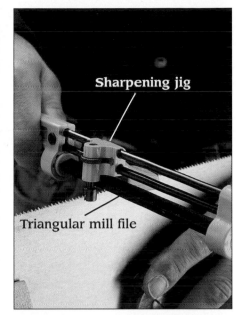

Sharpening jig

Triangular mill file

Saw jointing jig. File the points on all blade teeth to an even height using a flat mill file installed in a saw jointing jig. File in long, continuous strokes until the file just flattens the points of the teeth.

Saw set. Bend teeth to the proper angle on either side of the blade using a saw set. Calibrate the saw set to match the tpi of your saw. Position the saw set to bend only the top third of each tooth.

Sharpening jig. File the tooth points and cutting edges with a triangular mill file mounted in a sharpening jig. Set the tool to match the tooth angle for either rip or crosscut saws. Sharpen from toe to heel.

Sharpening rip and crosscut saws

Sharpening rip and crosscut hand saws involves three basic steps: jointing the teeth with a file so the tooth points are even in height; setting the teeth to the left and right of the blade body to establish the proper saw kerf width; and sharpening the tooth points and cutting edges.

Jointing teeth. As a saw dulls, the teeth can wear unevenly until the points of the teeth are no longer the same height. Use a bastard mill file installed in a *saw jointing jig* to flatten the points of the saw teeth until they are even along the length of the blade. The jig holds the file steady and perpendicular to the blade. Clamp the saw blade upside down in a vise with the heel of the blade facing you. Set the blade deep enough in the vise so it won't flex as you work on the teeth. Then, slide the jointing jig in long continuous strokes along the blade until the file just flattens the points of the teeth. Two to three strokes should be sufficient.

Setting teeth. Once the teeth are jointed, use a *saw set* to bend the teeth to the proper angle on either side of the blade body. Saw sets come with a numeric dial calibrated to match the tooth sets, ranging from 4 to 12 teeth per inch (tpi). Set the dial to match the *tpi* of your saw. Turning the dial rotates a graduated anvil inside the tool. When you position the saw set over a tooth and squeeze the tool handles, a small punch advances forward and pushes the saw tooth against the anvil.

To set the teeth, start with the first tooth facing away from you on the blade heel. Set each tooth that faces away in the same fashion until you reach the blade toe. Flip the blade around in the vise and set the second row of teeth that now face away from you. To avoid breaking off saw teeth, set only the top third of each tooth for either rip or crosscut saws.

Sharpen teeth. Finally, sharpen the tooth points and refine the tooth bevels with a *sharpening jig.* A saw sharpening jig is a sliding frame that fits over the saw teeth and holds a triangular mill file. The jig is outfitted with a saddle that rests on the saw blade and sets the file into proper orientation for filing rip or crosscut teeth. For ripping teeth, the file sits perpendicular to the saw blade and files teeth straight across. Crosscut teeth, which are beveled on the leading edge of each tooth, are filed at about a 30° angle toward the heel of the blade and about 15° down from horizontal. Follow the setup instructions that come with your jig.

To sharpen the teeth, select the proper saddle setting for your saw and install the jig on the blade near the toe. File each tooth that faces away from you until you reach the heel. The file should contact the leading edge of one tooth first, then the back edge of the tooth behind it as you push the file across the saw blade. Flip the blade end for end in the vise and sharpen the second set of teeth facing away from toe to heel. Use the same number of file strokes for each tooth. Saw teeth are sharp when their points reflect no glints of light.

Sharpening a cabinet scraper

Sharpening a scraper is a four-step process: removing the old burr, squaring and smoothing the edge, raising a new burr and turning the burr. Since each long edge of a cabinet scraper actually has two cutting edges, repeat each step for all four scraper edges before moving on to the next step.

Remove the old burr. To raise a fresh burr, start by filing away the old burr. Lay the scraper on a flat surface and use a fine single-cut mill file to shear off traces of the old burr. Hold the file nearly flat across the face of the scraper and work gently. Do not overwork the faces.

Square and smooth the edges. The long edges of the scraper must be smooth and straight, and the junctures where the faces and edges meet should be crisp and square. Clamp the scraper in a vise with a long edge up and run a mill file along the edge to flatten it, making sure to hold the file perpendicular to the scraper so the edge is perfectly square. Check for flatness along the edge with a straightedge. Polish out the file marks left on the edges with a fine oilstone; otherwise tiny serrations left by the file will leave marks on the wood. Stroke the scraper edges along the length of the stone, keeping the scraper perpendicular to the stone so the edges remain square.

Raise the new burr. For the next step, you'll need to work the flattened scraper edges with a burnisher. This is simply a length of polished steel rod, hardened to a higher degree than the scraper and attached to a handle. Burnishers are made with round, oval or triangular-shaped rods. Any of these burnisher shapes will do the trick. You can make your own burnisher using the back of an old gouge with the cutting edge ground off.

Place the scraper flat on your workbench and close to a bench

How to sharpen a cabinet scraper

1 *Remove remnants of the old burr.* Lay the scraper on a flat surface and use a fine single-cut mill file to shear off traces of the old burr. Hold the file nearly flat across the face of the scraper and work gently. A few broad strokes are all you should need to flatten the faces along the edges.

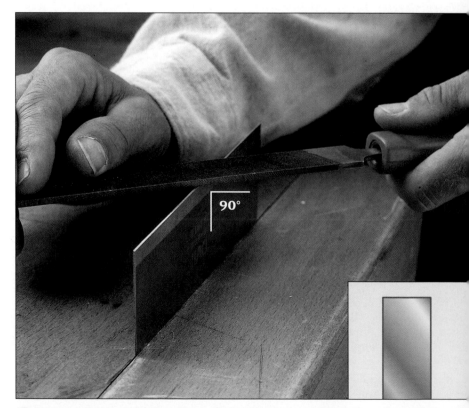

90°

2 *Square and smooth the edges.* Clamp the scraper vertically in a vise and run a mill file along the edge, holding the file diagonally to the length of the scraper and perpendicular to the face. Your goal here is to flatten the edges lengthwise and square them to the faces (See inset).

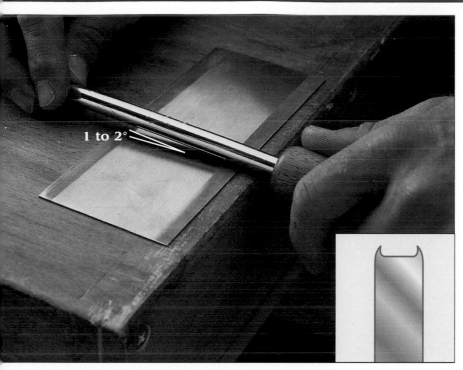

side. Lay the burnisher across the scraper and against a scraper edge, tipping the burnisher over the side of the bench a couple degrees down from horizontal. Stroke back and forth firmly along the edge of the face a few times. In doing so, you press out the steel along the edge and raise a burr.

Turn the burr. To ready the scraper for use, the last step requires bending the raised burrs over so they stand up along each scraper face. Clamp the scraper vertically in a vise and and run the burnisher along the raised edge, about 8° down from horizontal. Work in long, steady strokes. Repeat for the remaining three scraper edges. Burnishing is complete when you can run a fingertip across the faces and over the edges, feeling a slight and even "catch" along the full length of each scraper edge.

3 *Raise the new burrs.* Set the scraper flat on the workbench and close to a side. Lay the burnisher across the scraper and against an edge, tipping the burnisher over the edge of the bench a couple degrees down from horizontal. Stroke firmly along the edge of the face, back and forth a few times to raise a burr along each edge (See inset).

4 *Turn the burrs.* Clamp the scraper vertically in a vise and run the burnisher along the raised edge, about 8° down from horizontal. When done, you should be able to feel the burr evenly along the edge by running a finger across the face and over the edge (See inset).

Burnishing option

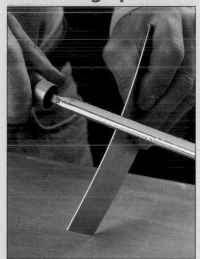

Freehand burnishing. Hold the scraper vertically, pushing one corner into a workbench, while flexing the scraper into a gradual curve. Burnish the edge with firm strokes down the edge, holding the burnisher slightly less than 90° to the face. Flex the scraper in the other direction to raise a burr on the opposite edge.

Index